Nation-States and Money

National currencies appear to be threatened from all sides. European Union member countries are abandoning their national currencies in favour of a supranational currency by the year 2000. Elsewhere, the use of foreign currencies within national economic spaces is on the increase, as shown by the growth of eurocurrency activity, and 'currency substitution' in many parts of the world. In the last decade, privately-issued sub-national 'local currencies' have also proliferated in a number of countries, and some predict the emergence of private electronic monies in the future.

In the light of these transformations, this book asks what the future holds for national currencies. The first half of the volume addresses issues relating to money leading up to, and during, the formation of national currencies. Ranging widely in their historical and geographical context, the articles problematise the relationship between money and nation-states by examining alternative forms and uses of currencies during this period. The second half of the book looks at contemporary challenges faced by national currencies.

This volume suggests that the future of national currencies is very much implicated in how money, nations and states have been interrelated in the past. Money, it suggests, is not solely an economic phenomenon but also a geographical, historical, political, social and cultural phenomenon. Bringing together a number of interdisciplinary experts, *Nation-States and Money* provides a very topical, varied perspective on the past and possible future between money and nation-states. It is written for students and researchers in economics, international relations, international political economy, sociology and geography.

The editors: **Emily Gilbert** is Assistant Professor, and Social Sciences and Humanities Research Council Postdoctoral Fellow at Queen's University, Canada. **Eric Helleiner** is Associate Professor in the Department of Political Studies at Trent University, Canada. He is the author of *States and the Reemergence of Global Finance: From Bretton Woods to the 1990s*, and editor of *The World of Money*.

Routledge/RIPE studies in global political economy

Series editors: Otto Holman, Marianne Marchand and Henk Overbeek

Research Centre for Internation Political Economy, University of Amsterdam

This series, published in association with the *Review of International Political Economy*, provides a forum for current debates in international political economy. The series aims to cover all the central topics in IPE and to present innovative analyses of emerging topics. The titles in the series seek to transcend a state-centred discourse and focus on three broad themes:

- the nature of the forces driving globalisation forward
- resistance to globalisation
- the transformation of the world order.

The series comprises two strands:

Routledge/RIPE studies in global political economy is a forum for innovative new research intended for a high-level specialist readership, and the titles will be available in hardback only. Titles include:

1 **Globalization and Governance**
Edited by Aseem Prakash and Jeffrey A. Hart

2 **Nation-States and Money**
Edited by Emily Gilbert and Eric Helleiner

The **RIPE Series in Global Political Economy** aims to address the needs of students and teachers, and the titles will be published in hardback and paperback. Titles include:

Transnational Classes and International Relations
Kees van der Pijl

States and Sovereignty in the Global Economy
Edited by David A. Smith, Dorothy J. Solinger and Steven C. Topik

Nation-States and Money

The past, present and future of national currencies

Edited by Emily Gilbert and Eric Helleiner

Routledge
Taylor & Francis Group
LONDON AND NEW YORK

First published 1999
by Routledge
2 Park Square, Milton Park, Abingdon, Oxon, OX14 4RN

Simultaneously published in the USA and Canada
by Routledge
270 Madison Ave, New York, NY 10016

Reprinted 2002

Transferred to Digital Printing 2005

Routledge is an imprint of the Taylor & Francis Group

Typeset in Baskerville by
MHL Typesetting Ltd, Coventry

British Library Cataloguing in Publication Data
A catalogue record for this book is available
from the British Library

Library of Congress Cataloging in Publication Data
Nation-States and money: the past, present and future of national currencies/edited by Emily Gilbert and Eric Helleiner.
p. cm. – (Routledge/RIPE studies in global political economy)
Includes bibliographical references and index.
1. Money. 2. Money–Political aspects. I. Gilbert, Emily, 1969– . II. Helleiner, Eric, 1963– . III. Series: RIPE series in global political economy.
HG221.N335 1999 99-32332
332.4–dc21 CIP

ISBN 0-415-18926-8

Printed and bound by Antony Rowe Ltd, Eastbourne

This book is dedicated to
Jennifer, Zoe, Jamie and Nicholas

Contents

Figures and tables

Figures

Tables

Contributors

Benjamin Cohen is the Louis G. Lancaster Professor of International Political Economy at the University of California, Santa Barbara. He is author of numerous articles and books, including *The Geography of Money* (Cornell, 1998), *Crossing Frontiers: Explorations in International Political Economy* (Westview, 1991), *In Whose Interest? International Banking and American Foreign Policy* (Yale, 1986), *Banks and the Balance of Payments* (Allanheld, Osmun, 1981), *Organizing the World's Money* (Macmillan, 1977), *The Question of Imperialism* (Basic, 1973) and *The Future of Sterling as an International Currency* (St. Martin's, 1971).

Nigel Dodd is Lecturer in Sociology at the London School of Economics and Political Science. He is author of *The Sociology of Money* (Polity Press, 1994), *Social Theory and Modernity* (Polity Press, forthcoming), and numerous articles on money, regulation and society.

Emily Gilbert is an Assistant Professor and Social Sciences and Humanities Research Council Postdoctoral Fellow at Queen's University. She is currently undertaking comparative research on the historical development of national currencies in England, Canada, South Africa, and Australia. Preliminary studies on Canadian paper money have been published in *Environment and Planning D: Society and Space*. She has also published a number of papers in journals and edited volumes on symbolic literary landscapes.

Eric Helleiner is Associate Professor in the Department of Political Studies at Trent University. He is author of *States and the Reemergence of Global Finance* (Cornell, 1994), editor of *A World of Money* (a special issue of *Policy Sciences*, 1994) as well as many articles and book chapters on globalisation, international money and finance, and international political economy theory.

Virginia Hewitt is Curator of Paper Money at the British Museum and has worked extensively on the history of note design. Her publications include the edited volume *The Banker's Art: Studies in Paper Money* (British Museum, 1995), *Beauty and the Banknote: Images of Women on Paper Money* (British Museum, 1994) and *As Good as Gold, 300 Years of British Bank Note Design*, co-authored with

Michael Keyworth (British Museum, 1987). Recently, much of her research has focused on colonial note issues in the British Empire.

Andrew Leyshon is Reader in Geography at the University of Bristol. He has published numerous articles and book chapters on money and banking, including papers on the City of London, Japan's postwar growth economy, and the globalisation of finance. He is co-author (with Nigel Thrift) of *Money/Space: Geographies of Monetary Transformation* (Routledge, 1997).

Makoto Maruyama is Associate Professor of political economy in the Department of Advanced Social and International Studies at the University of Tokyo, Komaba. His main research interests lie in an ecologically viable, human-scale economy and in decentralised, local money-use. He has published a number of articles and book chapters on these topics.

Matthew Rowlinson is Associate Professor of English at Dartmouth College. He is author of articles on Victorian poetry and fiction, and of *Tennyson's Fixations: Psychoanalysis and the Topics of Early Poems* (University Press of Virginia, 1994). He is currently writing a book on literature, allegory and paper money in nineteenth-century Britain.

Nigel Thrift is Professor of Geography at the University of Bristol. He has authored and edited numerous books, including, most recently, *Money, Power and Space* (Blackwell, 1994 – co-edited with S. Corbridge and R. Martin), *Mapping the Subject* (Routledge, 1995 – co-edited with S. Pile), *Spatial Formations* (Sage, 1996), and *Money/Space: Geographies of Monetary Transformation* (Routledge, 1997 – co-authored with Andrew Leyshon).

Amy Verdun is Assistant Professor of Political Science at University of Victoria. She was recently a Jean Monnet Fellow in the European Forum, European University Institute, Florence and has published a number of papers on European monetary integration.

Viviana Zelizer is Professor of Sociology at Princeton University. She is the author of *Morals and Markets: The Development of Life Insurance in the United States* (Columbia University Press, 1979); *Pricing the Priceless Child: The Changing Social Value of Children* (Basic Books, 1985) and *The Social Meaning of Money* (Basic Books, 1994). During the academic year 1996–7 she was a Member of the Institute for Advanced Study at Princeton and a John Simon Guggenheim Foundation fellow.

Series editors' preface

We live in a rapidly changing age as we at times become painfully aware. Familiar truths are disappearing at a much faster rate than the rate at which new familiarities are being established. Globalisation is usually blamed.

One of the certainties disappearing rapidly is that of the national currency. On 1 January 1999, eleven European countries gave up their independent national currency and jointly adopted the Euro. In the transition period until January 2002 (when Euro coins and bills are introduced) the old coins and paper currency will continue to exist, but only as (odd) denominations of the Euro. In recent times, various discussions have raised the possibility of Argentina officially dollarising its economy, and of Russia adopting the Euro as its official internal currency. Now, these proposals are of course in one sense only extreme examples of things we have known much longer: many economies around the globe use the US$ as currency, and in much of Eastern Europe and the Balkans the German DM has been the unofficial currency since 1989. It is however significant that high-ranking politicians and officials are publicly debating the wisdom and desirability of trading in the national currency for a foreign one.

This raises fundamental questions with regard to the one-to-one correspondence between nation-state and currency that has been assumed to be 'natural' for many decades. *Nation-States and Money* puts into historical perspective this presumed identity and shows how exclusive national currencies really only emerged in the course of the nineteenth century. The emergence of national currencies was intimately related to the emergence of the 'nation' itself: the creation of national currencies was one way of bolstering nascent national identities. With the processes of global restructuring since the late 1970s, the rising challenges to the nation-state are matched by emerging challenges to the exclusivity of national currencies. *Nation-States and Money* deals with these issues. It shows how globalisation reconstitutes the roles and functions of national monies, and evokes different forms of resistance to their universal use as well as movements for alternatives both at sub-national and at supranational levels. The book considers in detail the forces and actors involved.

The chapters in this volume are from a great diversity of disciplinary backgrounds, and offer a wide variety of approaches and insights. The book is very timely and will, we are sure, make a major contribution to both specialist and more general debates about the de-nationalisation of money and its economic, political, cultural and ideological implications.

Otto Holman
Marianne Marchand
Henk Overbeek

Preface and acknowledgements

Around the world, interest in the future of national currencies has been sparked by diverse phenomena such as the EMU project in Europe, the emergence of sub-national local currencies, the rapid growth of eurocurrency activity and 'dollarisation' as well as the looming prospect of new kinds of privately issued electronic monies. Why are national currencies facing these challenges today and what is their significance for the nation-state? Why have nation-states traditionally sought to maintain a national currency and what is the nature of the historical relationship between national currencies and nation-states?

These are questions that we have both become interested in from different disciplinary standpoints, one of us from cultural geography and the other from political science. In the course of our respective research, we have also been struck by the absence of significant attention to the relationship between nation-states and money in the existing academic literature. A key reason may be that this issue requires an examination of money not just as an economic phenomenon but also as an historical, geographical, political, social and cultural one. And while economists have often been wary of examining the non-economic dimensions of money, scholars outside economics have often steered their attention away from the study of money.

In the last few years, however, we have both been encouraged by a small but growing number of scholars from a variety of disciplines who are beginning to fill this gap in the literature. It is the work of these scholars that we have brought together in this volume. In so doing, we hope that this volume encourages further interdisciplinary research on the relationship between money and nation-states. Moreover, by bringing this variety of approaches together in this one volume, we hope to introduce this innovative research to a broader audience, both within academia and beyond.

We would each like to thank the Social Sciences Research Council of Canada for providing financial assistance for the project. We are also very grateful to two anonymous referees for their very helpful comments as well as to Patrick Proctor and Victoria Smith at Routledge for their advice and support. The volume could not, of course, been pulled together so smoothly without the helpful co-operation of all the contributors, whose enthusiasm for the project only increased our own. And most importantly, we would like to thank Jennifer, Zoe, Jamie and Nicholas for their patience, their company and their insights.

1 Introduction – nation-states and money

Historical contexts, interdisciplinary perspectives

Emily Gilbert and Eric Helleiner

Introduction

Historically, most nation-states have sought to maintain a distinct currency that is both homogenous and exclusive within their territorial boundaries. Indeed, it is widely believed that these national currencies (or 'territorial currencies', as some authors prefer) are a clear indicator of a nation-state's sovereignty. And yet, in the late twentieth century, it appears that national currencies are facing an increasing number of challenges. In Europe, for example, most member countries of the European Union have committed themselves to abandoning their national currencies in favour of a supranational currency. Elsewhere, the use of foreign currencies within national economic spaces is on the increase as evidenced by the growth of eurocurrency activity as well as extensive 'currency substitution' in many parts of the world. Privately issued sub-national 'local currencies' have also proliferated within many countries during the last decade and some predict the emergence of private electronic monies in the future.

What is the significance of these challenges to national currencies? Why are they taking place in the current era? And what do they tell us about the relationship between nation-states and money? Most existing literature addressing contemporary monetary transformations has been written by economists who are inclined to view money primarily as an economic phenomenon. This approach, however, has its limitations. For example, if money served only an economic purpose, it is unlikely that it would have been traditionally organised largely along national lines. After all, almost no country in the world represents the kind of 'optimum currency area' that economists suggest is best served by a single currency. Similarly, understanding money solely as an economic phenomenon makes it difficult to explain fully phenomena such as the nationalist sentiment recently generated in countries like England and Germany when faced with the prospect of losing their national currencies. Examining money from a more interdisciplinary perspective may help to elucidate the significance of national currencies for nation-states as well as the challenges to these monetary structures in the contemporary age. The objective of this volume is to provide such a perspective, demonstrating that national currencies, and money more generally, need to be examined not just as an economic phenomenon but also in terms of their geographical, political, social and cultural dynamics.

Included in this interdisciplinary perspective is also a focus on national currencies as an historical phenomenon. Existing literature on current monetary developments usually lacks much of an historical perspective; indeed, it is sometimes assumed that territorially homogenous and exclusive national currencies are a 'natural' way of organising money. As we will illustrate in more detail below and throughout the volume, a longer historical perspective quickly dispels this assumption. National currencies are a relatively recent historical creation that accompanied the emergence and the spread of nation-states during the nineteenth and twentieth centuries. Indeed, their creation resulted only from what Viviana Zelizer (1994: 205) describes as the 'painstaking and deliberate activities of public authorities'. An historical examination of national currencies not only draws out the ways that they have been deliberately constructed but also how they have never been as totalising or homogenous as is sometimes assumed. Studies of the historical relationship between nation-states and national currencies, and of alternatives to national currencies that predated and were coterminous to them can help us to interpret contemporary monetary transformations, a point that Eric Helleiner returns to in Chapter 12.

This volume draws together scholars from a wide range of disciplinary backgrounds who bring to the study of nation-states and money their historical, geographical, political, social and cultural perspectives. The volume is divided into two parts. The chapters in the first part each address issues relating to money in the period leading up to and during the formation of national currencies. Ranging widely in their historical and geographical context, these chapters grapple with the role of the nation-state in the development of national currencies and problematise this relationship by looking at alternative forms and uses of currencies during this period. While many of the chapters in Part II are also sensitive to an historical perspective, they turn towards the contemporary challenges faced by national currencies. Here the chapters address a wide range of issues, from the supranational currency project in Europe to the growing use of foreign currencies in national economic spaces.

The variety of perspectives adopted and the complexity of the issues addressed herein make it impossible to be exhaustive in the treatment of the relationship between money and nation-states in the past, present and future. In this introductory chapter and the concluding chapter, therefore, we seek to contextualise the many issues that are raised in the contributions to the volume. This introductory chapter begins by outlining some key historical issues concerning the emergence of national currencies and the relationship between this process and the construction of nation-states. It then considers in some detail the variety of approaches to money that are adopted in this volume and draws out the implications of these to our understanding of national currencies. The concluding chapter turns to address some of the issues arising from the contemporary challenges to national currencies. Its goal is to draw on the themes of the volume and to highlight the causes and implications of these challenges for the nation-state. While the contents of the various contributions are touched upon in both the introductory and concluding chapters, they are not summarised; instead, brief introductions to the two parts of the volume provide summaries of the chapters and indicate how they are linked with the themes of that part.

Construction of national currencies: forging connections between money, nations and states

To date, remarkably little academic literature has been devoted to the relationship between the historical origins of national currencies and the construction of nation-states. A look through the considerable and rapidly growing literature on the history of nation-state formation, for example, shows little mention of the importance of, or role played by, currency structures in this process. To be sure, some prominent scholars in this area – including Anthony Giddens (1985), Gianfranco Poggi (1978: 93) and Eric Hobsbawm (1992: 28) – have mentioned in passing that the emergence of national currencies took place alongside that of the nation-state, but they have not explored this association to any extent. If we turn to the scholarship on the history of money, we also find little assistance. The economic historians who dominate this area of study have tended to steer their attention away from the relationship of monetary change to the broader political, socio-cultural, and spatial processes associated with the construction of nation-states in the nineteenth and twentieth centuries.

This gap in the historical literature is unfortunate not only from the standpoint of historical interest but also because it inhibits our understanding of the changing nature of money in the contemporary era. The chapters in the first part of this volume – as well as many of the chapters in the second – begin to fill this gap in the historical literature by examining different aspects of the historical relationship between states, nations and currencies in specific contexts. In this section, we draw on their arguments and other sources to develop very briefly some broader themes.

How national currencies were established

Before turning to the role of the nation-state in the construction of national currencies, it is important to recognise the extent to which currency structures before the nineteenth century differed from the 'national' model with which we are so familiar today (Helleiner 1997, 1999). One difference was that the poor in many countries predominantly used low-denomination tokens or copper and bronze coins, often privately issued, that were not easily convertible into the official monies used by the more wealthy. The result was a tiered monetary order, rather than a coherent national one, in which a fluctuating and unclear 'exchange rate' existed between the respective forms of money used by these two classes. Equally important, official state currencies usually faced considerable competition from other monies within their own borders. One source of competition came from local currencies issued by private or sub-state authorities, as in the case of the Japanese feudal lords discussed in Chapter 4 by Makoto

Maruyama. Foreign coins offered a second kind of competition, as they were often a prominent means of exchange in domestic circulation.

Yet even the state-issued official forms of money that circulated among the more wealthy were not homogenous. Coins and notes were frequently very uneven in quality, not only because of the technological inferiority of their production by today's standards, but also because old and worn forms of money were not withdrawn regularly and counterfeiting was widespread. Furthermore, the relationship between the value of the two dominant types of coins in circulation in most parts of the world – silver and gold – was also subject to change because of their intrinsic metallic value; fluctuations of rates frequently caused the sudden disappearance of one or the other coin from domestic circulation. The increased use of paper monies further contributed to this complexity for many different private and public institutions issued their own notes in numerous denominations each with their own design; these paper currencies also had varying degrees of acceptance across the economic space of each country. Finally, to cope with this lack of uniformity in the domestic monetary system, abstract units of account were often used – in medieval and early modern Europe, for example – to value the many forms of money in circulation. Although they helped to reduce the confusion at the level of accounting, these 'ghost monies' also contributed to the monetary complexity by creating yet another monetary instrument with which the public had to contend.

The creation of territorially homogenous and exclusive national currencies required numerous changes to this chaotic monetary situation. Part of the process involved the production, for the first time, of large quantities of high-quality 'petty coins' for the poor, coins that were fixed in a clear relationship to the other official forms of money. Governments also began to replace 'full weight' silver and gold coins with well-made token coins, the value of which was set by the state rather than derived from an intrinsic metallic value. This helped to eliminate the use of and need for internal exchange rates, 'ghost monies' and foreign coins. Equally important were the initiatives to create a single homogenous banknote, to remove foreign coins from domestic circulation, and to integrate new forms of bank deposit money into the new national currency framework. At the same time, more concerted and effective efforts were launched to stamp out private unofficial money, counterfeiting and old, worn forms of money.

The forging of national currency structures out of a heterogeneous and complex monetary system was a central project undertaken by states across the world in the nineteenth and twentieth centuries (as discussed in Chapters 2, 3, 4, 5, and 8). England was the early pioneer in this process, building an homogenous and exclusive national currency primarily during the first half of the nineteenth century. Some other Western European countries, the United States, and Japan followed its lead, completing the consolidation of their monetary systems along the new 'national' lines in the decades leading up to the First World War. A third wave of countries – including the British Dominions, some countries in Europe and Asia, and much of Latin America – began the construction of national currencies during the nineteenth century, but did not create fully homogenous and exclusive currencies until the interwar period. And it was not until they gained independence after the Second World War that most formerly colonised countries in Africa and the rest of Asia established national currencies.[1]

Emergence of national currencies and nation-states

If national currencies are a relatively recent historical creation, why did they suddenly emerge as a model for monetary organisation in the nineteenth and twentieth centuries? And in what ways was this development linked to the emergence of the nation-state in this same period? Although the experiences of individual countries differed considerably, Nigel Dodd (1994, and Chapter 10) suggests that the creation of national currencies was part of a number of broader processes relating to the formation of nation-states. One such process was the centralisation of the state's administrative machine which gave the state considerable capability to influence and directly regulate the forms of money used by the inhabitants of its territory. The development of nation-wide policing structures, for example, enabled the enforcement of legal tender laws in a comprehensive fashion for the first time. Also significant was the deepening of the state's role in the daily economic life of the people that it governed which was made possible by the spread of national networks of post offices, state-regulated banks and railway stations, as well as national military conscription and the emergence of consolidated taxation system (e.g. Weber 1976). These changes enabled the state to influence the money used within its territory by proclaiming which forms of money would be accepted at public offices and which would not (e.g. Knapp [1905] 1924). They also increased people's 'trust' in the new national currency as the state's commitment to buy and sell token forms of money at fixed rates was made more real and credible. Also enhancing 'trust' in the new state-controlled national money was the introduction of more representative forms of government, as well as, in some instances, emerging nationalist sentiments, as Chapter 3 highlights.

The emergence of industrial capitalism also played a significant role in the formation of national currencies. In part, this was because the application of new industrial technologies to the manufacture of money made possible the mass production of standardised coins and notes (e.g. Hewitt and Keyworth 1987; Doty 1986; Mackenzie 1953). This change dramatically improved the uniformity of the money in circulation and, especially important, it enabled public authorities to produce large quantities of high-quality, low-denomination coins and notes for the poor for the first time. Counterfeiting also became more difficult in the face of technological advances which reduced the number of fraudulent monies in circulation. This in turn facilitated the use of homogenous 'token' monies on a mass scale which had been hitherto very difficult as counterfeiters were invariably tempted to produce large quantities of fraudulent money, given the enormous profits to be made (Redish 1990).

Industrial capitalism also created larger economic spaces at a national scale that were no longer well served by the older monetary systems. Commercial actors operating across the new national economic space, as well as the public authorities seeking to promote such activity, became increasingly frustrated at the transaction costs created by the heterogeneous money supply within the territory of the state. As the poor became further incorporated within a national monetary economy, they too began to protest the inadequate quantity and quality of 'small denomination' money. In an age when the masses were recognised as 'national citizens', their protests had considerable influence, and they often acted as an important impetus for monetary reforms ranging from the monopolisation of the paper money supply to the creation of a modern token coinage (Helleiner 1997).

The boundaries of economic trade in the industrial age did not, of course, stop at national borders, and neither did the push for national currencies. Indeed, as the world economy became increasingly integrated during the nineteenth and early twentieth centuries, foreign commercial interests and governments from 'core' regions had an increased interest in seeing more 'orderly' and 'modern' domestic monetary systems resembling those at home introduced in countries with which they had trading and investment relationships. It is then of little surprise that key monetary reforms, such as the introduction of modern token coinage systems based on the gold standard or the monopoly of note issues, were introduced with their prodding – and with the assistance of externally oriented domestic groups – in regions such as Latin America and Eastern Europe and under their more direct influence in the colonial regions of Africa and Asia (e.g. Drake 1989; Rosenberg 1985; Ofonagoro 1979). Indeed, at various moments in the late nineteenth and early twentieth centuries, more ambitious proposals were also advanced for a creation of a universal form of money that could circulate in all nations as a means of reducing transaction costs globally, although only more limited regional monetary unions of this kind among some European countries were created in the pre-1914 period (e.g. Neilsen 1933).

The age of industrial capitalism also created a demand for national macroeconomic management as money came to permeate all levels of economic life and as token forms of money, especially bank notes and bank deposits, proliferated. This, in turn, often encouraged the creation of a nationally homogenous and standardised currency. During the era of the gold standard, policymakers were most concerned with the macroeconomic goal of maintaining the external convertibility of their currency. The monopolisation of the note issue, for example, was frequently driven by the desire to control the supply of this form of money in order to ensure that it conformed to the requirements of the gold standard. Indeed, it was not just domestic policymakers who had this objective. So too did external figures concerned with the maintenance of stable exchange rates and the integrity and smooth functioning of the international gold standard. For this reason, in the pre-1914 period and the 1920s, private economic actors and policymakers from leading commercial and financial powers strongly encouraged the establishment of central banks with a monopoly in more peripheral regions (see Chapter 2).

Although the objective of macroeconomic control was thus an important one in driving monetary reform in the era of the gold standard, it was also a relatively limited objective in that period. Economic liberals who then dominated policymaking simply sought to ensure that the new token forms of money would be managed in a fashion that closely resembled the automatic market principles by which commodity money had been regulated. Many critics of this liberal approach during the nineteenth century, however, saw the broader potential of national currencies to bind state and nation in the industrial age. They advocated a monetary system in which a national token currency was actively managed by the state with the more inward-looking objective of promoting domestic industrial growth (see Chapter 8). Their vision was often linked to a broader political project which called for inhabitants of a territory, in their new role as 'national citizens', to make direct claims on the state to provide certain political rights and economic benefits.

This alternative monetary vision finally came to fruition on a large scale initially during the 1930s when industrial capitalism appeared close to collapse and then in a more systematic way after the Second World War with the triumph of Keynesian economics. To a greater extent than ever before in history, the state came to harness money as a way of linking itself to the inhabitants of the territory it governed. And this benefit became a central concern of the newly independent countries after the Second World War who sought to create national currencies. National currencies were seen as a key tool for their project of managing the national economy to promote rapid industrial growth and development (e.g. Basu 1967).

A further motivation for the 'nationalisation' of money was the growing fiscal needs of the state in an era of mass warfare and rapid economic development. The seignorage gains to be realised by monopolising the currency offered an easy source of revenue, particularly to states whose capacity to tax or borrow was limited (Smith 1990). More broadly, the creation of a single homogenous currency also greatly reduced the transaction costs associated with the administration of taxation and the running of modern bureaucracy associated with the nation-state. For this reason, initiatives to consolidate the currency often took place at the same time as modern accounting, taxation and financing systems were introduced into government (e.g. Piva 1992).

National currencies also came to be seen as significant for bolstering nascent national identities (Helleiner 1998). The goal of reducing transaction costs within the nation, for example, was sometimes conceptualised as something that would help citizens feel that they were a part of the same political community. Money was thought to be like language, a tool that would facilitate 'communication' among members of the nation. Moreover, in its role as a common and stable standard of value over time, a national currency was seen as a means through which members of the national community were linked to their common past and collective future. The goal of macroeconomic control was also often linked to national identities. Control over national currency became, for example, a key component of the notion of 'popular sovereignty' that was crucial to the new nationalist sense of political identity. The consolidation of money along national lines by the leading economic powers also came to be seen as an important model to emulate. The creation of a central bank with monopoly note issue, or the exclusion of all foreign money from domestic circulation, emerged as symbols for formative nation-states, regardless of their more concrete economic purposes (e.g. Basu 1967: 66).

Equally important, in a period when money penetrated across social relations at all levels of society, policymakers recognised that currencies could act as important carriers of nationalist imagery, particularly if their supply were monopolised. As money is 'among the most mass-produced objects in the world' (Hewitt 1994: 11) and the new national currencies circulated amongst most of the population, its communicative potential was at least as extensive as literary or journalistic representations. Policymakers inspired by nationalist thinking took full advantage of advances in printing technology in the nineteenth and twentieth centuries to provide detailed imagery of their vision of the nation on their coins and notes, as Chapter 2 on the Canadian experience demonstrates. These images, it was believed, would act as an everyday reminder to citizens that they were members of a larger community which nationalists tried to characterise as shared and homogenous.

While the creation of national currencies was closely associated with many of the historical developments that accompanied the emergence of nation-states during the nineteenth and twentieth centuries, it is also important to recognise that even as national currencies were consolidated, alternative forms of money persisted. This is clearly evident in colonial regions where, at the same time that they were consolidating national currencies at home, colonial powers were imposing foreign monetary systems on those regions that remained under their rule until the second half of the twentieth century. This process usually involved the coercive removal of the local currencies of these regions (such as the important and sophisticated cowry currencies in Africa – see Ofonagoro 1979) and the introduction of completely new monetary structures which were closely linked to that of the colonial country. And while the construction of national currencies at home was associated with nation building, the construction of homogenous colonial currencies abroad was intricately connected with colonial objectives: the promotion of trade with the home country, the extraction of an economic surplus from the colonies, the cultivation of international power and prestige, and the promotion of colonial ideologies among colonised peoples (e.g. Balogh 1966). The symbolic role of these currencies to the British colonial authorities is addressed in Chapter 6.

Alternatives to national monies could also be found in the 'core' regions of the world economy. In periods of monetary instability or inflation, for example, the use of foreign currencies or privately issued local currencies often proliferated rapidly (Carothers 1930). Moreover, as Chapter 5 illustrates, the standardisation of money did not prevent the public from differentiating money at a micro-level in all kinds of important ways, and thereby disrupting monetary uniformity. Thus, even when national currencies were consolidated, money was rarely fully homogenous. That alternative monies persisted not only during the formation of national currencies but after their consolidation is an important point to remember when we turn to the challenges that these currencies now face.

Recognising the historical roots of national currencies provides a useful perspective on contemporary challenges to national currencies. It reminds us, for example, that the historical novelty of some of the emerging alternatives to national currencies that are discussed in the second part of this volume should not be overstated. As we have outlined here, the growing use of foreign currencies within countries – as witnessed in the currency substitution trend and the growth of eurocurrencies – is similar to a practice that was very common before national currencies were created. Similarly, supporters of 'local currencies' today are promoting forms of money that in some respects parallel the inconvertible kinds of money commonly used by the poor prior to the emergence of national currencies. We might also mention here the other local forms of currency that have persisted, particularly in times of monetary instability, even after the consolidation of national currencies. Even contemporary initiatives to create to supranational forms of money, such as that in Europe, find partial precedents in nineteenth-century monetary union initiatives and also in the vast common currency zones imposed by colonial powers across a number of political jurisdictions that they governed. If national currencies are being challenged in these various ways, then, it may be more accurate to talk of a move 'back to the future' rather than a step forward into uncharted monetary waters.

This brief exploration of the historical origins of national currencies might also prove useful in explaining contemporary challenges to these monetary structures. The emergence of new currency arrangements in recent years may reflect a reconfiguration of the relationships between money and nation-states as they have developed historically in the ways outlined above. This issue will be taken up again in the conclusion to this volume where the contemporary challenges facing national currencies are considered in more detail. What we have sought to do here is simply to outline the historical trajectory of the formation of national currencies and the systematic procedures that were undertaken towards their realisation. In the following section we turn to consider the advantages of examining national currencies not only as an economic phenomenon but from an interdisciplinary perspective.

Past, present and future of national currencies from an interdisciplinary perspective

As noted above, current challenges to national currencies have been examined largely from an economic perspective in the existing academic literature. As should be clear from our brief contextualisation of the history of the relationship between money and nation-states, we advocate a much broader examination that takes account of historical, geographical, political, social and cultural factors. This is further emphasised in that the contributions to this volume range across numerous disciplines, offering a variety of methodological approaches to a study of national currencies. In this section of the Introduction we briefly outline how money has begun to be examined from these diverse perspectives and draw out the implications of these types of analyses for a study of national currencies. Again, where appropriate, we weave in the contributions to this volume to our discussion. In so doing, it will become clear that these perspectives are neither exclusive nor fixed and that many chapters effectively integrate a variety of approaches.

Historical perspective

As should be clear by our above contextualisation of the development of national currencies, we suggest that an historical examination of the relationship between money and nation-states is necessary to our understanding of contemporary monetary structures. Indeed, this emphasis is reiterated in the structure of the volume as a whole. We have also noted, however, how historians of both the nation-state and of money have been less productive in examining this historical relationship than might be expected. To be effective, an historical perspective on the relationship between money and nation-states must be willing to explore monetary transformations in a broader political, spatial and socio-cultural context.

While economic historians of money have been less inclined to adopt this comprehensive approach, some sociological studies of money have looked to history to provide a more integrated perspective. These studies, however, have been overly abstract and have not explicitly looked at national monetary structures. Karl Marx, for example, began *Capital* with a history of commodities and the money form; his objective, however, was to situate the historical development of money squarely at the centre of his theories of capitalism (Marx, 1974). Likewise, Georg Simmel attended to money's historicity, casting changes to the money form of his era as a peak of historical development, an idea that Max Weber continued to develop (Simmel 1991: 280; Weber 1978: 86). Even the many more recent postmodern accounts of money retain this evolutionary model of monetary history. Brian Rotman, for example, draws upon Jean Baudrillard to describe his own concept of 'xenomoney,' what he calls the monetary acme of financial capitalism, by correlating shifts in the money form – from gold, to paper to electronic currencies – to changes in forms of signification – from representation (gold), to mimesis (paper), to simulacrum (electronic currencies) (Rotman 1987).

In that they generalise and even romanticise monetary transformations, however, these sociological approaches do not usefully contribute to our understanding of the historical relationship between money and nation-states. What is necessary, therefore, are more specific historical studies rooted in concrete examples. The recent proliferation of histories of money largely geared towards a lay audience suggest that there is a wider demand for this kind of research (i.e. Chown 1994; Davies 1994; Weatherford 1997; Williams 1997). Yet these histories, while acknowledging social and cultural aspects of monetary developments, are more factual than analytical, and again, offer little in the way of detail on the formation of national currencies. Some work in this area, however, has indeed begun. As noted in the previous section, Dodd, for example, has elsewhere argued that the nationalisation of currencies was implicated within a complex framework of social and political transformations that included territorial centralisation, the expansion of capitalist enterprise, growing military strength, and an intensification of fiscal administration – much as we do herein (Dodd 1994: 35; see also Leyshon 1996; Helleiner 1997).

Dodd's analysis is especially useful because of its two important implications, ones that we wish to emphasise here. First of all, Dodd suggests that a historical examination of national currencies illustrates that the relationship between money and nation-states is not a necessary one; in other words that there is no intrinsic reason why monetary responsibility should be the (sole) domain of the nation-state. This is especially clear when we turn to examine the deliberate strategies used by the state in the historical formation of national currencies (see Chapters 2–5).

While this relationship is not necessary, Dodd's second point, which is of equal importance, is that there is nonetheless a functional relationship between money and nation-states (Dodd 1994: 26). Thus, while the relationship between money and nation-states may not be necessary, we cannot ignore that it has existed and continues to do so, even as the relationship is continuously modified. Thus history is not only useful to our understanding of the past, but equally can inform our understanding of contemporary monetary transformations. Indeed, the chapters in the second part of this volume highlight that many of the contemporary challenges that national currencies now face relate to the ways that states and nations are being reconfigured. At the same time, however, historical analysis also indicates that national currencies have never been as completely homogenous as has been imagined (see Chapter 5). These insights from history reveal that the alternatives to national currencies that are emerging today have, in fact, a much longer genealogy. Thus, a more detailed understanding of the historical development of national currencies ensures a better understanding of their future.

Geographical perspective

If national currencies need to be contextualised historically, they equally need to be situated in terms of space and place. Indeed, geographical approaches to national currencies have provided substantive analyses of the spatiality of modern monetary networks. In so doing, they have posed a challenge to social theorists such as Marx, Simmel, and Giddens who suggest that modern money forms are disembedded from place even as, or rather because, they bring distant places near. To these theorists, money plays an active role in the time–space compression associated with modernity and in fact they suggest that what makes money so useful is precisely its ability to separate and extend subjects and objects, sales and purchases in time (past and present) and space (here and there), for it is this separation across time and space that liberates transactors from the constraints of barter exchange (Dodd 1995; Simmel 1991; Harvey 1989). Money, especially as it became homogenised and standardised, was thus believed to play a constituent role in the annihilation of space by time; so much so that Simmel averred that 'Owing to the abstractness of its form, money has no definite relationship to space: it can exercise its effects upon the most remote areas' (Simmel 1991: 504). Giddens builds upon this theory to suggest that money, a means of time–space distanciation which extends social relationships in time and space, is a 'symbolic token' and thus a disembedding mechanism associated with modernity (Giddens 1990: 22).

Simply, these social theories consider abstract money to be both cause and consequence of the reconfiguration and even dilution of space that is associated with modernity (Turner 1986: 97). A geographical perspective on money, by contrast, offers some corrective to this totalising interpretation, as exemplified in the research on the consolidation of money in specific places, especially that on financial centres and world cities (e.g. Leyshon and Thrift, 1997; Black, 1996; Corbridge, Thrift and Martin, 1994). The role of space, place and money in restructuring of the global political economy is a central focus of the volume *Money, Power and Space* (Corbridge, Thrift and Martin, 1994). More than just adding space to studies of money and stirring, geographers (and the geographically inclined) have grounded their ideas in actual case studies; included in that volume are wide-ranging sections dealing with geopolitics, the intersections of financial and industrial capitals, and the technological, cultural and aesthetic dimensions of money (Corbridge and Thrift 1994: 4). Moreover, they do not treat the relationship between money and space as simplistic, but more along the lines of Simmel's more nuanced understanding of money as both 'unifying' and 'disintegrating' (Simmel 1991: 345).

Attending to money's geography is particularly useful to a study of national currencies for it directs us not to undermine money's specificity but to recognise that national currencies have emerged at different points in time in different places (see above) and that we can expect the contemporary challenges to national currencies to manifest themselves differently in different parts of the world (see Chapter 12). Moreover, while it is possible to generalise with respect to the processes involved in the formation of national currencies, a geographically sensitive approach to money illustrates that these ideas rarely cohere with how the formation of national currencies is actually played out in specific contexts (compare the chapters in the first part of this volume). The role of territorial consolidation to the formation of national currencies is yet another element accentuated when space and place are emphasised (see Chapter 2). But perhaps more significant has been the recognition that '*money is itself a geography*' (Leyshon and Thrift 1997: 3; emphasis in the original). The implications of this statement are twofold; that money, as a circulating medium, is necessarily on the move, but that it is equally rooted in specific places. Thus, even in the face of what appears to be the increasing dematerialisation of money in the contemporary context, place matters. In this volume, for example, Leyshon and Thrift (Chapter 9) while dealing with alternatives to national currencies from eurocurrency to LETS (local exchange trading systems), retain a focus on the City of London, again illustrating the need to examine the role of specific international financial centres. Indeed, the dematerialisation of money and its trans-national circulation has resulted not in the overcoming of place, but what has been called a 'new geography' of money (Chapter 7).

Political perspective

Some of the contributions to this volume take a more political approach to our understanding of national currencies (see, especially, Chapters 7, 8 and 11). This research is part of a larger body of literature produced by political scientists since the 1970s which seeks to make prominent the political dimensions of world monetary orders. This interest arose initially primarily out of the breakdown of the Bretton Woods monetary system in the early 1970s, which underlined, for economists and political scientists alike, the importance of the political foundations of monetary orders as well as their political consequences. Much of the initial political science literature sought to explore the important role of states in constructing the conditions in which a stable world monetary system could exist. Particular attention was given to the role of hegemonic states with respect to certain functions including the enforcement of rules, the provision of long-term lending and the willingness to act as a lender of last resort (e.g. Kindleberger 1973). Equally important, scholars examined the political consequences of different monetary orders, showing, for example, how currencies used at the international level served not just economic purposes but also the political interests of some states over others (e.g. Strange 1971).

More recently, analyses of the politics of world monetary orders have moved beyond the state-centric focus of the earlier work. Some political scientists have shifted attention away from the state level by analysing how various domestic interests – classes, sectors, and regions – profit or are at a disadvantage from different monetary arrangements, as well as the ways that these interests seek to promote their own interests in the arena of monetary policymaking (e.g. Frieden 1991). Another challenge to state-centrism has come from those analysing the implications of the recent globalisation of financial markets. Work of this kind has focused on the ways that national policy autonomy – and even the legitimacy of national governments – is being undermined by financial markets and private forms of authority within them, such as banks and credit-rating agencies (e.g. Pauly 1997, Cohen 1996).

Despite this shift away from the state-centrism of their early work on money, it is only very recently that political scientists have begun thinking about a world in which national currencies are threatened. Previously, with the exception of some literature on the eurocurrency market, most analyses made the assumption – although rarely made explicit – that every state maintained its own territorially homogenous and exclusive currency. Even work analysing challenges to the nation-state in this age of globalised finance shared this assumption, as the focus was primarily on the challenges that capital mobility posed to the macroeconomic policy autonomy of states. Two developments have helped political scientists finally begin to question this assumption. One is the political prominence of various challenges to national currencies today, and the second has been the wider questioning of the assumption of 'territoriality' within the fields of international relations and political science today (e.g. Ruggie 1993).

As attention has begun to focus on the challenges to national currencies, political scientists have been able to draw on previous analyses to raise important questions about the political dimensions of these monetary transformations such as: What powerful interests and political ideologies are promoting challenges to national currencies? What roles are states playing in encouraging the 'denationalisation' of money? What are the implications of alternative currency arrangements for the power and legitimacy of states, and which societal groups are benefiting and losing from these arrangements? (see Chapters 7, 8 and 11). These kinds of questions – which have begun to be addressed by the contributors to this volume and others (e.g. McNamara 1997) – highlight the quite distinctive perspective that political scientists bring to the study of money from that of economists. The latter usually define money according to its uses, of which economists traditionally list at least three: a medium of exchange, a store of value, a unit of account. But a political approach to money insists on a wider definition that recognises how money is also an instrument of power.

Social perspective

Another source of new thinking about money has come from scholars in sociology. As hinted above, the roots of economic sociology can be traced primarily to Marx, Simmel, and Weber. These figures were central in reacting to classical political economy and its 'dominant utilitarian understanding of money' (Zelizer 1989: 343) in that they incorporated individual and social elements into their analyses of exchange relationships. Simmel's role is most frequently singled out in that he brought together localised analysis with a broader social critique. And yet, by promoting uniformity, precision and calculation, Simmel argued that the spread of money depersonalises and standardises social life. He spoke of the 'complete heartlessness of money' as well as 'colourlessness', its 'uncompromising objectivity' and its ability to 'become a denominator for all values' (Simmel 1991). Similarly, Marx characterised money as a 'radical leveller' that 'does away with all distinctions' associated with traditional social relations (Marx 1974: 132). For these figures who bridged economics and sociology, money thus was a powerful vehicle for the commodification of social life.

The publication in 1985 of Mark Granovetter's paper, 'Economic action and social structure: the problem of embeddedness', set the agenda for a renewed and burgeoning interest in economic sociology (Granovetter 1985; see also Ingham 1996a: 266; 1996b). Although Granovetter does not himself discuss money, his paper presages the foci of the recent sociology of money, that is, the embeddedness of the economy in social relations, the relevance of social networks, and the importance of trust. Since then, there has been a continued interest in sociological studies of money that have emphasised the social nature of money, markets, and market economies more generally (Swedberg, Himmelstrand and Brulin 1987; Ganßmann 1988; Baker and Jimerson 1992; Mizruchi and Stearns 1994). How this approach differs from comparable economic accounts is suggested by Mark Mizruchi and Linda Brewster Stearns in their review of the literature in this area; they indicate that sociological accounts of money, banking, and finance are culturally embedded; attend to the effects of social networks; and recognise the workings of both social and political power (Mizruchi and Stearns 1994: 313). Dodd brings these ideas of bear in his analysis of the relationship between money and the nation-state as he attends to the networks of social relations that enable the transaction of money, that is, the rational, fiduciary, and political relationships among transactors that exist above and beyond these transactions (Dodd, 1994; see also Chapter 10).

In her contribution to this volume as well as in her book *The Social Meaning of Money* (1994), Zelizer also shows the potential contribution of this kind of approach to the study of nation-states and money. She criticises the views of the classical writers cited above, arguing that, while money undoubtedly has the capacity to transform social values and relations, those same values and relations also have considerable reciprocal power to transform money and invest it with meaning and social patterns. As Zelizer remarks in Chapter 5, money is not a culturally neutral or socially anonymous object, but rather is 'profoundly marked by varying cultural and social structures'. Many of the contributors to this volume share this perspective, but they examine how money has been linked to nation- or empire-building. By contrast, Zelizer highlights how people also make every effort to embed money in particular times, places and social relations. Thus Zelizer shows that in the midst of the standardisation and homogenisation of national currencies, people continually disrupted monetary uniformity by differentiating money at a micro-level through earmarking and the creation of special forms of currency. She concludes in her contribution to this volume: 'There is no single, uniform, generalised money, but multiple monies'.

The work of Giddens presents yet another focus for economic sociology. Giddens draws upon Parsons's description of money as 'a symbolic token,' although the former suggests that money's symbolism comes from its social circulation and the trust invested in it necessary to its circulation (see Zelizer 1994: 11). The relevance of this perspective to the study of nation-states and money is brought out briefly by Giddens who argues that the token forms of money that make up modern national currencies were made possible only when a more direct relationship between state and society was created with the rise of the nation-state. This direct relationship not only gave the state the ability to regulate the forms of money used by the population. It also encouraged the use of token forms of money by cultivating the 'trust' of the population in the state's ability to manage the value of this form of money (see Chapter 2). In this way, Giddens succeeds in showing how his sociological understanding of money helps to link the rise of national currencies to that of the nation-state. The relationship between trust and money is not merely an historical phenomenon but, as a number of the chapters in this volume indicate, persists as a constitutive element of contemporary monetary networks (see Chapters 7, 9 and 10).

Cultural perspective

Although certain forms of economic sociologies allude to the cultural aspects of money, these are rarely developed. There is, however, a growing literature on the culture of money. Many of these studies are on the discursive representation of money in literature (and more recently in visual media) which build upon earlier analogies between money and language. Marc Shell and Jean-Joseph Goux, for example, examine the 'isomorphic patterns' of economic, symbolic and metaphoric transformations in terms of their textual manifestations. Shell's *Money, Language and Thought* (1982), for example, examines the role of money in writings ranging from the search for the Holy Grail to Martin Heidegger's *Being and Time.* Couching his argument in terms of the shift from gold, to paper, to electronic monies, Shell suggests that 'new forms of metaphorisation or exchanges of meaning accompanied the new forms of economic symbolisation and production' and that these 'were changing the meaning of meaning itself' (Shell 1982: 4). Goux has traced this historical transformation through specific literary texts, including those by André Gide and Georges Bataille (Goux 1994). Drawing upon Jean-Paul Sartre's uncovering of an 'economic rupture at the beginning of the twentieth century ("dematerialization of wealth") and the ethical orientation of Gide's work', Goux concludes that Gide's novel, *The Counterfeiters*, 'in its very nature, coincides in an exemplary way with the transition from one form of exchange, dominated by gold-money, to a form in which the new phenomenon of inconvertibility appears' (Goux 1988: 18, 24).

The importance of these studies arises from Goux's assertion that economic exchange is linked with the cultural and symbolic practices of metaphors, symptoms, signs and representations. While Goux and Shell look at how money has been represented in art and literature, there have also emerged a growing number of studies that have turned to examine the representations on the money form (e.g. Hewitt 1994, 1995; Gilbert 1998). Much like economic sociological approaches to money, much of this kind of research draws upon anthropological literatures of money and their attention to the cultural symbolism of pre-modern money forms (Baker 1987; Zelizer 1989). Such studies illustrate that the actual form that money takes can have a significant influence on the ways in which money is used and even understood. Even anthropologists, however, have shied away from applying this kind of analysis to modern money forms, thus reinforcing the presumed distinctions between 'primitive' and 'modern' monies and tangentially an economic understanding of money as anonymous, neutral and immaterial. Those studies of the images on money that have appeared argue, by contrast, that it is through their design and production that the social production of modern monies has become so taken for granted.

As Chapters 2 and 6 suggest, the issuers of money have sought to harness specific iconographies to support their social and political aspirations. In the case of national currencies, paper and coins provided a popular and effective medium through which the state could promote its project of nation-building, to which the text, writing and images on money could each be harnessed (Mugnaini 1994). But it is not only that the images of money communicate a nationalist ideology, but that, as Christina McGinley indicates, it is through money that national subjects are constituted (McGinley 1993). Drawing upon the diverse figures of Teresa de Lauretis and Louis Althusser and their mediations on 'the production of subjects as subjects', McGinley looks specifically at the role of money as a general equivalent in the formation of subjects; in her words, 'Because all commodities must identify themselves by means of the general equivalent, and the lines between people, things, and commodities become blurred (as Marxist notion of alienation and commodity fetishism indicate), individuals also identify themselves via the general equivalent' (McGinley 1993: 248). National currencies, and the images thereupon, become a means through which 'citizens are authorised to "see" and to "be"' (McGinley 1993: 249).

How individuals come to identify with their national currencies, while mediated through iconography, depends upon the role that money plays in integrating society as a medium of circulation. As Rowlinson explains in Chapter 3, monetary communities are reinforced by the networks through which money is exchanged. The participants in paper money transactions, he suggests, particularly when paper was a relatively recent medium of circulation, 'identified with one another – one accepts paper money on the assumption that there are others like oneself who will also accept it'. This is tied back into the notion of trust introduced in the above discussion of economic sociology, for in that they share 'a delimited space with other subjects with whom they also share an immediately negotiable currency', people are 'situated' in specific communities of exchange largely based around trust (Rowlinson, Chapter 3; see Helleiner 1997, 1998). But, as Chapter 11 makes clear, the connection between national identity and national currencies is not solely an historical phenomenon, but equally apparent today at suggestions that national currencies are to be supplanted by a pan-European currency. Moreover, as we noted above, in areas where nation-states are in the process of being constructed, national currencies have become one of the means through which national identities are both produced and reproduced.

Conclusion

National currencies are not in any way a 'natural' monetary phenomenon. As we have illustrated, before the advent of national currencies money was organised quite differently. Moreover, the emergence of national currencies was a result of deliberate state policies arising from a specific historical period during which nation-states were also constructed and consolidated. We have also argued that the parallels between these developments were not coincidental. Many of the historical processes that encouraged the emergence of nation-states also were crucial in promoting the formation of national currencies; equally, the formation of national currencies contributed to the authority and legitimacy of the nation-state. By examining the historical formation of national currencies we can begin to understand how deeply enmeshed nation-states and money have become. And yet, that national currencies appear to face so many contemporary challenges further underlines that they are not the natural apex of monetary development, but a fragile, historically specific construction. It is precisely to uncover this kind of complexity that in this volume we have juxtaposed historical accounts of the formation of national currencies with papers on the contemporary challenges that these national currencies now face. Indeed, the future of national currencies is very much implicated in how money, nations, and states have been interrelated in the past.

Despite the importance of an historical analysis, we also argue that fully to understand the interrelationship between money and nation-states – whether in the past, present or the future – requires that we also take into account the geographical, political, social and cultural dimensions of money. The chapters in both parts of this volume, in that they offer a wide variety of possible interpretations to the relationship between money and nation-states, underline and engage with these debates. On their own, the chapters contribute valuable insights into the past, present and future of national currencies; taken together, they provide us with a much more nuanced perspective from which we might reflect upon the relationship between money and nation-states. Indeed, it is a central goal of this volume to highlight the many different positions from which these issues can be examined. By bringing together a wide range of disciplinary backgrounds, temporal perspectives and geographical vantage points, we intend to stimulate a new kind of interdisciplinary dialogue that will contribute constructively to these contemporary debates by raising many more issues and provoking many more questions.

Notes

1 Often, the construction of more territorially homogenous and exclusive currencies in these regions had in fact been started by colonial authorities in the late nineteenth and early twentieth centuries. But its completion – particularly involving the break-up of large regional common currency zones of the colonial period – did not come until independence. The most striking exception to this pattern involved most of the ex-colonies of France in Africa which maintained the common CFA franc zones of the colonial period.

Bibliography

Baker, W.E. (1987) 'What is money? A social-structural interpretation' in M. Mizruchi and M. Schwartz, eds *Intercorporate Relations: The Structural Analysis of Business*, Cambridge: Cambridge University Press: 109–44.

Baker, W.E. and J.B. Jimerson (1992) 'The sociology of money' *American Behavioral Scientist* 35: 687–93.

Balogh, T. (1966) 'The mechanism of neo-imperialism' in T. Balogh, *The Economics of Poverty*, London: Weidenfeld and Nicolson.

Basu, S. (1967) *Central Banking in Emerging Countries*, Bombay: Asia Publishing House.

Black, I.S. (1996) 'The London Agency System in English Banking, 1780–1825' *London Journal* 21 (2): 112–30.

Carothers, N. (1930) *Fractional Money*, New York: John Wiley and Sons.

Chown, J.F. (1994) *A History of Money: from AD 800*, London and New York: Routledge.

Cohen, B. (1996) 'Phoenix arisen: the resurrection of global finance', *World Politics* 48: 268–96.

Corbridge, S. and Thrift, N.J. (1994) 'Money, power and space: introduction and overview' in S. Corbridge, N.J. Thrift and R. Martin, eds, *Money, Power and Space*, Oxford: Basil Blackwell.

Corbridge, S., N.J. Thrift and R. Martin, eds, (1994) *Money, Power and Space*, Oxford: Basil Blackwell.

Davies, G. (1994) *A History of Money: From Ancient Times to the Present Day*, Cardiff: University of Wales Press.

Dodd, N. (1994) *The Sociology of Money*, Cambridge: Polity.

Dodd, N. (1995) 'Whither mammon? Postmodern economics and passive enrichment' *Theory, Culture & Society* 12: 1–24.

Doty, R. (1986) 'Matthew Boulton and the coinage revolution, 1787–1797' *Rare Coin Review* 61: 34–6.

Drake, P. (1989) *The Money Doctor in the Andes*, Durham: Duke University Press.

Frieden, J. (1991) 'Invested interests' *International Organization* 45: 425–52.

Ganßmann, H. (1988) 'Money – a symbolically generalized medium of communication? On the concept of money in recent sociology' *Economy and Society* 17 (3): 285–316.

Giddens, A. (1985) *The Nation-State and Violence*, Cambridge: Polity.

Giddens, A. (1990) *The Consequences of Modernity*, Stanford, CA: Stanford University Press.

Gilbert, E. (1998) '"Ornamenting the façade of hell": iconographies of nineteenth-century Canadian paper money' *Environment and Planning D: Society and Space* 16: 57–80.

Goux, J.-J. (1988) 'Banking on signs' *Diacritics* summer: 15–25.

Goux, J.-J. (1994) *The Coiners of Language*, Norman and London: University of Oklahoma Press.

Granovetter, M. (1985) 'Economic action and social structure: the problem of embeddedness' *American Journal of Sociology* 91: 481–510.

Harvey, D. (1989) *The Condition of Postmodernity: An Enquiry into the Origins of Cultural Change*, Oxford: Basil Blackwell.

Helleiner, E. (1997) *One Nation, One Money: Territorial Currencies and the Nation-State*, Arena Working Paper no. 17, Oslo: ARENA.

Helleiner, E. (1998) 'National currencies and national identities' *American Behavioural Scientist* 41, 10: 1409–36.

Helleiner, E. (1999) 'Historicizing territorial currencies: money and the nation-state in North America' *Political Geography*.

Hewitt, V. (1994) *Beauty and the Banknote*, London: British Museum Press.

Hewitt, V., ed. (1995) *The Banker's Art: Studies in Paper Money*, London: British Museum Press.

Hewitt, V. and J. Keyworth (1987) *As Good as Gold: 300 Years of British Bank Note Design*, London: British Museum Publications, Inc.

Hobsbawm, E. (1992) *Nations and Nationalism Since 1780*, 2nd edn, Cambridge: Cambridge University Press.

Ingham, G. (1996a) 'Critical survey: some recent changes in the relationship between economics and sociology' *Cambridge Journal of Economics* 20: 243–75.

Ingham, G. (1996b) 'Review essay: the "new economic sociology"' *Work, Employment and Society* 10: 549–64.

Kindleberger, C. (1973) *The World in Depression, 1929–39,* Berkeley: University of California Press.
Knapp, G. (1924[1905]) *The State Theory of Money* translated by H. Lucas and J. Bonar. London: Macmillan.
Leyshon, A. (1996) 'Dissolving distance? Money, disembedding and the creation of "global financial space"' in P. Daniels and W. Lever, eds, *The Global Economy in Transition*, London: Longman: 62–80.
Leyshon, A. and N.J. Thrift (1997) *Money/Space: Geographies of Monetary Transformation*, London and New York: Routledge.
McGinley, C.L. (1993) 'Coining nationality: woman as spectacle on 19th century currency' *American Transcendental Quarterly* 7 (3): 247–69.
Mackenzie, A.D. (1953) *The Bank of England Note: A History of Its Printing*, Cambridge: Cambridge University Press.
McNamara, K. (1997) *The Currency of Ideas,* Ithaca: Cornell University Press.
Marx, K. (1974 [1867]) *Capital: A Critique of Political Economy,* vol 1; New York: International Publishers.
Mizruchi, M.S. and L.B. Stearns (1994) 'Money, banking, and financial markets' in Neil J. Smelser and Richard Swedberg, eds, *The Handbook of Economic Sociology*; Princeton, NJ: Princeton University Press: 313–41.
Mugnaini, F. (1994) 'Messages sur billets de banque: la monnaie comme mode d'échange et de communication' *Terrain* 23: 63–80.
Nielsen, A. (1933) 'Monetary unions' *Encyclopedia of the Social Sciences* 10: 595–601.
Ofonagoro, W. (1979) 'From traditional to British currency in southern Nigeria: analysis of a currency revolution, 1880–1948' *Journal of Economic History* 39: 623–54.
Pauly, L. (1997) *Who Elected the Bankers?* Ithaca: Cornell University Press.
Piva, M. (1992) 'Government finance and the development of the Canadian state' in A. Greer and I. Radforth, eds, *Colonial Leviathan: State Formation in Mid-Nineteenth Century Canada*, Toronto: University of Toronto Press.
Poggi, G. (1978) *The Development of the Modern State*, Stanford: Stanford University Press.
Redish, A. (1990) 'The evolution of the gold standard in England' *Journal of Economic History* 50: 789–805.
Rosenberg, E. (1985) 'Foundations of US international financial power: gold standard diplomacy 1900–1905' *Business History Review* 59: 169–202.
Rotman, B. (1987) *Signifying Nothing: The Semiotics of Zero*, Stanford, CA: Stanford University Press.
Ruggie, J. (1993) 'Territoriality and beyond: problematizing modernity in international relations' *International Organization* 47: 139–74.
Shell, M. (1982) *Money, Language, and Thought: Literary and Philosophic Economies from the Medieval to the Modern Era*, Baltimore: The Johns Hopkins University Press.
Simmel, G. (1991 [1907]) *The Philosophy of Money,* Boston and London: Routledge & Kegan Paul.
Smith, V. (1990[1936]) *The Rationale of Central Banking,* Indianapolis: Liberty Press.
Strange, S. (1971) *Sterling and British Policy,* London: Oxford University Press.
Swedberg, R., U. Himmelstrand and G. Brulin (1987) 'The paradigm of economic sociology: premises and promises' *Theory and Society* 16: 169–213.
Turner, B.S. (1986) 'Simmel, rationalization and the sociology of money' *The Sociological Review* 34: 93–114.
Weatherford, J. (1997) *The History of Money: From Sandstone to Cyberspace*, New York: Crown Publishers, Inc.

Weber, E. (1976) *Peasants into Frenchmen: The Modernization of Rural France 1870–1914*, Stanford: Stanford University Press.

Weber, M. (1978 [1920]) *Economy and Society*, 2 vols, eds, Guenther Roth and Claus Wittich, Berkeley: University of California Press.

Williams, J., ed. (1997) *Money: A History*, London: The British Museum Press.

Zelizer, V.A. (1989) 'The social meaning of money: special monies' *American Journal of Sociology* 95: 342–77.

Zelizer, V.A. (1994) *The Social Meaning of Money*, New York: Basic Books.

Part I

Nations, states and currencies in historical perspective

Introduction

The chapters in the first part of this volume provide some historical perspective on contemporary challenges to national currencies. In addition to investigating aspects of the historical relationship between money and nation-states, they highlight the ways that alternatives to national currencies have existed and have flourished in the not-so-distant past. The chapters are not intended in any way to provide a comprehensive discussion of these issues in either a thematic, historical or geographical sense. (The introductory chapter to the volume and some of the chapters in Part II – particularly Chapter 8 – also provide further discussion of many of these historical issues.) Rather, each of the chapters in this part of the volume tackles a particular issue and examines it within a specific historical and geographical context.

This part of the volume begins with Emily Gilbert's chapter on the formation of a Canadian national currency, initiated in the mid-nineteenth century and finally achieved a century later. This chapter draws upon many of the themes set out in the Introduction and applies them to a specific case study. By drawing upon a specific example of national currency formation, Gilbert is able to examine the ways that money was implicated in both the state-making and nation-building activities of the Canadian nation-state in their articulation of community and territorial boundaries. In so doing, the deliberate practices that are involved in the formation of national currencies, as they emerged in one specific instance, are clearly illustrated. Moreover, as the Canadian case study reveals, national currencies have not only been a constituent component of nation-state formation, but national currencies in effect lent authority to and even legitimised the nation-state.

Chapter 3 turns to another time and place: Britain in the seventeenth and eighteenth centuries. It traces the emergence of paper instruments of credit, and even national currencies, out of the heterogeneous metallic circulation characteristic of early modern states. But Rowlinson's attention is more narrowly focused on the ways that these paper instruments were discursive performances conferring upon their users, for example, a new sense of geographical situatedness that articulated new relations between the domestic and the foreign, and between the metropolis and the provinces. In so doing, he builds towards a discussion of the crisis occasioned by the Restriction Act of 1797, when for the first time national sentiment was mobilised in the pound's defence – this at a date when the pound had no material existence in anything like a uniform national currency, but circulated only in a bewildering variety of local paper monies and credit instruments.

It is this bewildering variety of currencies that is the focus of the remaining chapters in this part of the volume in that they each highlight the various monetary alternatives that have persisted alongside emergent national currencies. Chapter 4 deals with the Tokugawa period, before Japan emerged as a modern nation-state. He calls attention to the significance of the various local currencies of that era and suggests that these currencies, which were eliminated after the Meiji Restoration of 1868 as part of the creation of a modern Japanese nation-state, were often useful in promoting local economic development. By way of conclusion, he speculates upon how a historical understanding of *hansatsu* may shed light onto how local currencies may be revitalised for a similar purpose as part of the current tendency towards decentralisation in Japan.

Chapter 5 describes the active role of the state in the creation of a homogenous and standardised national currency in the United States, a process that took place largely between the mid-nineteenth century and the years leading up to the First World War. But while recognising the important role of the nation-state, she highlights how the public continually disrupted the emerging monetary uniformity by differentiating money at a micro-level for various social purposes. Even in the age of national currencies, then, Zelizer illustrates that money has in fact rarely been fully homogenous. This historical analysis prompts her to challenge the view that the growing use of money depersonalises and standardises social life. Zelizer argues instead that, while money undoubtedly has the capacity to transform social values and relations, those same values and relations also have considerable reciprocal power to transform money and invest it with meaning and social patterns.

Chapter 6 is concerned with how national currencies were challenged in yet another way, colonialism. During the nineteenth and early twentieth centuries, European policies of colonisation and imperialism encouraged the spread of western-style banking and paper money across the world. This paper focuses on Britain's overseas territories, and looks at the role of private commercial banks; the changing attitudes of British government, from mercantile ambitions to political pragmatism; different and changing attitudes within the colonies; and, above all, the designs printed on the notes. As this chapter illustrates, the formation of national currencies was not only a domestic affair, but implicated in wider social and political processes, as illustrated here in terms of the shifting arguments and allegiances between the government in Britain, officers in colonial government, native populations, and British settlers.

2 Forging a national currency

Money, state-making and nation-building in Canada

Emily Gilbert

Introduction

Until recently it has been 'axiomatic' that money is the right and responsibility of the nation-state and that state intervention in this realm is both 'constant and constitutive' (Rotstein and Duncan 1991: 416; Leyshon and Thrift 1997: 56). While the role of economic factors in the formation of nation-states has long been alluded to (e.g. Hobsbawm, 1990; Smith, 1986; Gellner, 1983), it is ironically only now that national currencies appear to be threatened by contemporary monetary transformations that attention has begun to turn more specifically to the interrelationship between money and nation-states. That the role of national currencies appears to be fading means that an historical analysis of their development is more, not less, important, for understanding the contingency of their evolution means that we will be better able to assess the contemporary challenges to them and the emergence of alternative forms of exchange that are appearing on the horizon.

It is this contingency of national currency formation that will be at the centre of this chapter. Hence, I will be concerned with delineating the processes and practices involved in the formation of national currencies, in terms of both nation-building and state-making (Smith, 1986). As I will illustrate, the nationalisation of money has been implicated in a range of state-making processes such as the centralisation of bureaucracy and the territorialisation of state power (Helleiner, 1996a, 1996b; Anderson, 1992; Smith, 1986; Gellner, 1983).[1] The organisation of money into national currencies, for example, made possible the centralisation of the supply and issue of money and, consequently, became a means through which the state became involved in the daily life of the public (see Weber, 1978; Hobsbawm 1990: 81). The standardisation of currencies, whether with respect to their production or to the removal of foreign currencies, in turn facilitated trade and its expansion throughout the state (Helleiner 1996a: 11, 16). Moreover, money was yet another means through which state sovereignty was expressed, in the sense that it participated in the regulation of activities, people and objects across territorial borders (Gupta 1992: 71). National currencies thus provided territorial coherence not only internally but also externally, for example, *vis-à-*

vis the maintenance of monetary boundaries and borders with respect to standards of convertibility (Helleiner 1996a: 12).

Of equal interest to the role of money in state-making, is how money produces and reproduces on a national scale what Benedict Anderson has called 'imagined communities', whether through the use of the links that money forges among its transactors or through nationalist iconographies (Anderson, 1992; see also Helleiner, 1996a, 1996b; Dodd, 1995, 1994; Giddens 1990). The state's ability to guarantee the legitimacy of its money – facilitated by the homogenisation of the currency, centralisation, as well as the rise of policing capabilities (see Johnson, 1995) – made possible the use of token currencies such as paper money that are of no intrinsic value but which circulate because of the economic and political power inscribed upon them by their issuing institutions. Money's relationship to the state was thus mutually reinforcing for not only did this trust lend the state legitimacy, but it also compelled the public to become dependent upon the state's authority for fulfilling their financial obligations (Helleiner 1996a; Dodd, 1994; Giddens, 1990). Moreover, the public was further linked together through the currency in that it was a simple and effective medium for the communication of national symbols which, from the mid-nineteenth century onwards, increasingly predominated on the currencies as their production became increasingly centralised (Hewitt, 1994; 1995). The same innovations to printing technologies that enabled the mass production of written materials and their widespread dissemination also made possible the mass production of money and its dissemination across the nation-state (Anderson, 1991). Thus money, as with other 'invented traditions' of the period such as flags, ceremonies, and music, was harnessed to reflect a growing 'sense of identification' with a 'community and/or the institutions representing, expressing or symbolising it as a nation' (Hobsbawm and Ranger 1983: 11–12).

These issues will be fleshed out in this chapter as I examine money's role in the articulation of community and territorial borders with specific reference to the protracted development of a Canadian national currency, an idea that was introduced in the 1840s but not achieved until the mid-twentieth century. By explicating the deliberateness of state involvement in demarcating political and territorial monetary boundaries, and the insertion of this process into the national imaginary, I will call into question our assumption that the evolution of monetary organisation into national currencies has been natural or necessary.

Forging a Canadian national currency

Canada as case study

As with nation-states, it is possible to speak of national currencies in general terms, but the terms under which they are theorised rarely cohere with their actual formation (c.f. Smith, 1986). In this chapter, therefore, I focus specifically on the formation of a Canadian national currency. But let me be clear that I use Canada here as an example of the interrelationship of money and national identity, not as exemplary. Thus, as with many discussions of nation-states, there is both a generalisability and particularity about my discussion; the interpretations of iconography, for example, cannot be transposed to another context, although it is certainly the case that other national currencies reflect the state's efforts to forge certain national identities.

Canada offers a particularly useful example of the development of national currencies for the simple reason that it has had an interesting monetary history. As noted above, over a century passed between the introduction of the idea of a national currency and its actual implementation; while a Canadian mint opened in 1908 – and produced coin for all provinces but Newfoundland, which did not join Confederation until 1949 – it was not until the 1940s that Canada had a single, homogenous paper currency issue. Before that time, as I will illustrate in more detail below, all kinds of currencies were in circulation, issued by a number of individuals and institutions including governments, banks and merchants. The monetary system was further complicated by the country's enduring ties with Britain and proximity to the United States; no doubt the political, economic and cultural influences of these two leading monetary powers contributed to the late development of a Canadian national currency. These factors and others will be addressed in more detail below as I examine how a single, homogenous national currency arose from this monetary heterogeneity. To do so I will explore the ways that the formation of a national currency was implicated in both state-making and nation-building practices.

Money and state-making in Canada

In 1841, proposals were first introduced to enact a single government currency in the Province of Canada. The Province had just come into existence, a product of the unification of the British colony of Upper Canada and the predominantly French Lower Canada, and among the many issues facing the new government was how to resolve the financial difficulties arising from large debts (especially in Upper Canada), the lack of local capital from which to raise revenue and funds, and an 'excessive dependence upon the money markets in London, England' (Ryan 1995: 5). That the colony was just emerging from the financial crisis of 1837 made monetary problems especially pressing. A single currency, it was suggested, would help raise revenue internally as well as pay for public works, thus helping to remedy the new government's mounting debts (Watts 1972: 20). It was to this end that Lord Sydenham, the Province's first Governor General, proposed the establishment of the Provincial Bank of Canada which would issue and redeem notes, although not carry out other banking functions (Ryan 1995: 8).

Sydenham's proposals differed from other government initiatives into money matters precisely because he was suggesting that the state become solely responsible for the issuing of currency in the Province.[2] Thus while the proposed monetary reforms were designed to generate public revenue, they would also result in the homogenisation and standardisation of what was in effect a very complex monetary situation. Indeed, to understand the magnitude of Sydenham's proposals it is necessary to understand the great variety of formal currencies such as coins and notes that were then in circulation which would be aggregated by a single currency.[3] By the 1840s, when Sydenham introduced his proposals, paper monies were the most popular form of exchange as coin currencies were problematic for two main reasons. First, the coin in circulation was of diverse origin; by the eighteenth century, not only were French, English, Spanish and Portuguese coins in circulation, but also the Spanish-American dollar, which became the most important coin in North America (Haxby 1986: 28; Bank of Canada 1990: 6; Cross 1997: 23). The situation was equally complex in the early nineteenth century, for as one critic writing in the 1830s observed:

> The silver and copper coins we have in circulation are a disgrace to any civilised nation . . . All the antiquated cast-off rubbish, in the whole world, finds its way here, and remains. This Colony is literally the Botany Bay for all the condemned coins of other countries (quoted in Bliss 1987: 151).

Yet coins were not only problematic because of their diversity, but because they were continually scarce due to hoarding, rising merchant activity, and the need for specie to settle foreign accounts. By the early nineteenth century there were some domestic coins – merchant coins, bank tokens or 'sous' and provincial coppers – in circulation to ease these problems, but these were unreliable and insufficient to accommodate the expanding trade of the colony (Haxby 1986: 34).

These persistent problems with coin currencies, typical of colonial settler societies, enabled paper monies to become the most prevalent medium of exchange by the early nineteenth century.[4] Like coin, paper monies also had a long history in Canada, although their development was uneven. The first domestically issued paper currency was that circulated by the French Intendant, Jacques de Meulles, in Quebec in 1685 – the first paper money to be issued in North America. The money actually consisted of playing cards, cut into various sizes for the different denominations, and imprinted with the official seal. This playing card money, and its later incarnation as card money, was popular among the public (although less so with the French King), and continued to be circulated, off and on until the mid-eighteenth century. In addition, other more formalised government currencies, such as the French *certificat*, the *ordonnance*, and the *lettre de change* came into circulation in the early eighteenth century.

This whole monetary system, however, came crashing down in 1759 under the rule of Intendant Bigot. While Bigot had improved the monetary system by standardising and regulating the card money, he was also responsible for devaluing the paper currency to prop up his lavish and corrupt expenditures. Thus, just at the moment that the British acquired the colony from the French, the paper currency was almost worthless, with neither the French nor the British willing to redeem the currency at face value. The devaluation of paper currencies and their final redemption at a quarter of their face value, as well as the ensuing confusion and financial difficulties, dissuaded further use of paper currencies until the early nineteenth century. It was only in 1812, when the United States declared war on Great Britain, that Sir Isaac Brock sought to reintroduce paper currencies to what was then Upper and Lower Canada, since Canada's access to specie – which was primarily through the United States – was curtailed by the war just as preparations against American attack required additional military spending. Brock's Army Bills proved to be popular while they circulated, but more importantly, it has been suggested that their full redemption at the end of the war in gold and silver renewed the public's confidence in paper currencies and opened the way to the introduction of banknotes soon thereafter (McCullough 1984: 85).

Thus, in 1817, shortly following the full redemption of the Army Bills, the Montreal Bank (which was granted a charter as the Bank of Montreal in 1822), became the first bank to open and circulate notes. While the Montreal Bank's provision of new and sound currency did ameliorate the monetary situation in Upper and Lower Canada somewhat, it also added to its complexity in that its formation paved the way for the establishment of other banking institutions. The following year the Quebec Bank opened in Quebec City, and by 1825 banks were in operation in Lower Canada, Upper Canada, New Brunswick and Nova Scotia. The Bank of Montreal, as government agent, was the leading financial institution, but the banks were generally successful, so much so that their notes soon came to be the most prevalent medium of exchange. The number of banks continued to increase so that in the decade leading up to Sydenham's proposals, a record number of fifty-two banks had opened, in addition to the eight already in operation; many of these new banks, however, survived less than three years, lending further instability to the monetary system.[5]

Although banknotes were the predominant medium of exchange, there were also other paper currencies in circulation; some municipalities and local governments issued notes, but more important were the merchant notes or *bons* that made up a large part of the small change in circulation at this time (Bank of Canada 1990: 14). Merchant notes were particularly useful and prevalent during times of financial crisis; they had been quite common in the years following British conquest, and one merchant noted in 1792 that in settling a debt of £25 he received bills from twelve different people across Upper Canada (McCullough 1984: 77). After the War of 1812, merchant notes were again popular when they and American banknotes were the only paper currencies in circulation. But the heyday of merchant notes came during the financial crisis of 1837, just prior to Sydenham's proposals, when banknotes were made irredeemable in specie, and merchants such as the Molson family began to issue their own currency (seventeen years before they were to open their own bank). Although in response to their ubiquity legislation of the late 1830s and 1840s generally limited or prohibited these private issues in Upper and Lower Canada, merchant notes continued to persist, especially in areas not serviced by the banks where they could be found right up until the twentieth century (McCullough 1984: 247; Neufeld 1972: 166; Denison 1966: 350).

A final complicating factor in the monetary situation of the early nineteenth century, and especially during the financial crisis of 1837, was the circulation of a wide range of counterfeit currencies. There is evidence, for example, that Bank of Montreal tokens were frequently forged at this time (McCullough 1984: 102). But it was paper currencies that were especially prone to counterfeiting in at least three ways. First, and most simply, there were legitimate notes that were altered, either by changing the name of the bank on the note or by 'raising' the note so that it would appear to be of a higher denomination. This was usually done by cutting a counter for a higher denomination from the note of a failed bank and adhering it to a low denomination note of a legitimate bank. Secondly, facsimile copies were made of legitimate notes; from the crude hand-engraved note, to a photographic print of a real note sometimes supplemented with coloured ink, to notes produced on a printing press by letterpress, intaglio or lithography. Finally, there were the spurious notes issued by illegitimate banks, also known as 'phantom' and 'wildcat' banks, which had no intention of redeeming their notes. About a third of the banks that opened in the 1830s, for example, were fraudulent institutions. As this figure suggests, counterfeiting was not a minor problem; indeed, comparable estimates in the United States suggest that at mid-century about 40 per cent of the notes in circulation were counterfeit, with one estimate as high as 80 per cent (Nygren 1988: 135; Johnson, 1995).

Simply, as I have detailed, the monetary situation in the first decades of the nineteenth century was extremely complex, with hundreds of varieties of money in circulation – legitimate and illegitimate. In light of this heterogeneity, it is possible to comprehend how Sydenham's proposals for a single government note issue would have completely transformed the monetary system. A single currency would have standardised and homogenised the medium of circulation across the Province of Canada and centralised monetary responsibility into the hands of the new central government. As a result, the security of the money supply would have become greater in that 'phantom' or 'wildcat' banks would have been eradicated and in that the standardisation of money production and distribution would have in and of itself provided additional security.[6] Sydenham's proposals would thus surely have been of some benefit to the public. But benefits were equally to be had by the state. In that a single currency would have provided the government with a source of revenue, it would also have strengthened its financial standing, and consequently its political power. The state would also have benefited in terms of internal matters in that the accrued money was to contribute to public works and other infrastructural matters. Moreover, this shift with respect to the state's role and responsibilities would have furthered the public's dependence on the state, just as this dependence would have been increased through the public's reliance on the state for the supply of money, and its regulation, valuation and security.

The banks, however, rejected Sydenham's proposals as they stood to lose their issuing privileges, and his recommendation was defeated in the Legislative Assembly. But while a single currency did not arise in 1841, there were some initiatives made towards standardisation. That year a fixed unit of account was formally adopted in the Currency Act of the newly formed Province of Canada. There was some debate as to whether dollars or sterling should be adopted, and the government, merchant and banking authorities who responded to a survey on this matter were nearly evenly split between the two options. As a result, the Halifax money that was already prevalent as a unit of account in both Upper and Lower Canada was retained with some adjustments made to standardise the exchange rates (McCullough 1984: 103).[7] Although no new unit of account was decided upon, the process nevertheless had the effect of unifying the colonies, as once in place 'the value of a uniform currency soon became apparent', and 'nothing did more to promote economic unity, and therefore, to a considerable extent, political harmony between the naturally antagonistic sections of the new Canadian province' (McIvor 1958: 42).

Measures towards monetary standardisation continued in the late 1840s and early 1850s. Foremost among these was the move towards decimalisation. The need to homogenise the circulating currency (rather than simply the unit of account) was becoming more pressing with the growth of the Province. Customs collectors, for example, had problems establishing 'reasonable equivalents of value' for the multiple forms of currency that passed through their hands; also, there were often problems in redeeming the notes at the banks, some of them of questionable value (Piva 1992: 268). At the same time, the dollar was increasing in popularity; nearly half of those polled in 1841 had favoured the dollar, but its appeal was growing as trade links with the United States were expanding. Thus, the interest-bearing debentures issued by the government in 1848 were in dollar denominations (with their equivalent in sterling also inscribed in small letters) as were most of the banknotes in circulation. In 1851 representatives from the Province of Canada, Nova Scotia and New Brunswick agreed to hash out a common currency system based on the dollar. This was partly realised in 1853, after being delayed by the British government which was at the time trying to persuade its colonies to embrace a system based on pounds, shillings and pence; that year a compromise in the Legislature incorporated the pound, dollar, shilling, penny and cent as units of currency.

The point is not simply that the currency was being homogenised but that this was part of deliberate efforts to secure a domestic Canadian currency, especially in that foreign currencies were removed. Thus, in 1853, at the same time that the currency was standardised, all foreign coins (other than those issued by Britain) were made illegal tender (Helleiner 1996b: 14). By 1857, the dollar was firmly in place in the Province of Canada with stipulations that all government-related accounts be in dollars and cents, thus effectively doing away with sterling and Halifax money accounts (McCullough 1984: 110).[8] The adoption of the dollar as the medium of exchange was reinforced by the issuing of the first decimalised coinage for the Province of Canada in 1857, which was also a product of Francis Hincks's 'valiant efforts' to establish Canada's right to issue a national currency, in the face of the British Treasury which believed that 'the right to issue coinage and currency resided in the breast of the sovereign' (Bank of Canada 1990: 17).

In 1860, the idea for a single government currency was reintroduced by Alexander Tilloch Galt. His proposals followed on the financial crisis of 1857–59, the failure of two Toronto banks, and increased demand for government supervision of the banks just as 'difficulties in government finances made the prospect of a government note issue attractive' (McCullough 1984: 112). Galt, then Finance Minister and later Prime Minister, believed that currency 'properly belonged to the State' and proposed that a government currency be introduced and banknotes slowly withdrawn (Ryan 1995: 14). The banks, not surprisingly, resisted his proposals as they had Sydenham's, for again they stood to lose their note-issuing privileges upon the expiry of their charters. Galt's recommendations also failed. When Galt reintroduced his proposals in 1865 they were again unsuccessful, but in 1866, the passing of the Provincial Bank Act granted him some success. A government currency was introduced and the Province of Canada had its first issue of notes, to follow on its issue of interest-bearing debentures in 1848. With the introduction of the government currency, the banks were encouraged (but not obliged) to rescind their note-issuing privilege; only the largest bank, the Bank of Montreal, did so, in its capacity as official government bank. In total, over $4 million in Provincial notes were issued; only half of these notes actually circulated, however, for as they were legal tender they came to be used as part of a bank's reserve (McCullough 1984: 112–13).

These Provincial Notes were in effect the precursors of the present Canadian currency system, but while they marked the increasing role of government in monetary issues, the banks continued to issue notes. With Confederation in 1867 this began to change as the government 'assumed control of coinage and currency, banking, incorporation of banks, savings banks, bills of exchange and promissory notes, interest and legal tender, and the issue of paper currency, an arrangement which precluded provincial or local experiments with currency and banking' (Easterbrook and Aitken 1988: 462). First, in 1868 the redeemability of the provincial notes then in circulation was extended to Halifax and Saint John, in addition to Toronto and Montreal. Then, with the Bank Act of 1870 (revised slightly in 1871), a new Dominion of Canada government issue was authorised and that year notes for 25¢, $1 and $2 appeared, gradually followed by higher denominations. An important feature of this Bank Act, which sought to create a national currency, was that, for the first time, limits were imposed on the banknote issues; the government began to rescind the right of banks to issue notes for under $4. As a result, the lowest denomination notes – the $1 and $2 – which were used as 'hand-to-hand' currency by a large part of the population, moved solely into the hands of the federal government. A third policy was an extensive effort to remove all foreign silver coins from circulation (Helleiner 1996b: 5).

The decennial revisions to the Bank Act in 1881 further consolidated government control over note issues. Now all denominations under $5 became the sole responsibility of the state and all banknotes henceforth were to be issued in denominations divisible by five. As a result, the lowest denominations became increasingly homogenous and the monetary system as a whole became increasingly standardised with respect to what denominations were available. Later revisions to the banking act affirmed the state's growing appropriation of monetary control; while further restrictions to banknote issues did not come about until the formation of the Bank of Canada, the government continued to exert influence over the banks in ways that would contribute to the standardisation and even nationalisation of the currency. With the Bank Act of 1890, for example, banks were required to redeem notes at par in all of their branches across the country. Banks also became more national in scope as the largest banks, made larger still by the rush of mergers and acquisitions at the turn of the century, extended their branch networks across the country, from the Maritimes to British Columbia.

The First World War drew banks and state yet closer together, largely out of mutual necessity, so much so that 'Every branch of every bank had become a government agency' (Schull 1958: 122). As George Watts suggests in his history of central banking in Canada, the Finance Act put into place in 1914 'in effect constituted a highly permissive – if not an open-ended form – of central banking' (Watts 1972: 19). But it was actually only in the late 1920s that a small group of people began a real push for a national bank, prompted in part by criticisms of the financial system during the Depression and the belief in a centrally managed economy (Watts 1972: 16; Allan 1996: x).[9] The opening of a Canadian mint in 1908 certainly contributed to the idea of national monetary control. Moreover, at this time Britain was lending its support, and in fact actually encouraging, the formation of a central bank in Canada and throughout the empire. While this support for domestic banking appears to be a complete reversal of nineteenth-century British opposition to monetary independence for the colonies, the role of the Bank of England in the formation of a central Canadian bank belies precisely this same agenda; to maintain and exert monetary control throughout the Commonwealth, if not now through legislative control then at least through more subtle forms of suasion (Cain, 1996).

With the formation of the Bank of Canada in 1934 (which was made public in 1938), the *rapprochement* between the state, financial institutions and monetary control was sealed as the state consolidated its hold over monetary issues. As a result, the note-issuing privileges of other institutions were gradually rescinded – still to much opposition by the banks which were given ten years to reduce their notes in circulation to 25 per cent of their paid-up capital. In 1944 their right to issue notes was completely withdrawn except with regard to foreign issues, a right that was also removed in 1954. Thus, with banknotes out of circulation by 1950, the third series of notes issued by the Bank of Canada in 1954 in effect became the first series of notes to be issued as a single, homogenous and national currency. Sydenham's early attempts to centralise and standardise the currency were thus finally realised.

Money and nation-building in Canada

The iconography on the Bank of Canada note issue of 1954 differed significantly from that of earlier issues. Stylistically these notes were more streamlined, but while their modern look was important, even more significant was how the subject matter became more distinctly Canadian. Indeed, with the 1954 series, the Bank of Canada made a deliberate effort to create 'a prominent Canadian dimension [. . .] by replacing the earlier allegorical figures with Canadian landscapes' (quoted in Millard 1993: 28). Each denomination within the series featured a specific, and even identifiable Canadian landscape, based upon photographs from actual locations.[10] These scenes were as follows: the $1 features the Western prairie and sky of Saskatchewan; the $2 a rural scene from Richmond, Quebec; the $5 a stream, deciduous conifers, and rolling hills located at Otter Falls at Mile 996 of the Alaska Highway in Northern Canada; the $10 the Rocky Mountain peak of Mount Burgess in Alberta; the $20 a winter scene in the Laurentian hills; the $50 the crashing seas on the Atlantic coast; the $100 a mountain valley and the Okanagan Lake in British Columbia; and the $1000 a rural idyll from Anse St Jean, Saguenay River, Quebec (Allan 1996; Millard, 1993).

Clearly, an effort has been made to represent key Canadian landscapes from across the country; the rugged mountains to the North and West, the sprawling prairies, rural landscapes from central Canada as well as the Laurentians, and the crashing shores associated with the Maritime provinces – with Quebec places, representative of rural and central Canada, slightly over-determined. Even some of the seasonal variations associated with the country are alluded to in the contrast provided by the winter scene in the Laurentian mountains. More importantly, as Laura Millard points out, unlike earlier images, a human presence on the landscape is visible on only half the notes, and even then there are no traces of urbanisation or industrialisation; this itself draws upon the idea of an impenetrable natural world that had long been a trope in the Canadian national imagination, typified, for example, in the paintings of the Group of Seven (see, for example, Frye, 1971; Atwood, 1972; Osborne, 1992). In typical Canadian style, much as Brian Osborne has described Canadian representations of landscape around the turn of the century, the nature that is depicted on the 1954 Bank of Canada notes is 'bucolic rather than heroic, mundane not mythological' (Osborne 1992: 167).

The 1954 Bank of Canada notes thus evoked Canadian nationalism in a number of ways: by depicting landscapes specific to and typical of Canada; by making the representation of Canada's regions representative; and by drawing upon the kinds of natural images that have long fed the Canadian imagination. Yet although the 1954 series could be said to mark a peak in the use of nationalist iconography, some kinds of national symbols had in fact appeared much earlier on government currencies, and earlier still on private note issues. Even the images on the first Canadian monies were proto-nationalist, featuring beavers and maple leaves, icons that have been associated with Canada since the seventeenth century (Marquis 1985: 32–3). The first paper notes produced (but not circulated) by the Canadian Banking Company in 1792, for example, featured a small vignette of a beaver gnawing at a stump, while the first decimal coins issued for the Province of Canada in 1857 each featured wreaths of sweet maple. Notably, these images persist today; the beaver, which was also the symbol used in the first Canadian stamp designed by Sandford Fleming and issued in 1851, may be found today on the five-cent coin and the maple leaf is depicted on the one-cent coin, as well as, of course, on the Canadian flag.

While there are early traces of local iconographies, it is really with the advent of state-issued currencies that we can chart the deliberate manipulation of national symbols. Certainly the interest-bearing provincial debentures issued in 1848 aspired to be distinctively Canadian. In a letter written to the engraving company of Rawdon, Wright, Hatch and Edson on June 5, 1848, Sir Francis Hincks gave the following instructions with regard to the steel plates for the $10 and $20 denominations:

> The large bill might have the Royal arms the other some Canadian design. They should be numbered on both sides of the Bill & the designation should [be] both in French & English, as usual in Canada notes. Perhaps you could furnish me with a design at once & let me know how soon the order could be executed (quoted in Ryan 1995: 10).

In a postscript to the letter, Hincks adds that he is enclosing a rough design for the $10, as well as the Royal Arms which were to appear on the $20, and the Provincial Arms for the $10; these are in fact the images that appear on these notes, with Britannia featured next to the Provincial Arms on the $10.

Canadian recognition on these notes is minimal but clearly the desire was there to grant the notes some local significance; moreover, the move to underline British imperial connections is perhaps, in light of the move towards dollar denominations, an attempt to differentiate Canada from the United States. Similarly, ten years later, the first Canadian decimal coins were struck and decorated, as noted above, with wreaths of maple leaves; a portrait of Queen Victoria also appeared on the obverse of each coin. With the emergence of formal government note issues around the time of Confederation, Canadian national identity becomes even more prevalent. This rise of nationalism on the currency accorded with the more general swelling of popular nationalism in the last third of the nineteenth century and the beginning of the twentieth century, a phenomenon evident in, but not restricted to, Canada. As Jim Burant observes, Victorian society in general came to see visual imagery as one of the most conducive media for the communication of nationalist beliefs (Burant 1984/85: 121). In Canada, it was a nationalism that was for a long time, and especially for the elite, framed in terms of membership within the British Commonwealth; the currency reflected this anglophilia in that local images were juxtaposed with portraits of the monarchy, symbols of Britannia, etc.

Thus, as had earlier state-issued currencies, the notes of the Province of Canada that began circulating in 1867 – just a few months before Confederation – depict local and imperial icons. Members of the British royal family, for example, were featured on some of the Province of Canada denominations, including youthful portraits of Queen Victoria (two versions), the Princess of Wales and Prince Albert, much as they were also featured on the banknotes of the time (as well as on stamps and coins). A significant departure from early notes, however, was that historical figures important to Canada's founding and settlement are also depicted on the notes of 1866. This was of critical importance as a statement for nation-building, for it is commonly recognised that one of the first steps in the construction of national identity lies in the delineation of a national genealogy, so that the present can be anchored in a 'viable past', which by 'linking the dead to the not yet born' can project a national consciousness into the future (Friedman 1992: 207; Alonso 1988: 50).

The $1 Province of Canada note issued in 1866 is a case in point, and of especial interest in that, as the lowest denomination, it would have had the widest circulation. Here we have the figures of Samuel de Champlain and Jacques Cartier surrounding the Coat of Arms of the Province of Canada.[11] Both Champlain and Cartier were crucial to the founding of Canada. Cartier has been accredited as the first European explorer of the St Laurence, claiming Gaspé for France in 1534, while Champlain, recognised as founder of New France, established the first permanent European settlement on Canadian land in 1608 near present-day Quebec City. The $50 of this series communicates and reinforces a similar narrative of discovery, exploration and settlement (combined with commerce); here, a male allegorical figure of Mercury holds a map of British North America, with harbour, ships and trains in the background.

Some of these themes and images are reiterated in the Dominion of Canada notes, the first series of paper money of the newly Confederated provinces, issued in 1870. While Champlain is dropped from the new $1, Cartier is retained, here featured alongside an allegorical woman who, in the presence of cherubs, points to Canada's place on the globe. The images on the $2 issued the same year present a quite different iconography, but they too also play into a nationalist narrative (Figure 2.1). Here the historical figures commemorated are General James Wolfe and the Marquis de Montcalm who fought one another on the plains of Abraham outside Quebec City in 1759. The battle was of enormous consequence for with Wolfe's victory, the title of Canada passed from the French to the British. That both Wolfe and Montcalm died in the battle made it possible for both leaders to be commemorated as heroes, and thus for both French and British peoples to be recognised.

The vignette that is placed between Wolfe and Montcalm on the $2 provides a further insight into the mechanisms of nation-building; here we have a vignette of a Native chief atop a bluff watching an oncoming train – a not-so-subtle reference to how the indigenous peoples were cast in the role of onlookers to an encroaching

Figure 2.1 Front image of the Dominion of Canada $2 note of 1870. (National Currency Collection, Bank of Canada. Photographer James Zagon, Ottawa.)

'civilisation'. This was not the first time this kind of motif had been featured on Canadian paper money; the $5 note of the Provincial Bank of Canada issued in 1856, for example, features a vignette of three Native people overlooking a town and its billowing smokestacks, again from their vantage point on a bluff. Indeed, the scene resonates with lithographs published in the first half of the nineteenth century, produced in both Upper and Lower Canada, that employ the same compositional use of the bluff and thus communicate a hierarchy of social order in their compositional division of native and settler, nature and civilisation (Poulter 1990: 13). In each of these examples, Natives are cast apart from the action, the encroaching future, while they – their past and their traditions – are disappearing. What is of interest here is how the vignette on the paper money effectively communicates how this encroaching 'civilisation' is implicated in a sense of burgeoning national identity and linked to the growing territorialisation of the state-issued currency.

The rhetoric of nationalism not only infused the images on the notes, but also their production. Certainly, it was within this rhetoric of nationalism that the Canadian-based British American Bank Note Company (BABNCo) was formed.[12] While domestic security over the production of money was one of the motivations behind the BABNCo's formation, in their promotional materials they appealed more directly to nationalist sentiment to gain banknote contracts from the government and the banks. A circular with specimens of engravings distributed in 1870 asked for 'your support for the enterprise in which we have embarked; we hope it may commend itself as one that proves good to the Country as well as in the advertisement of Art as in the encouragement of Home Industry' (Vaughan 1956: 5). Similarly, if we jump to the twentieth century, the formation of the Canadian Mint in 1908 was also thought to be an expression of Canadian nationalism, although in this case an expression of independence from Britain, not the United States. The minister of Public Works and Government Services, Alfonso Gagliano, who was also responsible for the Canadian mint, observed at the time that the government 'believed that by holding government and banking reserves in its own coinage it could take control of national finances. From the outset, therefore, the Mint was a symbol of young Canada's growing confidence, and its emerging independence from Britain' (Reback 1998: 776).

But to return to the nineteenth century, it was in the 1870s that the BABNCo became solely responsible for the Dominion of Canada notes issues, and images relating to national identity became a central feature of the money. These images were not just apparent on notes of low denomination. The $50 note, issued in 1872, features the same Mercury holding the map of British North America as had appeared on the $50 of the Province of Canada notes, while the $100 note of 1872 introduces an image of the newly constructed Parliament Buildings in Ottawa. But it would have been the representations on the lowest denomination notes that would have been especially important, for as noted above, it was in 1870 that the right of the banks to issue denominations of $4 and under was rescinded. The $1 and $2 government notes with their images of Cartier, Wolfe and Montcalm would have been the only notes of these values to circulate legitimately.

In 1878 the Dominion of Canada issued a second series of low-denomination notes. For the first time on government notes, living people are featured; the current, and popular, governor-general the Earl of Dufferin on the $2 and his wife the Countess on the $1. When the government issued a $4 note for the first time in 1882, having rescinded the right of banks to issue notes of under $5 just two years earlier, again it was the governor-general who was featured, the Marquis de Lorne, who held the position from 1878 to 1883. The continued appearance of governors-general on Canadian paper money right into the twentieth century reflects the Canadian nationalist sentiment of the time and was enmeshed with imperial associations, a sentiment whereby many nationalists believed that it was not by severing ties with Britain, but ironically by reinforcing them, that Canada would come into its own. Indeed, this second series of Dominion of Canada notes signals a move away from recognition of the French role in the formation of the country and an intensification of connections with the British home government. Jacques Cartier is relegated to the back of the note with a vibrant vignette of his arrival at Quebec, and while the image retains a sense of the role of the French in the country's history, it is notable that it is not longer the figure of Cartier that is celebrated but the act of discovery.

This emphasis on all things British remains the predominant focus on the remaining Dominion of Canada notes, with portraits of governors-general and their wives and members of the Royal family persisting until the first issue by the Bank of Canada in 1935. Amongst these symbols of empire emerge some more realist images particular to Canada including logging, fishing, and agricultural scenes: the Parliament buildings; the Sault Ste. Marie locks; and the Inter-continental Railway. The first Bank of Canada issue in 1935 brought with it some significant changes, although in some ways the new notes retained the spirit of earlier notes in that each of the denominations from $1 to $100 depict a portrait of a member of the Royal Family. The reverse of the notes, by contrast, signalled a return to the classical and allegorical images that were so popular in the first decades of the nineteenth century, with a few modern twists; among the themes reproduced were agriculture, transportation, electric power and modern inventions (Figure 2.2). As a result, the new notes were not particularly Canadian, indeed, the series as a whole has been described as 'foreign' (Millard 1993: 32). Only two notes stand out – the highest denominations, the $500 and the $1000 – in that they depict the former Prime Ministers, Sir John A. Macdonald and Sir Wilfred Laurier. And yet, now we know there was a set of essay notes produced which were even more overtly Canadian. As Hillel Kaslove describes, essay notes found in the Nova Scotia Public Archives indicate that other Canadian historical figures such as Sir Georges Etienne Cartier and Sir Charles Tupper were also contemplated for the notes (Kaslove, 1990). We can only surmise that the use of portraits of royalty not only reflected a persistent association of Canadian nationalism within imperial allegiance but also the significant role played by the Bank of England in the formation of the Bank of Canada. While nationalist sentiments were behind the formation of Canada, clearly the expression of this sentiment was restricted to certain forms as it struggled to articulate itself.

Figure 2.2 The French Canadian $2 note of 1935. (National Currency Collection, Bank of Canada. Photographer James Zagon, Ottawa.)

Simply, then, the first issue of the Bank of Canada (and a very similar issue two years later) expressed a kind of Canadian national identity but only began partly to differentiate itself from earlier government issues. As already noted, it was only with the 1954 note issue that the iconography becomes more distinctly Canadian. Yet even in 1954, the colonial influence lingers – as it does today – in that Queen Elizabeth II appears on the face of the notes. Nevertheless, the 1954 series of notes had a much clearer Canadian iconography than ever before. One reason for this shift may be the fading importance of British empire in the 1950s, as Canada became further consolidated with the entry of Newfoundland into Confederation, and as the Prime Minister Louis St Laurent began to 'firmly if discreetly' remove signs and symbols of British bonds from the public scene (Morton 1983: 221).

But while British affiliations were on the wane, it should also be recalled that the 1954 Bank of Canada issue was also the country's first series of notes issued as a single, national currency, with the right to issue notes now completely rescinded from the banks. Monetarily, therefore, this note issue marked the advent of a distinct Canadian currency, and the national symbols appear particularly appropriate. Indeed the landscape images on this series of notes thus not only reinforce the connections between the official forms of the state and the historical role of landscape and nature in the Canadian imagination, but they also – especially in their comprehensive inclusion of distinct Canadian regions – reflect the territorial cohesion brought about by the Bank of Canada notes. That every issue of the Bank of Canada since 1954 has retained the focus on landscapes that are representative of the country's regions, as have recent commemorative coin issues (with significant variations in the actual images used), reinforces the importance of this kind of iconography to the Canadian imaginary, and indeed is perhaps the only kind of iconography that can accommodate growing regional factionalism (Figure 2.3).

Figure 2.3 Front image of the Bank of Canada $2 note of 1954. (National Currency Collection, Bank of Canada. Photographer James Zagon, Ottawa.)

More importantly, however, the landscape images strengthen the terms under which national currencies have been characterised in the Canadian context where, without a common religion, language or ethnicity, nationalism has become mediated through a 'civic ideology', that is, 'a framework of ideas and aspirations which expresses itself in allegiance to certain public policies and institutions' (Francis 1997: 10). It needs to be emphasised that what is taking place here is not only the projection of certain kinds of nationalist sentiments on the national currency, but that these appeals to this kind of national identity are among the best means available to the Canadian state through which it can produce and reproduce its own legitimacy. Simply, not only does the Canadian currency convey nationalist iconographies, but it is these iconographies that lend support to the construction of the Canadian state and thus, through an elegant tautology, the iconographies on the national currency affirm and even justify the organisation of money along national lines.

Conclusions

In this chapter I have set out the long process of national currency formation in Canada in terms of both state-making and nation-building. What I have sought to underline is the role that money plays in the integration of people, places and institutions into the distinctive, social, territorial and political unit known as the nation-state. In so doing, I have very much attended to the dominant narratives associated with the formation of national currencies and have paid little attention to the porousness of either the actual circulation of money or its myth-making capabilities. For despite the narratives of homogeneity, national currencies are never completely pure. In Canada, for example, not only have foreign currencies circulated across national borders – particularly American currencies, from the seventeenth century until the present day – but Canadian currencies have also circulated outside of Canada, as they did right up until mid-century in the Caribbean. Moreover, I have only briefly touched upon the ways that the construction of national identity expressed on Canadian currency has been exclusionary, dependent, for example, upon a notion of progress and 'civilisation' which delayed the participation of Native peoples within a monetary economy, but also in the sense that the representations on the national currency have masked the economic marginalisation of the Quebecois population who have historically been under-represented by Anglo-Canadian banking institutions (Rudin, 1985).[13]

That national currencies were and are porous, however, only reinforces my general point that national currencies are deliberately invented, just as national narratives have been shown to be social constructions by attending to their partiality and ambivalence (see, for example, Bhabha, 1990; Renan, 1990). But rather than focus on the permeability of national currencies, in this chapter I have sought instead to underline the fragility of their construction. As I have outlined, more than one hundred years elapsed between the first proposals for a single, government currency in Canada and its actual realisation. The Canadian context thus provides an example of how the centralisation of money into the hands of the state necessitated a variety of manoeuvres including standardisation, homogenisation, and the increasing presence of the state in the daily life of the public.

As I described above, in Canada early measures towards this centralisation included the removal of foreign currencies and 'ghost' monies. Units of account and rates of exchange then became standardised of the Province of Canada, with the aim, in part, to facilitate trade across the expanding territory. In the 1870s, the right to issue notes was gradually rescinded from the banks as the government became responsible for the lowest denomination notes which circulated as 'hand-to-hand' currency among the public. These processes were furthered with the setting up the Canadian Mint in 1908 (which became independent of the Royal Mint in 1931) and the formation of the Bank of Canada in 1934, which were both understood as expressions of state sovereignty and increasing monetary independence.

The consolidation of a single, national currency in the 1950s was an expression of internal and external territorial coherence, reinforcing national borders both domestically and with respect to foreign powers. But if the circulation of money along national lines is an expression of territorial coherence, so too have the images of money advanced official ideologies of the nation-state to itself as well as to outsiders. Generally speaking, the innovations to printing technology in the mid-nineteenth century made possible the mass production and dissemination of paper currencies and states began to take advantage of this popular medium to communicate certain kinds of national identities. Indeed, the fact that currencies are, in most cases, regularly modernised through the issuing of new designs, means that they are an effective communicator of national identity for the state for they are able, as I have described above, to accommodate and assimilate the subtle shifts that national identities undergo over time.

The actual exchange of money furthered the bonds between transactors expressed through the iconography in that the public increasingly came to participate in a national economy. Moreover, by way of their everyday transactions, the public became further linked to and even dependent upon the state and its official forms of national currencies. Indeed, the power of the representations on money lies not only with the iconographies that they communicate, but also with the fact that these narratives forge links between the past, present and future. They do so through the daily routines and practices associated with money (c.f. Hobsbawm and Ranger 1983: 11–12). Indeed, money is necessarily performative, that is, money needs to be exchanged – symbolically or materially – in order to be effective. Moreover, this exchange is invariably repetitive and routine within the context in which the money circulates; for money needs to move (or have the potential to move), from person to person, in order to be effective. Thus it is through exchange that individuals are linked within specific territorial communities, communities that are not limited to the geographies of the participants in any given transaction (although these are important too), but also to the wider networks – of people and institutions – upon which these transactions depend. Finally, money draws together the past, present and future, not only as discussed above, through the iconographies that it depicts, but also in the sense that all money is a form of credit, a promise to pay in the future (Ingham, 1996).

Money thus becomes a medium through which social consensus, social integration and territorial borders are produced and reproduced. The use of the official currency, therefore, becomes a daily affirmation of the nation-state; a legitimisation of its authority, its jurisdiction and the history that it projects (cf. Renan 1990: 11). Clearly, therefore, money has functioned as 'an artefact of boundary-drawing activity' in that it draws together people and territory, nation and state (Bauman 1992: 677). National currencies have not just emerged as a product of nation-state formation, but have been a constituent element in the articulation of state sovereignty (Helleiner 1996a: 11, 16). Moreover, the formation of national currencies are clearly not the 'natural' or inevitable evolution of monetary organisation, but deliberately 'forged' through strategies and policies relating to state-making and nation-building.

Acknowledgements

Many thanks to Jim Duncan, Paul Glennie, Derek Gregory, Andrew Leyshon, Brian Osborne, and Nigel Thrift, as well as the participants in the historical-geography seminar organised by Aidan McQuillan, who have commented upon some of the ideas in this chapter as they have appeared in other forms. Especial thanks go to Eric Helleiner whose work in this area has been formative to my own thinking. The Bank of Canada has graciously supplied the illustrations for this chapter. Finally, I am grateful to the Social Sciences and Humanities Research Council for supporting this research.

Notes

1 My discussion of state-making phenomena is greatly indebted to the framework set out by Helleiner (1996a, 1996b).
2 The idea of a government note-issuing bank, for example, had already been broached by William Hamilton Merritt in 1824 (Ryan 1995: 5). Merritt's proposal, however, unlike Sydenham's, did not require that the government notes replace those issued by the banks.
3 There were also, of course, numerous informal currencies such as wampum and barter that added to the monetary complexity of the time. For more information on these see, for example, Bank of Canada (1990) Shortt (1986), and McCullough (1984).
4 As Agnes Dodd illustrates, settler colonies faced two specific monetary difficulties: (1) establishing a currency that would circulate domestically rather than be used to settle foreign accounts and (2) designing a currency that could accommodate rapid economic and industrial growth (Dodd 1911: vi). Paper monies, which were easily produced and had only a local circulation, addressed both these difficulties.
5 At the time of Sydenham's proposals there were still at least twenty-one legitimate banks issuing notes functioning in Lower Canada, Upper Canada, Nova Scotia and New Brunswick.
6 The raising or altering of notes may also have become more difficult as the notes of failed banks would be less available.
7 The Halifax currency system was actually a 'ghost' unit of account that had no corresponding medium of exchange and which was based on a fixed exchange rate between British sterling and the dollar.
8 Nova Scotia soon followed by adopting decimal currency in 1859, New Brunswick and British Columbia in 1860; Newfoundland in 1864 and Prince Edward Island in 1871 (Haxby 1986: 38).
9 Although there were some earlier gestures in this direction: in 1913, W.F. MacLean proposed a central bank modelled on the Imperial Bank of Germany in the House of Commons; in 1914 two leading bankers also made a similar proposal for a central bank; and in 1917 and 1918, E.L. Pease of the Royal Bank of Canada (Watts 1972: 20).
10 With the acknowledgement that 'Because of some of the technical and aesthetic considerations of Bank note design, the illustrations may vary slightly from the actual locations depicted' (Millard 1993: 28).
11 A portrait of Cartier had earlier appeared on a 10-shilling stamp issued in 1851. Both images were based on an 1837 painting by F. Riss.
12 Until the 1860s, most Canadian security documents were produced by American engraving companies, and increasingly, by specialised American banknote companies, although some small note issues were produced locally, and some Maritime notes were produced by engraving companies in Britain. For a more detailed examination of the production of Canadian paper money and monetary iconographies see Gilbert (1998a, 1998b).
13 There are, of course, other groups that are excluded that I have not mentioned at all; women, for example, have continually been objectified on currencies as symbolic representations of fertility and fecundity, but seldom granted status as economic or national subjects (see Hewitt, 1994; McGinley, 1993).

Bibliography

Allan, Walter D., ed. (1996) *The Charlton Standard Catalogue of Canadian Government Paper Money*, 9th edition, Toronto: The Charlton Press.

Alonso, Ana Maria (1988) 'The effects of truth: re-presentations of the past and the imagining of community' *Journal of Historical Sociology* 1 (1): 33–57.

Anderson, Benedict (1992) *Imagined Communities: Reflections on the Origin and Spread of Nationalism*, London and New York: Verso.

Anderson, Patricia J. (1991) *The Printed Image and the Transformation of Popular Culture, 1790–1860*, Oxford: Clarendon.

Atwood, Margaret (1972) *Survival: A Thematic Guide to Canadian Literature*, Toronto: Anansi Press.

Bank of Canada (1990) *The Story of Canada's Currency*, Ottawa: The Bank of Canada.

Bauman, Zygmunt (1992) 'Soil, blood and identity' *The Sociological Review* 40 (4): 675–701.

Bhabha, Homi (1990) 'Introduction: narrating the nation' in Homi Bhabha, ed. *Nation and Narration*, London: Routledge: 1–7.

Bliss, Michael (1987) *Northern Enterprise: Five Centuries of Canadian Business*, Toronto: McClelland and Stewart.

Burant, Jim (1984/85) 'The visual world in the Victorian age' *Archivaria* 19: 110–21.

Cain, P.J. (1996) 'Gentlemanly imperialism at work: the Bank of England, Canada, and the sterling area, 1932–1936' *Economic History Review* 49 (2): 336–57.

Cross, W.K (1997) *The Charlton Standard Catalogue of Canadian Coins*, Toronto: The Charlton Press.

Denison, Merill (1966) *Canada's First Bank: A History of the Bank of Montreal*, vol. I, Toronto and Montreal: McClelland and Stewart Limited.

Dodd, Agnes F (1911) *History of Money in the British Empire and the United States*, London, New York, Bombay and Calcutta: Longmans, Green, and Co.

Dodd, Nigel (1994) *The Sociology of Money: Economics, Reason and Contemporary Society*, New York: Continuum.

Dodd, Nigel (1995) 'Money and the nation-state: contested boundaries of monetary sovereignty in geopolitics' *International Sociology* 10 (2): 139–54.

Easterbrook, W.T. and Hugh G.J. Aitken (1988) *Canadian Economic History*, Toronto: University of Toronto Press.

Francis, Daniel (1997) *National Dreams: Myth, Memory and Canadian History*, Vancouver: Arsenal Pulp Press.

Friedman, Jonathan (1992) 'Myth, history, and political identity' *Cultural Anthropology* 7 (2): 194–210.

Frye, Northrop (1971) *The Bush Garden: Essays on the Canadian Imagination*, Toronto: Anansi Press.

Gellner, Ernest (1983) *Nations and Nationalism*, Oxford: Blackwell.

Giddens, Anthony (1990) *The Consequences of Modernity*, Stanford, CA: Stanford University Press.

Gilbert, Emily (1998a) *Circulating Values: Cultural and Historical Geographies of Nineteenth-Century Canadian Paper Money*, Unpublished PhD thesis, the University of Bristol.

Gilbert, Emily (1998b) '"Ornamenting the façade of hell": iconographies of nineteenth-century Canadian paper money' *Environment and Planning D: Society and Space* 16: 57–80.

Gupta, Akhil (1992) 'The song of the nonaligned world: transnational identities and the reinscription of space in late capitalism' *Cultural Anthropology* 7 (1): 63–79.

Haxby, James A. (1986) *Striking Impressions: The Royal Canadian Mint and Canadian Coinage*, Canada.

Helleiner, Eric (1996a) 'Historicizing territorial currencies: monetary structures, sovereignty and the nation-state,' paper presented at the 1996 Annual Meeting of the International Studies Association, San Diego, 17–20 April.

Helleiner, Eric (1996b) 'Money and the nation-state in North America', paper presented for the Annual Meeting of the Canadian Political Association, St. Catharines, Ontario, 2–4 June.

Hewitt, Virginia (1994) *Beauty and the Banknote: Images of Women on Paper Money*, London: British Museum Press.

Hewitt, Virginia (1995) 'Soft images, hard currency: the portrayal of women on paper money' in Virginia Hewitt, ed. *The Banker's Art: Studies in Paper Money*, London: British Museum Press: 156–65.

Hobsbawm, Eric (1990) *Nations and Nationalism Since 1780: Programme, Myth, Reality*, Cambridge: Canto.

Hobsbawm, Eric and Terence Ranger, ed. (1983) *The Invention of Tradition*, Cambridge: Cambridge University Press.

Ingham, Geoffrey (1996) 'Money is a social relation' *Review of Social Economy* 54(4): 507–29.

Johnson, David R. (1995) *Illegal Tender: Counterfeiting and the Secret Service in Nineteenth-Century America*, Washington and London: Smithsonian Institution Press.

Kaslove, Hillel (1990) 'Bank of Canada essay notes for the 1935 issue' *Canadian Paper Money Journal* 26(4): 102–10.

Leyshon, Andrew and Nigel Thrift (1997) *Money/Space: Geographies of Monetary Transformation*, London and New York: Routledge.

McCullough, A.B. (1984) *Money and Exchange in Canada to 1900*, Toronto and Charlottetown: Dundurn Press.

McGinley, Christina L. (1993) 'Coining nationality: woman as spectacle on nineteenth-century American currency' *American Transcendental Quarterly* 7(3): 247–69.

McIvor, R.C. (1958) *Canadian Monetary Banking and Fiscal Development*, Toronto: The Macmillan Company of Canada Limited.

Marquis, Yvon (1985) *La monnaie canadienne*, Toronto: The Unitrade Press.

Millard, Laura (1993) 'Images of Canada: Canadian bank notes' *Border/Lines* 28: 30–5.

Morton, Desmond (1983) *A Short History of Canada*, Edmonton: Hurtig Publishers Ltd.

Neufeld, E.P. (1972) *The Financial System in Canada: Its Growth and Development*, Toronto: MacMillan.

Nygren, Edward J. (1988) 'The almighty dollar: money as a theme in American painting' *Winterthur Portfolio* 23 (3): 129–50.

Osborne, Brian S. (1992) 'The iconography of nationhood in Canadian art' in Denis Cosgrove and Stephen Daniels, eds, *The Iconology of Landscape: Essays on the Symbolic Representation, Design and Use of Past Environments*, Cambridge: Cambridge University Press: 230–54.

Piva, Michael (1992) 'Government finance and the development of the Canadian state' in Allan Greer and Ian Radforth, eds, *Colonial Leviathan: State Formation in Mid-Nineteenth-Century Canada*, Toronto: University of Toronto Press: 257–83.

Poulter, Gillian (1990) 'Representation as colonial rhetoric: the image of "the Native" and "the *habitant*" in the formation of colonial identities in early nineteenth-century Canada' *The Journal of Canadian Art History* 16(1): 11–26.

Reback, Marilyn (1998) 'Canada's mint: making change for the future' *The Numismatist* 111(7): 775–7.

Renan, Ernest (1990) 'What is a nation?' in Homi Bhabha, ed. *Nation and Narration*, New York: Routledge: 8–22.
Rotstein, Abraham and Colin A.M. Duncan (1991) 'For a second economy' in Daniel Drache and Meric S. Gertler, eds, *The New Era of Global Competition: State Policy and Market Power*, Montreal and Kingston: McGill-Queens University Press: 415–34.
Rousseau, Lyse and Emanuel Darnell (1997) *Darnell Stamps of Canada*, Montreal: Darnell Publishing.
Rudin, Ronald (1985) *Banking en français: The French Banks of Quebec, 1835–1925*, Toronto: University of Toronto Press.
Ryan, Christopher D. (1995) 'The quest for a government paper currency in the Province of Canada' *The Canadian Paper Money Journal* 31: 5–23.
Schull, Joseph (1958) *One Hundred Years of Banking in Canada: A History of the Toronto Dominion Bank*, Vancouver: Copp Clark.
Shortt, Adam (1986) *Adam Shortt's History of Canadian Currency and Banking 1600–1880*, Toronto: The Canadian Bankers' Association.
Smith, Anthony D. (1986) 'State-making and nation-building' in John A. Hall, ed. *States in History*, Oxford: Basil Blackwell: 228–63.
Tomasko, Mark (1996) 'Security for the world' *Friends of Financial History* 55: 17–25.
Vaughan, A. Murray (1956) *Ninety Years of Security Printing: The Story of the British Bank Note Company Limited: 1866–1956*, Ottawa: British Bank Note Company.
Watts, George S. (1972) 'The origins and background of central banking in Canada' *Bank of Canada Review* 16–26.
Weber, Max (1978 [1920s]) *Economy and Society*, 2 vols. eds, Guenther Roth and Claus Wittich, Berkeley: University of California Press.

3 'The Scotch hate gold'

British identity and paper money[1]

Matthew Rowlinson

Introduction

In Volume 3 of *Capital*, Marx argues that a contradictory understanding of money is endemic to capitalism. Obscuring the social origins of value in labour, the economic theorists of capital, with what Marx satirises as 'beautiful . . . dualism', throw themselves alternately into the error of believing that the extension of credit can create value and into that of believing that value is an intrinsic property of legal tender:

> As long as it claims to treat 'of capital,' enlightened economics looks down on gold and silver with the utmost disdain, as the most indifferent and useless form of capital. As soon as it deals with banking, however, this is completely reversed, and gold and silver become capital *par excellence*, for whose preservation every other form of capital and labour have to be sacrificed. (Marx 1981: 707)

In our own time, with the passing of the gold standard and the progress of late capitalism toward the monetisation of all values, Marx's beautiful dualism has become a pluralism. In calculating the money supply central banks now use several different figures, each including assets of different degrees of liquidity, depending on the purpose of the calculation.[2]

The apparently homogenous money supply of the modern nation-state thus comprises a number of heterogeneous circulations. Arguing from the early history of the first modern monetary system, that of Britain, I shall in what follows explain how this became so. In so doing, I will take a hint from another passage of Marx, in which he satirises the money-faith of capitalism as one that, like Christianity, tends to fall into schism:

> The monetary system is essentially Catholic, the credit system essentially Protestant. 'The Scotch hate gold.' As paper, the monetary existence of commodities has purely a social existence. It is *faith* that brings salvation. Faith in money value as the immanent spirit of commodities, faith in the mode of production and its predestined disposition, faith in the individual

> agents of production as mere personifications of self-valorizing capital. But the credit system is no more emancipated from the monetary system as its basis than Protestantism is from the foundations of Catholicism. (Marx 1981: 727)

Marx's fugitive reference to Scotland's proverbial preference of credit money to legal tender reminds us that within Britain even in the mid-nineteenth century, the inhomogeneity of currency was most visible in regional and national disparities, both in the medium of circulation and in banking practice. It would be an error to regard these disparities as relics of an era prior to the unification of Britain in a single state and to the hegemony of sterling. On the contrary, I shall show that their appearance was part of the process that made of sterling a national currency, and that made it possible to mobilise patriotic sentiment in its support. Scotland's national preference for paper money dates from after the abolition of the Scottish state and of its currency. We shall see that the formation of national identities around money in general depended on the circulation of money substitutes and was consequently, paradoxically, attended by variant and contradictory understanding of what is and is not money. The national identities thus formed themselves therefore appear as containing contradictions – as we shall see when we discuss how resistance to legal tender coin could come to be a mark of Scots difference while also marking the Scots bourgeois as arguably the paradigmatic British subject.

Determinate trajectory of paper money: the bill of exchange as mediator of heterogeneous specie circulations

My argument will concern a period of British history extending from the early seventeenth century to the late eighteenth in which the inland circulation of money for all purposes involving larger sums than retail trade came to be carried out primarily by paper instruments of credit. These instruments – bills of exchange and banknotes – were both introduced to Europe as devices by which different forms of specie could be exchanged with one another. It is thus a significant historical irony that they, and not the specie moneys coined by states, were the original forms from which modern national currencies evolved. National currencies evolved as it were in the interstices between the legal tender currencies of Europe's pre-national states. In demonstrating this, I will be less concerned with the economic function of bills and notes than with their discursive structure. As directions and promises to pay, bills and notes were in their origin discursive performances. Their function as money or money-substitutes depended on complex effects of address, signature, reference, and reception. They bore value constituted as travelling between subjects whom they represented as signifiers – signatory, addressee, bearer, and so forth – and situated in a formally determinate though open-ended series of relations to one another. Which is to say that the paper note or bill in general occupies a position in a chain of signifiers, in which it also situates the subjects who use it. It is for this reason that it constitutes social relations within which can be formed subjects identified by class, place, and nation.

For centuries, the most important form of credit in European trade was the bill of exchange, whose use began in twelfth-century Italy but did not become general among English merchants until the late fourteenth century at the earliest (De Roover 1953: 110–11). The earliest English court cases establishing bills' enforceability as debts date from the beginning of the seventeenth (Scammel 1968: 25–6). Two fundamental points about the circulation of bills distinguish it from that of the metallic currencies in which they were ultimately redeemed. The first is that a bill circulates in a given direction from one specific place and time to another. The circulation of a coin may be subject to temporal and spatial limits – it may only be current within certain political boundaries; it will wear away as it circulates – but within these limits its value appears to be immediate and inalienable. A bill, on the contrary, offers value at a time and place different from those of the transactions in which it takes part; indeed, its value derives partly from its capacity to articulate and set a price on the differences of time and place that bring it into being. The second crucial point about the circulation of bills is that it articulates and sets a price not only on the abstractions of time and place, but also on that of money itself.

I shall expand on these claims. Well before the seventeenth century the bill of exchange had become the principal means by which traders in one European country would pay debts contracted, for instance by the purchase of goods, in another. The bill was thus an instrument for the transferral of debt between places, and consisted in its most basic form of an instruction from a creditor, who drew the bill, to another person, who accepted it, to pay a specified sum to a third person at a given place and time. Once the bill was accepted, it became a legally enforceable obligation on its acceptor. (For a fuller definition and history, see Scammell 1968: 21–2.) Bills' capacity to transfer debt between places depended upon the confidence with which they could be bought and sold by traders at either end of the route along which they circulated. To give a very simple example, if a London trading house owed money for commodities purchased in Amsterdam, it would normally not export specie to pay the debt, but would seek to buy a bill accepted in Amsterdam from another London house that had sold goods there. This second house would sell a bill drawn on Amsterdam to the first at a price agreed upon in London, whereupon it would be returned across the North Sea to be redeemed by one Amsterdam trader upon another. This simple example considerably understates the complexity of the system as it evolved during the seventeenth century. By 1651, when the practice is mentioned by John Marius, it had become usual in London for bills to circulate by endorsement (De Roover 1953: 112). The circulation of bills by endorsement also appears in the Low Countries between 1610 and 1640 (De Roover 1953: 99), and somewhat later in other parts of the Continent. No longer simply the means of making a payment in a single transaction, the bill eventually became a negotiable instrument that could be repeatedly bought, sold, or exchanged for commodities, bearing a value determined by the state of trade between the place where it was sold and that on which it was drawn.

No later than the end of the seventeenth century, then, there existed in each major European trading centre a well-defined market in bills drawn on the others. These markets were the beginning of the world-wide currency market as it exists today. They were also, more importantly, the first instance of a form of circulation that came over the next two hundred and fifty years to define the norm for money in general as a circulation of paper credit in principle redeemable in legal tender coin, but in which in practice coin only appeared as a symptom of a major imbalance or of the imminent breakdown of the system. Eighteenth-century writers on the subject, such as David Hume and Adam Smith, assert that the price of bills on foreign currencies was in the last instance regulated by the cost of exporting coin – that is to say that a company in England would not choose to pay a foreign debt by buying a bill when it could pay the same debt more cheaply by sending coin abroad (Hume 1955: 64; Smith 1976: 499). The cost of foreign bills thus could not rise beyond a theoretical maximum determined by the cost of transport. But it seems reasonable to assume that the system was in most cases self-regulating before such exports became widespread. If we use the same simple bipolar model of trade that I sketched out a moment ago, we can imagine the nature of a circulation between London and Amsterdam when trade between them was perfectly in balance, i.e. when the same value of commodities passed between them in each direction over a given period of time. Under such conditions, the bills drawn in each city upon the other would also normally balance one another out; that is to say, the number of people in London seeking to buy bills on Amsterdam in order to buy goods there would normally equal the number who had such bills to sell as a result of export transactions.

A similar situation would prevail in Amsterdam with respect to bills on London. In such a situation, the exchange between London and Amsterdam was said to be at par, which is to say that currency could be exchanged between them through the medium of bills at precisely the same rate – barring whatever commissions accrued to the bill dealers – as if the moneys represented by the bills were actually to encounter one another at a single place and time. Bills exchanged at par may thus be said virtually to abolish the spatio-temporal distance between the markets on which they are drawn.

But such exchanges did not by any means always operate at par. To understand why this was the case, we may imagine the effects of a trade imbalance in which, for instance, London over a period of time imported a greater value of commodities from Amsterdam than it exported to it. Under such circumstances London would experience a shortage of bills payable in Amsterdam, while in Amsterdam there would be a surplus of bills payable in London. The result would be that the price of the former would rise while that of the latter would drop, which would have the effect of making it cheaper for the Dutch to buy a given value of goods in England, and more expensive for the English to buy goods in Holland, and would thus tend to drive the exchanges back into balance without the need for any transfers of coin.

The theoretical case of an exchange at par should thus not be seen as the norm for a market in foreign bills. Far from mediating exchanges of currency as if there were no distance between their spheres of circulation, bills in any given market sell at a price that depends on the place where that market exists. A bill market is above all a situated market; it articulates an inhomogenous space and renders visible the differences between the various currencies on which it is based. In other words, the bill market makes it possible for the relative prices of, say, Dutch and English currencies to differ depending on whether they are exchanged in London or Amsterdam. And though this difference may in the last instance be limited by the cost of transporting and negotiating actual coin, in the short run it will be determined by, indeed will express the differing conditions of production, distribution, and consumption within the respective spheres of the two currencies' circulation.

The bill thus articulates the difference between two places – that where it is sold and that on which it drawn. Its essential function is to travel, by however circuitous a route, from one to another. As long as it circulates, it marks itself out as alien, foreign to an ideally homogenous space of circulation of the domestic currency in which, for instance, every English pound is equivalent to every other, wherever and by whomever it is held. (In fact, I shall argue below that this ideal of monetary homogeneity was a late development, which arose as a consequence of the bill's capacity to articulate a difference between domestic and foreign currencies.) And in so circulating, I suggest, the bill structured the subjects who dealt with it as themselves situated – as sharing a delimited space with other subjects with whom they also in principle shared an immediately negotiable currency, and distinct from foreign subjects with whom they traded through the medium of bills.

In the late seventeenth century such a sense of situatedness would not necessarily be associated with a nation or state. For one thing, not all currencies in that era were national; and for another, national currencies, particularly those of Britain, were not at that time homogenous in the sense in which I have been using the term. Nonetheless, I would want to argue that it would have been at least proto-national, and provided part of the foundation for the development in the eighteenth century of a specifically national bourgeois identity – this in spite of the fact that in eighteenth-century Britain itself, trade in foreign bills was widely seen as inimical to national loyalty. Here for instance is Joseph Harris, Assay Master of the Mint, writing in 1757:

> [The bill of exchange] was the greatest security to merchants both as to their person and effects, and consequently the greatest encouragement to commerce, and the greatest blow to despotism, of any thing that ever was invented. For, by this sort of correspondence, merchants can imperceptibly convey away their effects when and wherever they please; and this they will never fail doing, if they are in any wise molested or threatened with danger. But at the same time, that this is so beneficial to commerce, and to liberty, both in certain degrees, inestimable blessings; it weakens the attachments, and, as I may say, the allegiances of tradesmen to their mother-country.

> And I should not, for many reasons, chuse to have my abode where the chief property and the chief rule was in mercantile hands. (Harris 1966: 416)

Such views were commonplace throughout the eighteenth century, particularly though not exclusively among English Tories. That they proved quite wrong is in brief the salient fact for which this chapter seeks an explanation.

Why national currencies are abstract: the heterogeneity of specie money

A bill represents the command of a certain quantity of abstract exchange value payable at a certain place. What I have described as the situatedness of bill markets, and hence also of those who participate in them, already implies my second point about a bill circulation, that it materialises an abstract unit of exchange and constitutes it as a commodity. The drawer of a bill puts pounds in circulation, and constitutes the pound as a commodity that can change place with other commodities in its own person, as Marx might put it. For virtually all of English and Scots history in the medieval and early modern eras, the pound existed only as an abstract unit of account, equivalent at different times to varying quantities of the heterogeneous metallic currencies actually in circulation. Neither the royal monopolies on minting the precious metals that had prevailed in most European states since the feudal era, nor the legislation against the export of coins and precious metals enacted in England as elsewhere during the sixteenth century, ever succeeded in endowing the pre-national dynastic state with a uniform material medium of circulation.

To make a short story of an extremely complex history, the heterogeneity of early modern metallic currencies may be said to have been of three kinds: of origin; of material; and of quality. The idea of a national circulation is in fact in fundamental conflict with the basic principle of a currency minted from precious metal, which is precisely that the metal in question can be exchanged anywhere. Precious metal coin thus necessarily will and actually did circulate across state borders. René Sédillot provides a historical overview:

> The very concept of monetary frontiers is a modern idea. More correctly, although countries had thought for a long time of isolating their currencies, they have really managed to do so only recently. In ancient times, such as the feudal age and the era of monarchies, all currencies, *de facto* and often *de jure*, circulated everywhere. Greek, Persian, and Roman coins circulated well beyond the limits of the cities or the nations which had minted them. The English Esterlin [a silver penny, first minted in the thirteenth century, at the rate of twenty to the pound weight of metal. The term 'sterling' is probably derived from its name] . . . was accepted all over the Continent, which struck imitations and flooded England with them. Saint Louis paid his ransom in Bezants. The ancient trade fairs of the old province of Champagne were the favorite rendezvous of all contemporary currencies. Even during the

> centuries of triumphant mercantilism, payments were made in Austria with French Ecus, in France with Spanish Pistoles, in Spain with British Guineas, in England with Venetian Zecchini, and in Venice with Turkish Piastres. (Pick and Sédillot 1971: xv)

The coins Sédillot refers to in this last sentence were all of gold, and the transactions he mentions all involve payments across state borders.[3] After such transactions were completed, the coins in question might be reminted to the local standard or might circulate in their original form. Which of these things happened would depend on a number of factors, including the charges imposed by the mint for coining bullion into legal coin – a charge known as seignorage – the general balance of trade, and the degree of credit accorded to local coins relative to that given foreign ones. In a region where local coin was old, worn, clipped, or widely counterfeited, for instance, foreign coin would rapidly come to circulate at a premium. The composition of the currency would thus vary from region to region at different times, and it is difficult to generalise. It seems, though, that Spanish gold coins were widely acceptable throughout Europe at least until early in the seventeenth century. The English silver currency of shillings and pennies seems in England to have remained largely unmixed with foreign coin, at least after 1600.[4] English silver did, however, circulate widely abroad. Rice Vaughan asserts that in 1622 at Frankfurt '*English* shillings were current at a higher rate fineness for fineness and weight for weight, than their own *Dollars* coined in that town, so as in those times there was great profit by transporting *Dollars* out of Francfort, *Ryders* out of Holland, and *French* Crowns out of *France*, and carrying them back again coined in *English* coins' (Vaughan 1966: 49).

In countries lacking the precious metal to remint their currency as it degraded over time, however, the situation was different. There foreign coins would tend to circulate alongside the deteriorating local issue. This was clearly the case of Scotland in the seventeenth century; after the removal of the court to London in 1602, Scots coin was largely neglected. When at the Act of Union in 1707 the old Scots currency was abolished and its coinage called in to be reminted to the English standard, the total of the silver received was worth £411,117 10s. 9d. sterling, of which only £239,036 13s. 9d. was Scots coin. The remainder comprised £40,000 of English and £132,080 17s. of foreign coin (Graham 1911: 19). In fact, it seems likely that English units of account were used to reckon in this heterogeneous mass well before England and Scotland were actually united. By 1700, the Scots pound had come to be worth 1/12 of the English; a Scots shilling was thus equivalent to an English penny. In 1704 the Bank of Scotland began to issue what it recorded in its accounts as one pound notes, even though they bore on their face the denomination of £12 Scots (Graham 1911: 16). Ironically, the Bank of Scotland's one pound notes continued to bear this denomination well into the eighteenth century, for years after the shadow of a currency they ostensibly represented had been legally abolished (Figure 3.1).

If in Scotland the connection of the pound as an abstract unit of account with the coin actually in circulation was thus an extremely tenuous one, the situation in

Figure 3.1 1716 Bank of Scotland note. (Courtesy of the Governor and Company of the Bank of Scotland.)

England was in some respects clearer, as the pound could be described as a unit of account comprising twenty of the shillings that had been minted from different amounts of silver since 1504. But it should be recalled that silver was not the only legal tender in England, which also issued a baffling variety of gold coins at different weights and degrees of fineness. The value of these coins was set in the first instance by royal proclamation, which regulated the price at which the mint would buy gold for coining – this price tended to be set above the prevailing international value of bullion, as a way of discouraging its export. However, during the seventeenth century gold gradually rose to circulate at a premium over its proclaimed value, owing to the increasingly worn condition of the silver coinage with which it effectively competed. Thus in the second year of James I, the price of gold at the mint was raised by an eleventh, with the consequence that the value of the gold sovereign was raised by proclamation from 20s. to 22s., that of the angel from 10s. to 11s., and so forth. After the Restoration, James II issued a new gold coin at 20s., the guinea, so called because it was originally minted of gold imported from West Africa. Writing in 1695, however, William Lowndes observes that the guinea had circulated at a premium ever since it was first issued, and had by his time risen to a value of as much as 30s. (Lowndes 1966: 217).

Even in a country like England, then, whose circulating coin had largely issued from its own mint, that coin in the seventeenth century comprised several different circulations, whose relative values were subject to wide fluctuations. The consequence was necessarily a growing tendency in commercial practice for money to circulate in abstraction from any specific money commodity. The basic point was recognised by Rice Vaughan in the 1630s: 'The sum of a pound sterling is not restrained to any solid *species*, but is rather imaginary and abstracted from the matter guided according to the uncertain valuation of the *species* of Money, wherein the payment is made' (Vaughan 1966: 90–1). Vaughan is here discussing the disadvantage of payments in coin whose value varies; it must be remembered that the value of coin could be affected not only by changes in the market or at the mint, but also if it became worn or was clipped around the edges for bullion. English silver was not subjected to general re-minting between 1601 and 1696; by the time of the recoinage that began in the latter year, the metallic value of the silver in circulation had been reduced by almost half from the standard at which it had been minted (Shaw, 1967: 103). The rise in the value of the gold coinage as expressed in silver during the course of the century was largely the result of this depreciation.

The reminting of the silver currency from 1696 to 1699 did not solve the problem. The coin was reminted to its old standard; in effect the total face value of the silver circulation was reduced by close to half. The resulting shortage of coin was exacerbated by the fixing of the value of the gold guinea in relation to the new silver currency at 21s. 6d., which was reduced to 21s. in 1717. Even at this second value, and *a fortiori* at the first, gold was overvalued in relation to silver in terms of prevailing international rates. It thus proved profitable to export silver coin from England and use it to buy gold in foreign markets; the gold could then be imported back into England and minted into guineas at the proclaimed rate. The result was that shortages of silver were endemic in England for the next hundred years; moreover, because silver coin was exported to be sold as bullion, and not at face value, those coins that did remain in circulation were predominantly those that were under weight. By 1776, as Adam Smith observed, the replacement of silver with gold and the dilapidated state of the silver currency had effectively reduced silver to a token currency whose value was only sustained by its convertibility into gold (Smith 1976: 46–7). In effect Britain had passed on to a gold standard, a fact that was recognised by the parliamentary committee on the price of bullion in 1810 and ratified by the legislative enactment of a gold standard for the pound in 1817.

This enactment ended a twenty-year period during which, owing to the economic demands of the war with France, Britain's domestic circulation had been based on inconvertible paper, during which time the value of the pound had effectively not been tied to that of a precious metal. In one sense, therefore, the legislation of a gold standard and the issuance of the gold sovereign as the standard material form of the pound marked a return to an earlier currency regime. But in a larger historical view it marked the culmination of a two centuries-long process of the emergence of a single abstract unit of national currency from the heterogeneous and international metallic circulation of the early modern era.

We have already seen that as early as the 1630s Rice Vaughan recognised in the pound an abstract unit of account distinct from any particular form of specie. Commerce over the next two centuries developed a wide variety of ways to represent this abstraction and to circulate it independently of its material support.

The adoption of the gold standard did not reattach the pound's value and channels of circulation to those of some other commodity; rather, it transformed gold itself into an abstraction, which provided a single standard that enforced the mutual convertibility in Britain of all forms of currency and debt.

Inland bill of exchange as mediator of heterogeneous regional circulations

The historical process of the abstraction and rationalisation of British currency on a national basis, I re-emphasise, was not itself an abstract one. The abstraction of circulating credit from the metallic circulation was a material practice, or rather the sum of many material practices, which I have already argued had as one of their effects the reshaping of the space of circulation itself. We have already seen how international bills of exchange served to articulate and indeed to commodify the differences between their places of issue, at which they were sold, and their eventual destination, at which they operated as promises to pay. The effect of the international bill was to establish in London a circulating pool of obligations payable in pounds. It is not difficult to see how this circulation would come to extend beyond London, and come to mediate England's domestic trade as well as its trade with foreign countries. Merchants in England's provincial towns, wishing to purchase goods in London, would learn that they could avoid shipping specie by purchasing a bill payable in London using a bill of their own. In turn, ideally, their bill would be bought by a London merchant needing to make a payment in the provinces. For the circulation of commodities by means of bills to operate really efficiently, there needs to be a well-developed market in bills at both ends of any given transaction; such markets seem to have appeared throughout Britain during the period with which we are concerned.[5] John Marius, writing in 1655, asserted that inland bills had existed in England for the preceding 24 years (Nevin and Davis 1970: 11); in Edinburgh, there was a market in bills by 1660 (Smout 1963: 117). By 1721 Charles King in *The British Merchant* was able to describe as typical a complex series of transactions involving a textile wholesaler in London, retailers and tenants in Wiltshire, a retailer and a weaver in Norwich, and an importer in London, between whom payments could be made entirely by means of bills without any transfer of specie (King 1721, vol 3: 115–17). By the mid-eighteenth century, then, we may assume that the bulk of domestic commerce in Britain was transacted by means of bills.

Inland bills thus extended the sphere in which pounds could circulate as an abstraction of the legal-tender currency until it encompassed every major trading centre in Britain. Out of an heterogeneous metallic currency, then, the bill circulation articulated a homogenous national standard of exchange value. Even as it did so, however, it also articulated a new heterogeneity based on minutely calculated differentials of space and time. The function of a bill, I recall, is fundamentally to defer payment. For a metallic currency whose tender in Britain constituted by law an immediate discharge of debt, it substitutes a promise to pay at a specified time and place different from those at which it is issued. The spatio-temporal difference between the location where the bill is given in payment and that where it will become payable determines its value at any given moment. A bill payable at a future date, say thirty days, is naturally worth less than its face value. More importantly for my purposes, the value of a bill in any given market depends on the place where it will become payable. We have already seen how the price of international bills of exchange fluctuated in response to imbalances of trade between the countries among which they circulated. Precisely the same thing happened within Britain between different bill markets. In *The British Merchant*, King thus describes in a theoretical example how, if in the trade between London and Norwich, London were to purchase more in Norwich than it sold there, the result would be that bills on Norwich would be at a premium in London while those on London would be at a discount in Norwich (King 1721, vol. 3: 116–18). The trading surplus that King imagines Norwich as experiencing with respect to London probably reflects the conditions of trade at the time he wrote, when Norfolk was a major producer of textiles that were mostly shipped to the capital for processing or resale to other parts of the country. Other cities, particularly those that relied on London for supplies of manufactured and imported goods, would experience the opposite condition. The exchange with London seems for instance to have been against Edinburgh for most of the eighteenth century and to have become more so in times when imports to Britain rose in price.

Inland bills in the eighteenth century thus on the one hand articulated a single standard of value for the commodities they circulated; on the other they also articulated and to some extent determined the regional heterogeneity of this abstraction's material representatives. Bills on London, Norwich, Wiltshire, Edinburgh, and so forth expressed their value in a single unit of account, but they circulated along different trajectories to their ultimate destinations, a fact that was itself reflected in their price at any given time and place. The highly localised nature of bill markets partly reflected the highly localised circulation of the paper money for which bills were usually exchanged – a matter about which I shall have more to say below – but in some instances the local circulation of bills in fact rendered paper money unnecessary. We've already seen that a bill consists of an instruction addressed by the person who draws it to another person, who accepts it, and in so doing agrees to pay a specified sum to a third person at a specified time and place. This third person, the bill's payee, receives it as a promise of payment. On receiving a bill, a payee could hold it until it came due; more normally, the payee would either sell the bill at a discount to a bank or bill-dealer, effectively raising a short-term loan using it as security, or use it as money by giving it in exchange for commodities. In either of these two latter cases, the payee would transfer the bill and the debt it represented by endorsing it.

This last point is crucial to understanding the geographical specificity of a bill circulation. If when the bill fell due its original acceptor could not pay it, the debt would fall on its original drawer. If the drawer could not pay, it would fall in turn on each of the bill's endorsers. The debt represented by the bill thus became progressively more secure as it circulated, since with each successive transaction in which it changed hands it acquired another guarantor. For this reason, in some areas bills added to their original function of mediating long-distance trade that of serving as the principal local currency. Such a currency, I re-emphasise, was of necessity local, both because the value of bills is necessarily contingent upon their geographical location and, probably more importantly, because the credit of a bill is supported by the credit of its signatories. As they circulated, bills would link their successive holders in local networks of mutual obligation and credit. The most notable local bill circulation of this kind was in Lancashire, where after the collapse of a major early issue of banknotes in 1788 they were for many years viewed with suspicion (Ashton 1953: 41). Only a minority of Lancashire banks thereafter attempted a note issue, and Bank of England notes began to come into circulation only after 1797. As late as the middle of the 1820s, nine-tenths of the business of the Bank of Manchester was done in bills, and only one-tenth in gold or Bank of England notes (Ashton 1953: 39).

Determinate trajectory of paper money: the banknote

In most other areas of Britain – though not of Ireland – however, the bulk of the local commercial circulation by the end of the eighteenth century was in notes issued by regional banks. The practice of issuing banknotes in Britain began with the goldsmiths of London and Edinburgh, who from the early seventeenth century had doubled as changers of money, owing to their expertise in weighing and assaying precious metals. In the course of time they also came to function as moneylenders and also, especially after 1640, to take in coin and plate on deposit. For these deposits they would issue receipts, which gradually came to circulate as a means of payment in the place of the specie that they represented, functioning in effect as paper money. By the end of the Commonwealth, many members of the goldsmiths' guild in London were effectively in the business of large-scale finance (Nevin and Davis 1970: 15–32).

Though both are fundamentally instruments for the transfer of debt, banknotes differ from bills in certain crucial respects. To begin with, they are payable to bearer, which is to say that they can pass from one person to another without endorsement – a fact that in England, though not in Scotland, led to legal questions regarding their enforceability as debts (Graham 1911: 4–5). Further, they are normally payable on demand, rather than at a specified date; in principle, therefore, they will circulate at face value rather than at a discount reflecting the time left until they fall due. Finally, and most importantly for my purposes, unlike bills, which are drawn and paid by different persons, a banknote is a promise to pay that is redeemable only by the issuer. Consequently, while the trajectory of a bill's circulation is necessarily directed from its place of issue to a destination elsewhere, a banknote's trajectory must always be circular, returning it at the end to its point of departure. Credit money in the form of notes was in fact the first kind of money for which the term 'circulation' is truly a proper one – and indeed, the *OED* lists the first uses of 'circulation' and 'circulate' with respect to money as occurring in 1684 and 1691 respectively, a fact that may reflect the specific effect of note issue on economic discourse, or possibly the larger transformation in the monetary topography of Britain which I have argued began in the seventeenth century.[6]

The last decade of the seventeenth century saw the establishment of the first two institutions in Britain designed from the first to act as banks – the Bank of England and the Bank of Scotland, chartered by their respective parliaments in 1694 and 1695. Both were chartered as joint-stock companies whose partners' liability was limited to the amount of their investment. In England that investment took the form of a loan to the government, in return for which the bank was granted a perpetual monopoly on joint-stock banking; the Bank of Scotland, which was prohibited by its charter from lending money to the government, was granted a monopoly only for twenty-one years. The difference of these charters was to prove highly consequential in the development of banking in England and Scotland over the succeeding two centuries. In Scotland, the Bank of Scotland was by 1750 competing with two other chartered banks, the Royal Bank of Scotland and the British Linen Bank. Alongside these chartered banks operated ten or so private banks, which for the most part did not issue notes of their own but made loans in the notes of the larger joint-stock banks. Finally, by 1750 the chartered banks began to experience competition from joint-stock banks operating in trading centres outside Edinburgh without the protection of limited liability. These banks, which invariably issued notes, were to be in the second half of the eighteenth century the boom and bust sector of Scots banking.[7]

The consequence of the existence of competing note issues in Scotland was that the larger banks were unable to drive each other out of business and were eventually forced to accept one another's notes. Scotland thus enjoyed a national circulation in which the notes of all the major banks passed current everywhere north of the Tweed and indeed for some distance south into the English border counties. Competition between the banks to get their notes into circulation moreover led them to supply Scotland's chronic lack of coin by issuing notes in small denominations. We have seen that the first one pound note was issued in Scotland in 1704; in the 1750s not only banks but small merchants and shopkeepers began issuing notes, in some cases for amounts of less than a shilling. Notes for less than a pound were banned in 1765, but it remained the case that in Scotland paper formed a larger fraction of the total money supply than anywhere else in Europe. Smith estimated that in 1776 the circulation of Scotland was £2 million, of which no more than a quarter consisted of gold and silver (Smith 1976: 316).

In England, the Bank of England's monopoly was interpreted until the nineteenth century as prohibiting the formation of any bank with more than six partners. In consequence the issues of England's regional banks remained small and for the most part impossible to exchange with one another. English banknotes were rarely issued for less than five pounds and thus did not, as in Scotland, play a part in retail transactions, circulating rather in wholesale transactions among merchants and producers. More importantly, as they could not be exchanged at any bank other than that which issued them, their sphere of circulation remained limited to the immediate environs of the city or market town in which that bank was located. The Bank of England itself did not attempt to push its circulation outside London, where its notes mediated transactions between national and international traders and in the national money market. Whenever one of its notes did appear in the provinces, it would be returned to London for payment by the first bank into whose hands it fell.

By the end of the eighteenth century, then, the paper money of Britain consisted of a patchwork of distinct regional circulations. As the Earl of Liverpool complained in his 1805 *Treatise on the Coins of the Realm*:

> the Notes of . . . country Bankers have credit only within a certain extent or district; if a traveller passes from one district to another, he must provide himself with the Notes of other Bankers which have credit within the district on which he is entering; and an inconvenience to which travellers have hitherto been subject, in passing from one small independent state on the continent to another, is experienced by those who travel through Your Majesty's dominions, in passing from one district to another. (Liverpool 1966: 352–3)

Paper money transactions, even more than those involving bills, were thus in their very nature situated in a particular place. The participants in such transactions identified with one another – one accepts paper money on the assumption that there are others like oneself who will also accept it. And such regional or – in the case of Scotland – national identifications could be mobilised in the interests of bankers. The most notable instance occurred in 1826, when the British government proposed to abolish one pound notes, which in Scotland at the time made up 60 per cent of the paper circulation. Sir Walter Scott, who was at this time heavily in debt to the Edinburgh banks, published a series of letters in defence of the Scots pound note, and more generally of a regionally heterogeneous paper circulation. Here is Scott arguing that Britain's strength depends on the diversity of the nations that comprise it, and that that diversity is properly represented in its paper money:

> Would the British empire become stronger, were it possible to annul and dissolve all the distinctions and peculiarities, which, flowing out of circumstances, historical events, and difference of customs and climates, make its relative parts still, in some respects, three separate nations, though intimately connected into one empire? . . . For God's sake, sir, let us remain as Nature made us, Englishmen, Irishmen, and Scotchmen, with something like the impress of our several countries upon each! We would not become better subjects . . . if we all resembled each other like so many smooth shillings. (Scott 1841: 402–3)

Scott's Romantic Toryism leads him to see 'Nature' not in an inalienable human essence, which could be figured as the metal of a coin, but in the variables of history, landscape, and culture that 'impress' themselves upon the subject. The figuration of nationality as an 'impression' borne by money could refer either to the stamp of a coin or to the printed legend of a note; it nonetheless remains significant that this deployment of nationalism in defence of a particular material form of money should have been attached to paper rather than to metal currency.[8]

The regional nature of British banking was reflected in the variety of capitals that it employed. In different areas landed property, profits on mercantile or industrial capital, securities based on private or government debt, and a variety of other kinds of wealth could provide the capital that enabled a bank to begin issuing notes. But in their economic function, British banks in the eighteenth and early nineteenth centuries were to a remarkable extent as one. From the outset, their principal business was the issuance of short-term loans, which were transacted by the purchase at a discount of bills of exchange. Merchants or producers who had given commodities in exchange for a bill, if they needed cash immediately, would sell the bill at a discount to a bank, which would pay in its own notes. Under normal circumstances, then, banknotes did not represent a bank's fixed capital, but the value of a bill for which they had been exchanged. And the bill, in turn, represented and was in theory secured by the value of the commodities for which it had originally been given. These would typically have circulated out of the area in which the bill and the notes encountered one another at the same time as the bill circulated into it. Within any regional circulation, then, banknotes represent the exchange value of commodities that circulate elsewhere.

The heterogeneous paper circulations of eighteenth- and early nineteenth-century Britain thus *mediate* transactions that are in their very nature place-specific, and structure their users in local networks of obligation, credit, and mutual identification. But paradoxically these currencies *represent* a capital that is precisely not local and indeed has no specific place that is proper to it, since bills of exchange in their nature represent the value of commodities that are still in circulation.

The point may be clearer if we look at paper money not in terms of what it represents but in terms of its function. A bank can sustain a local paper circulation only on the condition that it is always ready to exchange its own notes for money that can be used elsewhere. The heterogeneous British paper currencies therefore articulated not only their differences from one another, but also their identity as *different instances of a single abstraction.* I have claimed that these currencies, as they passed from hand to hand, installed in their users regionally specific forms of class identity; to this claim we must add that in so doing regional notes nonetheless remained oriented towards another circulation external to their own, with respect to which they function as a sort of place-holder.

For most of the three-century history of British paper money, the abstraction whose place it holds could legally be compelled to appear at any time in the form of gold. But I have argued that the history of abstract units of exchange value is crucially distinct from that of legal tender coin, and that the nature of their circulation and the sites at which they become visible were determined by the formal characteristics of the paper instruments in which they found their earliest embodiments. The identification of monetary abstractions with particular regions, and ultimately with particular states, was occasioned by the trajectories of circulation that characterised credit money and not by those of coin.

Conclusion: national currency as the mediator of heterogeneous circulations and identities

It is thus apt that nationalist sentiment during the era of high capitalism typically mobilised around currency in the form of credit money rather than that of legal tender. The paradigmatic British instance occurred in February of 1797, when the Bank of England found that owing to the loans it had made to the government to pay for the war against France, its gold reserves had diminished to the point where it could no longer guarantee the convertibility of its notes. Afraid to suspend payment on their own account, the Bank's directors met with Pitt, the Tory Prime Minister, and asked him to intervene. He agreed to do so, and on Monday the 27th an order of the Privy Council was issued prohibiting the Bank from making any further payments in gold. It was immediately clear that no other financial institutions had the resources to do what the Bank could not, and in consequence the entire paper circulation of Britain at once became inconvertible. The result was an extraordinary series of displays of the class solidarity of the regional bourgeoisie, which manifested itself throughout as loyalty to Britain. On the afternoon of the 27th a meeting was called at the Mansion House of the City of London. I quote Cobbett's scathing account:

> consisting of *Merchants*, *Bankers*, and others, the Chairman being the Lord Mayor, whose name was Brook Watson, who then or very soon afterwards, filled the lucrative office of *Commissary General to the Army*, and who was, a very few years after that, made a *Baronet*. The persons assembled on this occasion proclaimed their resolution *not to refuse* bank notes in payment of any sums due to them, and to use their utmost endeavors *to make all their payments* in the same manner. (Cobbett 1815, vol. 1: 227).

In its commendatory report the following day, the *Times* congratulated the meeting's participants on their 'patriotism and loyalty' (Feb. 28, 1797). Over the next few days similar meetings took place in trading centres all over Britain. On Wednesday the news reached Edinburgh; Sir William Forbes, the city's leading private banker, describes in his memoirs how he met privately with representatives of all of the other Edinburgh banks and agreed with them that there was no alternative but to stop payment. Then followed a meeting 'of the principal inhabitants', at which 'a resolution was immediately and unanimously entered into by those present to give every countenance and support to the Edinburgh banks – including our firm – by receiving their notes in payment with the same readiness as heretofore, and a handbill to that effect was instantly circulated over Edinburgh, and inserted in all the newspapers' (Forbes 1860: 83).

These meetings assembled the networks of subjects whose regional identifications I have argued were supported by the interchange of local notes. It was necessarily these local notes that the meetings supported. Nonetheless, the use of banknotes was everywhere represented as testing a generalised British loyalty, as a contemporary print by James Gillray makes clear (Figure 3.2). Published on

Figure 3.2 James Gillray, etching, 1797. Henry C. Bohn folio, 1851.

March 1, the print shows John Bull deciding to accept banknotes in spite of the blandishments of the Whig MPs Sheridan and Fox, whom Gillray represents as French sympathisers.

Gillray's cartoon suggests, as well, the class basis of the campaign to support the paper circulation. The participants in that campaign were men who had assets in various forms of paper, whose negotiability they had an obvious interest in maintaining. The campaign did nothing for the mass of the population who bought and sold goods and earned wages with small sums of coin, and who discovered in the immediate aftermath of the stoppage of payment that coin had disappeared from circulation. After his account of the public meeting at Edinburgh, William Forbes describes the scene he encountered when he returned to his bank:

> Our counting-house, and indeed the offices of all the banks, were immediately crowded to the door with people clamorously demanding payment in gold of their interest-receipts, and vociferating for silver in change of our circulating paper. . . . They were deaf to any argument, and although no symptom nor threatening of violence appeared, their noise, and the bustle they made, was intolerable; which may readily be understood when it is considered that they were mostly of the lowest and most ignorant classes, such as fishwomen, carmen, street-porters, and butchers' men, all bawling out at once for change. (Forbes 1860: 83–4)

The shortage of coin diminished as the currency stabilised and hoarding became less prevalent; it was also alleviated by the eventual legalisation of notes in denominations as small as five shillings. These the mass of people accustomed to a metallic currency had to be persuaded to accept, especially in England; hence Gillray's representation of John Bull as a countryman slowly deciding to take the unfamiliar notes he is being offered.

Throughout the Restriction period, though, English resistance to notes persisted on a variety of grounds. Its major spokesman was Cobbett, whose *Weekly Register* mounted repeated attacks on the Restriction Act and on paper money in general. Cobbett's arguments are beyond my scope here but I offer an attack on him from the *Morning Post* in 1810 as an example of the over-the-top nationalist rhetoric that could at need be mobilised against him:

> He publishes weekly an *infernal register*, to excite *mutiny in the army and the fleet*, to seduce the *loyalty of British subjects*, to *confound the good sense of the yeomanry* by *cunning* and *artful sophistry*, and above all *to destroy Public Credit and Bank Paper, as the best bond of individual and public security, and the only medium of exchange to suit and exert the energies of an insular and commercial people.* (Cobbett 1815, vol 1: 175)

The attachment of the Tory press in England to bank paper during the restriction era of course expressed party political and class interests, and would not outlast the government's need for gold during wartime. But in promoting these interests, the *Post* puts into play the assumption that the nation's currency expresses its character, an assumption shared by Walter Scott with respect to Scotland, and indeed in a quite different way by Cobbett. Versions of this assumption continue to play a role in discussions of monetary questions down to our own time.

What makes such assumptions difficult to understand is the elusiveness of the object to which they are attached. Scott's sense of the Scottishness of the paper pound has nothing to do with the pound as a unit of account, or with its value, but with the distinctiveness of the Scottish banking system and of the pound's material embodiment in paper. In England from 1819 until the First World War national attachment to the pound was inseparable from its status as the representative of a certain quantity of gold, a status that was throughout the period expressed by its embodiment in the gold sovereign. The issue of notes for less than five pounds was banned in England from 1826, and throughout the nineteenth century paper money, particularly the notes of the Bank of England, often seem to have been invested with a tinge of the uncanny – although, particularly in the first half of the century and particularly in the North, there persisted strong regional attachments to local circulations of notes or bills.

By the 1830s, then, Britons could at different times and places have understood gold sovereigns, banknotes, or bills of exchange as the privileged local representatives of the pound. These forms of currency were not only materially different; they also served as money (or money-representatives) for very different reasons – gold because it was legal tender, notes because they were bank debts, and bills because they were individual debts theoretically secured by commodities. For these different reasons, each of these forms of currency could come to represent the abstraction that was a pound; none of them however could be viewed as embodying the pound in itself, or as being the form of money of which the others were only representations, since under the right circumstances it had become clear that the function of money could be served by any of the three without the others. On the contrary, the pound as an abstraction was constituted precisely by its capacity to assume these heterogeneous forms, since its existence as a national currency was determined by the mediations between them.

Notes

1 I gratefully acknowledge a grant from the American Council of Learned Societies, which has assisted in the completion of this chapter.

2 For an account of the different aggregates used to measure the money supply in the UK in the 1980s, see Sayer (1982) 66–72.

3 Gold, silver, and token coinages naturally had very different geographical circulations. For a more detailed account of these in the fifteenth and sixteenth centuries, see Spufford (1988): 319–39.

4 In the opening years of the eighteenth century, for reasons I shall discuss below, foreign gold coin again became common in England. King reprints a paper from 1713 stating that in that year almost no money was current in Exeter and the other trading cities of Devonshire and Cornwall but Portuguese gold (King 1721, vol. 2: 24). Isaac Newton's 1717 letter to the revenue commissioners, written in his capacity as Master of the Mint, states that

> In the end of King *William's* Reign, and the first years of the late Queen [Anne] . . . *Foreign coins abounded in* England. . . . The *Dollars* of *Scotland*, worth about 4s. 6d. Half-penny were put away in the North of *England* for 5s. and at this price began to flow in upon us: I gave notice therof to the *Lords Commissioners of the Treasury*, and they ordered the *Collectors of Taxes* to forbear taking them, and thereby put a Stop to the Mischief.
>
> At the same time the *Lewidors* of *France*, which were worth but 17s. and 3 farthings a piece, passed in *England* for 17s. 6d. I gave notice therof to the *Lords Commissioners of the Treasury*, and his late Majesty put out a Proclamation that they should go but at 17s. and thereupon they came to the Mint, and 1400001. were coined out of them. . . .
>
> Some years ago the *Portugal* Moydores were received in the west of *England* at 28s. a Piece; upon Notice from the Mint, *that they were worth only about 27s. 7d. the Lords Commissioners of the Treasury ordered their Receivers of Taxes to take them at no more than 27s. 6d.* (Newton 1966: 276–8)

These observations illustrate the circulation of foreign coin in England in the early eighteenth century; they also show the complex interaction of custom, legal decree, and intrinsic value that determined how any precious metal coin would circulate, and at what value, whether it was issued in England or abroad.

England was for most of its history exceptionally successful in maintaining a distinct national currency. The contrast with continental Europe is suggested by Fernand Braudel's assertion that in 1614, 400 different currencies were circulating in the Netherlands, while in France at the same date there were 82 (Braudel 1992:

196). Eric Kerridge argues that England's exceptionalism in this regard was important in determining the distinctive evolution of English banking (Kerridge 1988: 1–4). But, as the letter from Newton I have just quoted suggests, even England's coinage was not always single and unified as Kerridge proposes. His own survey of probate inventories between 1538 and 1660 shows that they occasionally included foreign coin (Kerridge 1988: 98).

5 Eric Kerridge argues that the inland bill of exchange originated in the second half of the sixteenth century as the network of regional fairs in which English trade had hitherto taken place was supplanted by a national market centred on London. He demonstrates that trade between London wholesalers and country producers was already in the sixteenth century conducted very largely on credit, and claims that as early as 1615 at major centres such as Norwich there existed a regular market for bills on London (Kerridge 1988: 46). He concedes, however, that before 1650 the system was far from perfect, and that for many purposes transfers of specie remained necessary (Kerridge 1988: 56). Kerridge does not, it seems to me, fully account for the fact that writers on exchange from Marius to Defoe concur in viewing the inland bill of exchange as a development of the outland bill.

6 The use of 'circulation' with respect to money derives from an analogy with the circulation of the blood, of which Hobbes provided the most influential early instance in *Leviathan* (1651) part 2, chapter 24 (Hobbes 1968: 300). An earlier physiology, in which the body suffered not from impediments to the circulation of blood, but from its excess or deficit, could also provide analogies with money, as in Gerard Malynes' *Lex Mercatoria* (1622): 'Money then (as the Blood in the bodie) containeth the Soule which infuseth life; for if Money be wanting, Trafficke doth decrease' (Malynes 1622: 253).

7 For a tabular presentation of this history, see Checkland (1975) 134–5.

8 Scott's campaign was successful, and the one pound note was allowed to continue in Scotland and Ireland after it had been banned in England. England resumed the use of one pound notes during the First World War and then replaced them with coins in 1983. In Scotland, the Royal Bank continues to issue them, and they are still valued as a marker of Scots difference. Thus Gerald Warner, writing in the *Sunday Times* in 1992: 'Since the English abandoned the pound note years ago, our retention of it joins the Kirk and our legal system as one of the institutions celebrating our separate identity. Indeed, since only 17 per cent of Scots now adhere to the Kirk, whereas 100 per cent feel a fervent attachment to the pound, it is arguably the supreme expression of national sovereignty within the Union.'

Bibliography

Anon (1966[1810]) *Report from the Select Committee of the House of Commons on the High Price of Gold Bullion*, reprinted in John R. McCulloch, ed. (1966[1856]) *A Select Collection of Scarce and Valuable Tracts on Paper Currency and Banking*, New York, Augustus M. Kelley: 403–74.

Ashton, T.S. (1953) 'The Bill of Exchange and Private Banks in Lancashire, 1790–1830,' in T.S. Ashton and R.S. Sayers, eds, *Papers in English Monetary History*, Oxford, Clarendon: 37–49.

Braudel, Fernand (1992) *The Wheels of Commerce*. Sîan Reynolds, trans. Berkeley and Los Angeles, University of California Press.

Checkland, S.G. (1975) *Scottish Banking: A History; 1695–1973*, Glasgow and London, Collins.

Cobbett, William (1815) *Paper Against Gold and Glory Against Prosperity*, 2 vols. London. Reprinted articles from the *Weekly Register* of 1810–11.

Cobbett, William (1821) *Preliminary Part of Paper Against Gold*. London. Reprinted articles from the *Political Register* beginning 1803.

De Roover, Raymond (1953) *L'Evolution de la Lettre de Change, XIVe–XVIIIe siècles*, Paris.

Defoe, Daniel (1732) *The Complete English Tradesman*, 3rd edn, in 2 vols, London.

Forbes, Sir William (1860) *Memoirs of a Banking House*, London and Edinburgh.

Graham, William (1911) *The One Pound Note In the History of Banking in Great Britain*, 2nd edn, Edinburgh.

[Harris, Joseph.] (1966[1757]) *An Essay upon Money and Coins. Part 1: The Theories of Commerce, Money, and Exchanges*, Reprinted in John R. McCulloch, ed. (1966[1856]) *A Select Collection of Scarce and Valuable Tracts on Money*, New York, Augustus M. Kelley: 339–429.

Hobbes, Thomas (1968) *Leviathan*. C. B. Macpherson, ed. Harmondsworth, Penguin Books.

Hume, David (1955) *Writings on Economics*, Eugene Rotwein, ed. Madison, University of Wisconsin Press.

Kerridge, Eric (1988) *Trade and Banking in Early Modern England*, Manchester, Manchester University Press.

King, Charles (1721) *The British Merchant; or, Commerce Preserv'd*, 3 vols, London.

Liverpool, 1st Earl of [Charles Jenkinson] (1966[1805]) *A Treatise on the Coins of the Realm*, reprinted in John R. McCulloch, ed. (1966[1856]) *A Select Collection of Scarce and Valuable Tracts on Paper Currency and Banking*, New York, Augustus M. Kelley: 351–9.

[Lowndes, William] (1966[1695]) *A Report Containing an Essay for the Amendment of the Silver Coin*, reprinted in John R. McCulloch, ed. (1966[1856]) *A Select Collection of Scarce and Valuable Tracts on Money*, New York, Augustus M. Kelley: 169–258.

Malynes, Gerard (1622) *Consuetudo vel Lex Mercatoria, or the Ancient Law Merchant*, London.

Marx, Karl (1981) *Capital*, vol. 3. David Fernbach, trans. Harmondsworth, Penguin Books.

Nevin, Edward, and E. W. Davis (1970) *The London Clearing Banks*, London, Elek Books.

Newton, Sir Isaac (1966) 'Representation Third to the Right Honourable the Lords Commissioners of His Majesty's Revenue.' London: 21 Sept. 1717, reprinted in John R. McCulloch, ed. (1966) *A Select Collection of Scarce and Valuable Tracts on Money*, New York, Augustus M. Kelley: 274–9.

Pick, Franz, and René Sédillot (1971) *All the Monies of the World*, New York, Pick Publishing Co.

Sayer, Stuart (1982) *An Introduction to Macroeconomic Policy*, London, Butterworth.

Scammell, W.M. (1968) *The London Discount Market*, London, Elek Books.

Scott, Sir Walter (1841) *Letters to the Editor of the Edinburgh Weekly Journal, from Malachi Malagrowther, Esq. on the Proposed Change of Currency, and Other Late Alterations, as they Affect, or are Intended to Affect, the Kingdom of Scotland*, reprinted in *Critical and Miscellaneous Essays*, Philadelphia, Carey and Hart, vol. 3: 333–422.

Shaw, William A. ed. (1967 [1896]) *Select Tracts and Documents Illustrative of English Monetary History 1626–1730*, reprinted New York, Augustus M. Kelley.

Smith, Adam (1976[1904]) *An Enquiry into the Nature and Causes of the Wealth of Nations, vol. 1*, Chicago, University of Chicago Press.

Smout, T.C. (1963) *Scottish Trade on the Eve of the Union*, Edinburgh and London, Oliver and Boyd.

Spufford, Peter (1988) *Money and its Use in Medieval Europe*, Cambridge, Cambridge University Press.

Warner, Gerald (1992) 'Taking Note of Scottish Identity.' *Sunday Times*, 25 Oct.

Vaughan, Rice (1966[1675]) *A Discourse of Coin and Coinage . . .*, reprinted in John R. McCulloch, ed. (1966[1856]), *A Select Collection of Scarce and Valuable Tracts on Money*, New York, Augustus M. Kelley: 1–119.

4 Local currencies in pre-industrial Japan

Makoto Maruyama

Tokugawa Japan was a pre-industrial society, which lasted between 1600 and 1868. Although its economy was largely based on agriculture, the growth of commerce in metropolises, castle towns and other local towns during the Tokugawa period was prominent. During the first several decades of the seventeenth century, it seems that the Tokugawa government managed to supply metal monies, such as gold, silver and copper, to the markets in metropolises, and, to some extent, in castle towns. However, during the 1660s, it became obvious that the money supply by the Tokugawa government was not sufficient to meet the needs of growing markets, especially the markets in the *han*, or fiefs, ruled by the feudal clans that had antagonised the Tokugawa family when they established the new regime. Also, since the Tokugawa government prioritised the regions ruled by their family members or hereditary vassals, other feudal clans suffered from financial difficulties from the very beginning of the Tokugawa regime.

The idea of issuing local paper currency had already been known to the merchants in the Ise area near Nagoya in the sixteenth century. They issued commercial bills among themselves for local transactions. Soon the bills became accepted by local people as a means of exchange in the area. During the 1660s, several feudal clans, which suffered not only from the shortage of a means of circulation in local markets but also from financial deficits, decided to apply the practice of Ise's merchants to their own fiefs. This was the beginning of the use of *hansatsu*.[1]

Hansatsu, which refers to a feudal clan note, was a kind of local paper currency which was issued by or authorised by feudal clans. In principle, *hansatsu* was allowed to circulate within each *han*, or fief, where *hansatsu* was issued. In most cases, *hansatsu* was backed by silver money. It was therefore crucial for feudal clans to hoard enough silver for reserves. As far as *hansatsu* stayed within the fief where it was issued, the Tokugawa government did not interfere, except during the period between 1707 and 1730 when the Tokugawa government imposed a nation-wide ban on the use of *hansatsu*, aimed at strengthening their hegemony over feudal clans. The result was disastrous. The sudden shrinkage of money in circulation caused nation-wide deflation and stagnation. The Tokugawa government had to lift the ban and allow the use of *hansatsu* in order to revive local economies.

The use of *hansatsu* spread rapidly among many fiefs. In 1707, when the Tokugawa government banned the use of *hansatsu*, 51 fiefs had already used *hansatsu*. After 1730, the number of fiefs that had their own *hansatsu* steadily increased; the figure was more than 100 in 1836, and reached more than 200 at the end of the Tokugawa regime.

It has been often argued that *hansatsu* was bad money. The evaluation of *hansatsu* in this manner usually stems from those instances where feudal clans rushed to issue their *hansatsu* without enough reserves. There were, as a matter of fact, many fiefs where *hansatsu* was abused by their governments, and sometimes such abuse of *hansatsu* caused turmoil in their fiefs. Nevertheless, *hansatsu* was not always hazardous. On the contrary, in most cases, local economies needed local currencies to sustain themselves, and *hansatsu* was a convenient tool for meeting the demand of local economies.

In this chapter, I shed light on three fiefs in the western part of Japan and illustrate how *hansatsu* was actually regulated in these fiefs and what kind of circumstances obstructed the circulation of *hansatsu*.[2] In my conclusion, I will refer to the problems of the modern, national currency which has suppressed the issue of local currencies for more than a century. I will also suggest the possibility of reviving local currencies in the form of Local Exchange and Trading Systems (LETS).

Hansatsu in Okayama-*han*[3]

Okayama-*han*, a middle-sized fief, facing the Inland Sea of Seto in the western part of Japan, was in financial difficulties after the bad flood in 1654.[4] In 1670, the government of Okayama-*han* compiled a handbook of *hansatsu*, and started a task force, which pursued the possibility of using *hansatsu* as a tool for financial reform. In 1673, another flood hit the castle town of Okayama. Also, in 1675, the Tokugawa government ordered the government of Okayama-*han* to contribute to the construction of the Emperor's Palace. These events forced the *han* government to accelerate financial reform.

In the middle of the 1670s, the task force of *hansatsu* extended their research on the concrete use of *hansatsu* by accumulating the data of other fiefs which had already put *hansatsu* to use. The *han* government, on their part, made efforts to hoard silver as reserves for future *hansatsu*. By the end of the 1670s, the preparation for the issuing of *hansatsu* was completed and the *han* government issued their first *hansatsu* in 1679. These *hansatsu* were called Empo notes, because they were issued in the seventh year of Empo.

The government of Okayama-*han* assigned two officials of the treasury department as the executives of the issuing section. Under their supervision, five government officials took charge of the manufacturing of *hansatsu*. The *han* government also chartered a local papermaker to supply the material for *hansatsu*, and ordered two merchants to administer the use of *hansatsu* on a practical level.

In order to compel the use of *hansatsu*, the *han* government forbade the use of silver within the fief, and urged the silver holders to change their silver with *hansatsu* at exchange offices throughout the fief. The silver that was brought from outside had to be exchanged for *hansatsu* at these offices. *Hansatsu* was exchanged for silver only when the *hansatsu* holders went outside the fief. Gold money could be exchanged for both silver and Empo notes, but people were banned from using gold to purchase goods. Copper money was allowed to be used as a means of exchange in small-scale transactions. The *han* government also accepted tax payments by *hansatsu* provided that the payment was originally specified to be made in silver. In this manner, the government of Okayama-*han* guaranteed the quality of *hansatsu* as legal tender in the fief.

The circulation of *hansatsu* had two channels. The first channel put *hansatsu* into circulation in exchange for gold and silver and took it out of circulation again by converting it into silver. Both transactions were made at exchange offices in the fief. The second channel supplied *hansatsu* to local markets through the government's expenditure and absorbed it from markets through tax payments. The government's expenditure included the payment of salaries to the warriors.

The exchange rate of silver against Empo notes was 100:101, whereas the rate of the latter against the former was 102:100. The difference of the two exchange rates was intentionally made to encourage silver holders to change their silver for Empo notes. There were several other devices to facilitate the use of Empo notes. Those who brought silver to the exchange offices to get Empo notes for the purpose of tax payment obtained the special premium of 2 per cent in addition to the regular rate. It was decided that debts were to be paid by Empo notes. If the debts predated the commencement of the use of *hansatsu*, the creditors could charge 2 per cent premium in addition to the ordinary interest. The warriors who had been paid salaries prior to the introduction of Empo notes also received the premium.

At the outset, the government of Okayama-*han* was advised by the task force of *hansatsu* that the amount of the issue of Empo notes should not exceed 4,000 *kanme*.[5] It also suggested that the government should hoard silver equivalent to at least 30 per cent of the issued Empo notes. In actuality, the *han* government issued Empo notes far beyond the maximum which the task force suggested. As a result, the excess notes were immediately returned to the *han* government, as Table 4.1 indicates.

Table 4.1 also suggests that the sum of Empo notes which remained in the markets was substantially smaller than the maximum amount which the task force originally set. This implies that the *han* government, together with the task force of *hansatsu*, overestimated the spread of Empo notes. Nevertheless, the sum of Empo notes in circulation increased gradually during the first three years.

Table 4.1 The sum of *hansatsu* in circulation in Okayama-*han*, 1679–1681 (*kanme*)

Year	*Issued by government*	*Returned to government*	*Remaining in markets*
1679	2,737	654	2,083
1680	6,379	4,097	2,281
1681	10,589	8,204	2,384

Source: Okayama-City (1966: 178).

Although Empo notes did not win popularity as fast as the *han* government expected, they began to find their own place in local markets.

During the last two decades of the seventeenth century and the early eighteenth century, the economic growth of Okayama-*han* was remarkable. The reclamation of new rice fields, which had already started before the use of Empo notes, was accelerated during the period (see Table 4.2).

The reclamation of the rice fields in the Kurata area, which was completed in 1679, was accompanied by the construction of a new irrigation channel. The opening of this irrigation channel contributed to the development of water transport. As for the existing rice fields, there was a depopulation problem during the 1660s and 1670s caused by the migration of poor peasants into the castle town and other local towns to be servants. However, during the 1680s, a new type of small-scale family farming increased, and the economic activities in the villages began to be revived. The number of working cattle and workhorses also increased from 3,428 in 1677 to 25,258 in 1710.

The expansion of agricultural production was followed by the commodification of home-made produce and handiwork, such as cotton and cotton products, colza and colza products, and rush and rush products. The brokers who received orders from the merchants of the castle town came to the villages and purchased these goods. Peasants also visited the castle town to sell their produce and handiwork to the merchants. The imported goods from other fiefs, such as tea, charcoal, Japanese star anise, and indigo plants, were allowed to be traded freely in Okayama-*han*, except that the *han* government monopolised the trade of indigo plants between 1696 and 1726.

Since the data on the use of Empo notes between 1681 and 1706 are not available, it is not certain to what extent the issuing of Empo notes contributed to the growth of the *han* economy. However, it can be at least suggested that the supplying of Empo notes into local markets in Okayama-*han* avoided the shortage of currency, which might have happened if Empo notes were not issued at all. It is also clear that the economic growth of Okayama-*han* in return contributed to the financial reform of the *han* government.

In 1707, when the Tokugawa government put a ban on the use of *hansatsu* nationwide, the government of Okayama-*han* converted the circulating Empo notes into silver. The conversion was done without delay and completed within the year. As a consequence, the *han* government had to turn its *hansatsu*-based spending policy into financial retrenchment.

Table 4.2 Reclamation of new rice fields in Okayama-*han*, 1664–1771 (*koku*)[6]

Year	*Newly reclaimed rice fields*
1664	34,265
1684	61,777
1711	104,597

Source: Taniguchi (1964: 172).

When the Tokugawa government lifted the ban on the use of *hansatsu* in 1730 (the fifteenth year of Kyoho), the government of Okayama-*han* resumed the issuing of *hansatsu*. The new *hansatsu* were called Kyoho notes, named after the year of Kyoho. This time, two senior officials were assigned as the executives of the issuing section. In order to hoard the silver reserve, the *han* government established a commission agent of cotton in 1731 and monopolised the cotton trade.

In actuality, however, the financial difficulties of the *han* government made it difficult to secure enough silver for reserves. The famine which attacked the western part of Japan in 1732 brought particularly serious damage to the *han* economy. As a consequence, the market rate of Kyoho notes fell between one-half and one-third of its face value in 1733. This resulted in the temporary suspension of the circulation of Kyoho notes.

In 1736, the conversion of Kyoho notes was restricted to particular purposes. In 1737, the *han* government absorbed the excessively issued *hansatsu* by borrowing Kyoho notes from its holders. The shrinkage of the circulation of Kyoho notes inevitably raised the problem of currency shortage. In 1742, the *han* government removed the ban on the use of gold and silver as currencies in local markets. In the meantime, the *han* government established a commission agent of Japanese sumac fruit in Osaka in 1739 in order to strengthen the hoarding of silver.

The method of the regulation of the use of Kyoho notes by the *han* government was remarkable. They did not resort to the most easy-going and hazardous manner which was chosen in some other fiefs, i.e., to suspend the conversion of *hansatsu* into silver and to make people use *hansatsu* by force. Instead, the *han* government continued on the one hand to absorb Kyoho notes from local markets, and on the other hand to supply silver to the markets. Whenever the excessive issuing of *hansatsu* undermined the acceptability of *hansatsu*, the *han* government intentionally borrowed it from its holders and disposed of it. In 1786, the government borrowed *hansatsu* which was worth 200 *kanme* and burned it completely. In 1788, when the market rate of Kyoho notes dropped to 40 per cent against its face value, the *han* government issued new *hansatsu* and retrieved the old one with its market value. The *han* government let the new *hansatsu* circulate in parallel with silver money in local markets.

Although there still existed a tendency toward the depreciation of *hansatsu* after 1788, it was not so serious as to abolish the use of *hansatsu*. Sometimes *hansatsu* even regained its purchasing power. Table 4.3 illustrates that the market rate of *hansatsu* remained relatively stable until 1851.

Under the circumstances, the local economy of Okayama-*han* grew significantly. During the latter half of the eighteenth century, local towns in the countryside were newly developed. As a consequence, the dominance of the commerce in the castle town was weakened. The monopoly of the commission agents of Okayama-*han* gradually gave way to the freer trade in local markets. Despite the efforts of the *han* government to strengthen the monopoly by extending the dealing area of the commission agents, the governmental monopoly of local produce and products had to be abandoned. In 1856, the largest monopoly of Okayama-*han*, i.e., the commission agent of cotton, was closed.

Table 4.3 Market rate of *hansatsu* against its face value, 1850–4 (%)

Year	*1850*	*1851*	*1852*	*1853*	*1854*
Market rate of *hansatsu*	77	90	n/a	64	10

Source: Kokusho (1928: 85), Shimbo (1976: 267).

The failure to maintain hegemony over the commercial sector by the *han* government deepened its financial difficulties since governmental revenue mostly depended on rice production, the growth of which was limited compared to the growth of the commercial sector. In addition, the *han* government was often asked to contribute a significant amount of resources in one form or the other to the Tokugawa government.

The financial difficulties of the *han* government became even worse in the middle of the nineteenth century. The debt of the *han* government, which was only 787 *kanme* of silver in 1831, swelled to 4,000 *kanme* by 1847. The government borrowed silver money from merchants in Osaka as well as from local merchants. Since the borrowing of silver from local merchants was done by means of purchasing silver by *hansatsu*, the excess issuing of *hansatsu* was also accelerated. The restoration of financial conditions by the *han* government was impaired completely by consecutive calamities, such as the famine in 1851, the flood in 1852, the call for the patrol of the coast near Edo (Tokyo) by the Tokugawa government in 1853, and the drought and earthquake in 1854.

The catastrophe of *hansatsu* in 1854 took place amidst such conditions. Between 1853 and 1854, the market rate of *hansatsu* dropped from 64 per cent to 10 per cent against its face value (Table 4.3). The sudden depreciation of *hansatsu* caused panic among local people. Some of them rushed to the exchange offices to protest. Although the *han* government could manage to prevent the rebellion against the destructive devaluation of *hansatsu*, they never succeeded in regaining the credibility of *hansatsu* after this. The conversion of *hansatsu* into silver money was thus suspended until the termination of the use of *hansatsu* in 1871.

Hansatsu in Choshu-*han*

In the middle of the seventeenth century, Choshu-*han*, located in the west end of the main island of Japan, also suffered from financial difficulties due to the loss of three-quarters of its territory at the beginning of the Tokugawa regime. In 1677, when the first *hansatsu* was issued in Choshu-*han*, the governmental debt reached 12,000 *konme* in silver. The *han* government issued *hansatsu* up to 11,000 *kanme*, out of which only 4,000 *kanme* actually circulated.[7]

Unlike the case of Okayama-*han*, no concrete data about *hansatsu* of Choshu-*han* during the years between 1677 and 1711 are available. All that is known is that the *han* government issued *hansatsu*, which was based on a silver standard, by lending it to their warriors who depended on the local markets in the castle town.

In 1681, the governmental debt increased to 20,000 *kanme*. During the 1680s, the *han* government resorted to raising taxes and to extending the lending of *hansatsu* to their people in order to cut the deficit in silver. The result was disastrous. Since the issuing of *hansatsu* lacked sufficient silver reserve from the outset, the market rate of *hansatsu* fell to one-fifth of its face value during the decade. The financial conditions of the *han* government continued to deteriorate through the 1690s and 1700s, and the governmental debt became 50,000 *kanme*. By the end of the 1700s, the market rate of *hansatsu* dropped to as low as 10 per cent against its face value.

In 1711, four years after the Tokugawa government's ban on the use of *hansatsu*, the circulation of *hansatsu* in Choshu-*han* was suspended. Unlike the case of Okayama-*han*, the use of *hansatsu* in Choshu-*han* between 1677 and 1711 ended with complete failure.

During the next two decades, i.e., the years of the suspension of *hansatsu*, the choice for the government of Choshu-*han* was very limited. All the *han* government could do without *hansatsu* was either to retrench their expenditure or to pursue paternalistic policies to regain the trust of local people. During the 1710s, the governmental debt declined from 50,000 *kanme* to 15,000 *kanme*, although it still remained higher than the debt of 1677.

In 1730, when the Tokugawa government lifted the ban on the use of *hansatsu*, the government of Choshu-*han* resumed the issuing of *hansatsu*. According to the document dictated by a senior official of the nineteenth-century Choshu-*han*,[8] the *han* government restricted the conversion of *hansatsu* into silver to the exchange offices in the *han*, as Okayama-*han* did. The exchange rates between *hansatsu* and silver were the same as those of Empo notes in Okayama-*han*. People were not allowed to use silver money inside the fief except the travellers who had to spent their money for travelling expenses while moving around Choshu-*han*. The *han* government also accepted tax payments by *hansatsu*. In 1731, the *han* government entrusted big merchants, mainly from Choshu-*han* to regulate *hansatsu*, and granted them annually 10,000 *koku* of rice to ensure silver reserves.

Unfortunately, the effort which the *han* government made to sustain the circulation of *hansatsu* was ruined by the famine in the western part of Japan in 1732. This famine caused the damage of 300,000 *koku* to Choshu-*han*, a figure which was worth the annual wealth of the *han* as a whole. The *han* government had to ask for a loan from the Tokugawa government and the merchants in Osaka. The loan pressed down so heavily on the financial condition of the *han* government that they could not even prepare for the financial reform. Under the circumstances, the *han* government had to keep on retrenching and persuading local people to reduce the outflow of silver money from the fief.

The sudden lifting of the ban on the local use of silver money in 1736 only resulted in people rushing to acquire silver money. The reserve of silver for sustaining *hansatsu* thus vanished. By the end of 1739, the use of *hansatsu* was again suspended.

During the 1740s, the *han* government devoted themselves to the financial reform which had been delayed for a long time. They resumed the emergency fund system which had not been in operation for several decades. By 1744, they stored 1,000 *kanme* of money and 8,600 *koku* of rice for emergency purposes. The *han* government also made efforts to develop the waste land and forestation.

The reform was, however, hindered by repetitive natural disasters. By 1751, the governmental debt had doubled. The credibility of the *han* government declined, and they had more difficulties in borrowing money from the merchants in Osaka. In addition, the decline in the prices of the major products of Choshu-*han*, rice and paper, intensified the stagnation of the *han* economy.

Despite these unfavourable conditions, the *han* government resumed the use of *hansatsu* for the third time in 1755, and banned the use of gold and silver monies in local markets. The governmental debt swelled continuously and reached as high as 41,000 *kanme* by 1758. The *han* government was forced to engage in further financial reform. During 1761 and 1762, they received the taxable fields and incorporated 42,000 *koku* of new resources into the existing financial resources.

In 1763, the *han* government, based on the new resources, established the Buiku-system, i.e., a system of charitable budgets which developed from the emergency fund system. The new system was independent from the government's regular budget. The purpose of the system included the relief of the poor, the renovation of armaments and public works including the development of the waste land, the promotion of wax production, and the lending of money to the regular budget of the *han* government.

The balance of the Buiku-system increased steadily and reached 78,000 *kanme* in 1840. It is estimated that 52,000 *kanme* out of the total balance was always kept in the safe and that the rest of the balance was actually used for the system. The growth of the Buiku-system was, as a matter of fact, linked with the increase of the debt of the *han* government. In a sense, the Buiku-system served as a reservoir for the *han* government. Even when the government experienced difficulties in borrowing money from the merchants in Osaka, they could now count on the Buiku-system. Supported by such a unique system, the *han* government finally succeeded in bringing the *han* economy into prosperity.

In accordance with the growth of the *han* economy, the sum of *hansatsu* in circulation increased from 3,000 *kanme* in 1755 to 30,000 *kanme* in 1840. The market rate of *hansatsu* fluctuated between these years, but there was no serious turmoil which would obstruct the circulation of *hansatsu*. On the contrary, *hansatsu* of Choshu-*han* was even accepted by the people in the neighbouring *han* as well as in Osaka. In Toyoura-*han*, for example, *hansatsu* of Choshu-*han* was widely used during the first few decades of the nineteenth century, despite the government of Toyoura-*han* having banned its use officially. In Osaka, the *hansatsu* of Choshu-*han* was used for the transactions between merchants and the *han*'s warehouse.

By 1840, the market rate of Choshu-*han*'s *hansatsu* stabilised around the level of 80 per cent of its face value, and this level was sustained until 1871. Choshu-*han* was one of the leading regions where radical reforms of the politico-economic system were executed during the 1840s and 1850s. During the 1860s, Choshu-*han* became one of the strongest leaders of anti-Tokugawa powers who finally defeated the Tokugawa government and accomplished the

Meiji Restoration in 1868. During the civil war between the anti-Tokugawa regions and the pro-Tokugawa ones in 1865, the peasants in the pro-Tokugawa regions welcomed the *hansatsu* of Choshu-*han*, and even asked the warriors and merchants of Choshu to give Choshu-*han*'s *hansatsu* in exchange for the ones that the peasants possessed.

Hansatsu in Hiroshima-*han*

Hiroshima-*han*, situated between Okayama-*han* and Choshu-*han*, would provide still another example of the use of *hansatsu*.[9] The government of Hiroshima-*han* first issued *hansatsu* in 1704. Their *hansatsu* was also based on a silver reserve, and the method of issuing was more or less the same as that of Okayama-*han* and Choshu-*han*. The *han* government obviously over-issued *hansatsu* before they ascertained the optimum amount of *hansatsu* in circulation. In 1707, when the Tokugawa Government declared the nation-wide suspension of the use of *hansatsu*, the *han* government had to call in *hansatsu*, but they could convert only 40 per cent of the circulating *hansatsu* into silver. The rest was replaced by the temporary note which was exchangeable only for the new *hansatsu* issued in 1730.

During the following hundred years, there were several occasions when the circulation of *hansatsu* was suspended. For example, the market rate of *hansatsu* dropped to 20 per cent of its face value in 1732, when a serious famine attacked western Japan and the silver reserve was consumed in purchasing rice from Osaka. The crisis was overcome in the next year, when the *han* government managed to borrow money from the merchants in Osaka. Accordingly, the market rate of *hansatsu* returned to the normal level.

There was a temporary suspension of the use of *hansatsu* in 1759, which instigated a rush to the exchange offices by people demanding the conversion of *hansatsu* into silver money. They were the victims of the wild rumour that the Tokugawa government would again forbid the nation-wide use of *hansatsu*. As a matter of fact, the Tokugawa government decided to ban the issuing of *hansatsu* only where the use of *hansatsu* had never taken place. When the rumour was cleared, the credibility of *hansatsu* was restored.

In 1764, the *han* government again replaced the circulating *hansatsu* with a new one, which was accepted by local people until the end of the 1820s without serious trouble. Although the expenses of the *han* government rapidly increased in accordance with the growth of local markets during these periods, they managed to keep the amount of *hansatsu* at a reasonable level.

The sudden change which was quite unfavourable to the use of *hansatsu* came in 1831. In this year, the *han* government turned their spending policy into a policy of retrenchment, and laid down restrictions on the conversion of *hansatsu* into silver. Henceforth, the *han* government allowed such conversion exclusively for the people who had to purchase rice from outside markets for subsistence. In this manner, the *han* government tried to save the silver reserves.

However, their intention was thwarted especially when famine prevailed across the nation between 1836 and 1838. The Tokugawa government required a relief fund from all fiefs, 2 per cent of their annual revenue. In consequence, the financial conditions of the government of Hiroshima-*han* further deteriorated. The *han* government then resorted to the least appropriate means, increasing the amount of *hansatsu* in circulation without enough reserves. Accordingly, the market rate of *hansatsu* declined to as low as 30 per cent of its face value in 1838.

The *han* government, being no longer able to issue additional *hansatsu*, sought an alternative. In 1841, they issued a kind of absolutely inconvertible note and compelled people to use it as local currency. The new note made the situation worse. Since the note was not backed up by any fund, people simply refused to accept it. The next step that the *han* government chose was to devalue *hansatsu* in order to make the official exchange rate of *hansatsu* closer to its market rate.

During the 1850s, the economy of Hiroshima-*han* seriously stagnated and suffered from deflation. The supplying of *hansatsu* into local markets did not function as a remedy for the recession at all. The *han* government never succeeded in restoring the credibility of *hansatsu* until 1872 when *hansatsu* was replaced with the new national currency.

Conclusion

The use of *hansatsu* in Okayama-*han* provides a good example of how *hansatsu* served as local currency in the pre-industrial economy. Although Empo notes – the first *hansatsu* of Okayama-*han* – were issued primarily as a remedy for financial difficulties, they also contributed to the growth of the local economy. The sum of *hansatsu* in circulation was strictly regulated in accordance with the demand of the local markets. This regulation was practised by means of recalling excess *hansatsu* by the *han* government. It is actually astonishing that the *han* government already recognised the basics of money supply at this early stage of the history of *hansatsu*. Many of the *han* which issued *hansatsu* tended to ignore the nature of the circulation of *hansatsu*.

In any case, Empo notes stayed in local markets to the sum of 2,000 *kanme*. The use of *hansatsu* enabled Okayama-*han* to expand its trade with other regions, a trade that required gold and silver as a means of payment. The growth of trade brought about the growth of local markets, in which *hansatsu* fitted as a means of circulation. The commodification of local produce, especially cotton, stimulated peasants in Okayama-*han* to use *hansatsu* for purchasing goods in the castle town. In this manner, the use of *hansatsu* before 1707 contributed to the economic development of Okayama-*han*.

Kyoho notes, by contrast, were always problematic for the discrepancy that existed between their face value and their market rate. Nonetheless, the *han* government was cautious enough to prevent the sudden depreciation of the market value of *hansatsu*. At least, as long as *han*'s monopoly of cotton trade functioned effectively, the *hansatsu* of Okayama-*han* was accepted by people as a relatively convenient means of local exchange.

The irony of the use of *hansatsu* in Okayama-*han* is that while it contributed to the development of the local economy as a whole, it also opened up freer trade which made the government's monopoly obsolete. With the decline of the hegemony of the *han* government over the local economy, the financial difficulties of the *han* government became serious. Accordingly, the *han* government had to give up their long tradition of issuing *hansatsu* prudently, and turn to temporary relief by excessively issuing *hansatsu* during the 1850s and 1860s.

Whether the excessively issued *hansatsu* during the period actually hindered the growth of the local economy of Okayama-*han* is open to question. What is clear is that, whereas the abuse of *hansatsu* by the *han* government caused the instability of money circulation, the supply of *hansatsu* into local markets helped to avoid a serious depression which might have occurred if *hansatsu* had not been issued at all.

Unlike the case in Okayama-*han*, it took time for the government of Choshu-*han* to become accustomed to the regulation of *hansatsu*. It was only after the Buiku-system was established that the *han* government was able to stabilise the circulation of *hansatsu*. However, once they took control over the circulation of *hansatsu*, they made better use of *hansatsu* than the government of Okayama-*han*, and managed to adapt themselves to the expansion of market transactions in the middle of the nineteenth century. In a sense, the success of the use of *hansatsu* in Choshu-*han*, gave good reason to the Meiji government to issue state paper currency.

By contrast, the case of Hiroshima-*han* in the middle of the nineteenth century typically illustrates the abuse of *hansatsu* which took place in various fiefs. During the middle of the nineteenth century – the period of transition from the Tokugawa regime to the Meiji regime – many *han* governments which had never issued *hansatsu* before started to issue *hansatsu* one by one, as a temporary remedy to their financial difficulties. Even the governments of Okayama-*han* and Hiroshima-*han*, which had experience in regulating *hansatsu*, were forced to issue excessively. The other *han* governments which were new to the use of *hansatsu* replicated the bad habits of these experienced governments. As a consequence, in many cases, *hansatsu* lost its meaning as local currency and became a tool for *han* governments to rescue themselves from financial catastrophes.

The ban on the issuing of *hansatsu* and the monopolisation of the issuing of paper currency by the Meiji government in 1872 was thus inevitable, because without a ban the economies of various regions would have collapsed due to the abuse of *hansatsu*. The Meiji government, which overthrew the Tokugawa government together with their feudalistic regime, established a modern, centralised nation-state. By means of a unifying national monetary system, the Meiji government not only provided relief for the local governments, but also subordinated local economies to the national economy. Although this process was necessary for creating a modern, national market, it apparently closed the door to the possibility of reviving local currencies in modern societies.

The centralised national economy in Japan functioned successfully until the end of the 1960s. It enabled the rapid economic growth and industrialisation from the macro-economic viewpoint. However, the same process also brought unprecedented environmental problems, and broadened inequality among people as well as regions. The economic boom during the 1980s temporarily concealed the problems as if they had already been solved. In actuality, the environmental and welfare problems became more serious than ever before. It has also become obvious that the centralised government system is no more efficient at resolving these issues.

In contemporary Japan, therefore, the decentralisation of the highly centralised and concentrated socio-economic institutions has become a focal issue. The central government itself has now begun to decentralise some of its functions, such as welfare. In this context, the government recently proposed the idea of spreading localised vouchers as gifts across families with children. It is almost certain that, in the near future, local governments will be more responsible for environmental and welfare issues as well as for the development of local economies.

In order for the local governments to be able to perform these tasks successfully, it is necessary to ensure that they have enough funds at their disposal. This can be done partly by earmarking certain portions of national funds for local and regional use. However, since the circulation of the national currency is not limited within the nation-state, no one can ensure that the money which is spent in a certain locality or region will always stay in the same place. It is therefore apposite to propose that local and regional governments should be able to use local and regional currencies, provided that the authorities that issue these currencies are independent of local and regional governments.

The reviving of local currencies in modern societies is, of course, not an easy task. Nevertheless, there are growing efforts in many parts of the world, such as in Canada and in the United Kingdom, to establish local currencies by setting up Local Exchange and Trading Systems (LETS). LETS is a system in which people reciprocate their goods and services by using their own local currencies. Unlike modern currencies, the local currencies used in LETS are usually not convertible into other currencies, and, therefore, remain within the LETS. Some local and regional governments are interested in using LETS for welfare and the environment. Although their immediate interest is to economise their budget in the areas of welfare and the environment, it is also expected that their support of LETS will contribute to the development of local economies.

In Japan, the experiments of LETS have just started in a few places. However, the idea of LETS seems to be constantly gaining popularity among those who are concerned with welfare and environmental issues. Since there are ample experiences of the use of *hansatsu* throughout Japan, the Japanese people will be able to take advantage of these experiences to understand how local currencies should be best regulated.

Acknowledgements

I would like to thank the editors for carefully reading my draft and for clarifying discussions of many points.

Notes

1 The earliest *hansatsu* was allegedly issued in Fukuyama-*han* in 1630 (National Archives 1993: xxiii–xxv). However, no sample has been found yet, and there is little material to explain how this *hansatsu* was used in Fukuyama-*han* (Higaki 1989: 135).
2 For an overview of the use of *hansatsu* in its socio-economic context, see Maruyama (1994).
3 This section is an abbreviation of Maruyama (1996).
4 The following data are based on Hara (1966), Kawade (1991), Kokusho (1928), Okayama-City (1966) and Taniguchi (1964).
5 The denomination of silver money was *monme*. One *kanme* was 1,000 *monme*. It is difficult to evaluate the silver money of the Tokugawa period according to today's monetary system. However, if we used rice as common measure, we could roughly figure out the value of silver money. Although the price of rice varied considerably according to places and years, we could assume one *koku* of rice was worth one *ryo* of gold, where *koku* was a traditional unit of capacity and one *koku* was about 180 litres in the metric system. Regarding *ryo*, it was the denomination of gold money. The official exchange rate between gold money and silver money in 1700 was that one *ryo* of gold equalled 60 *monme* or 0.06 *kanme* of silver. If we assume that one litre of rice weighs one kilogram, and one kilogram of rice equals 620 yen (Yano Kota Commemorative Society ed. 1997), one *ryo* of gold would be worth 111,600 yen, and one *kanme* of silver would be worth 1.86 million yen.
6 One *koku* is about 180 litres in the metric system.
7 The following data are based on Akimoto (1977), Misaka (1977) and Miwa (1938).
8 Kaneshige (1976).
9 The following data are based on Tshuchiya and Yamaguchi (1975) and Yamaguchi (1966).

Bibliography

Akimoto, H. (1977) 'Hagihan zaisei shushi to keizai seisaku' [The budget and the economic policy of Choshu-*han*], *Shakai keizai shigaku* [Journal of socio-economic history] 42(4): 341–63.

Hara, M. (1966) 'Bizen okayama hansatsu shoshi', [A history of *hansatsu* in Okayama-*han*], *Kahei* [Money] 10(5): 1–11.

Higaki, N. (1989) 'Hansatsu no hatashita yakuwari to mondaiten' [The role of *Hansatsu* and its problems], *Kinyu kenkyu* [Financial studies], 8(1), Tokyo: Institute of Financial Studies, Bank of Japan.

Kaneshige, S. (1976) *Choshu han zaiseishi dan* [Kaneshige's talk about the history of the budget in Choshu], Tokuyama: Matsuno Shoten.

Kawade, T. (1991) *Okayama han ni okeru hansatsu no kenkyu* [A study of *hansatsu* in Okayama-*han*], Tokyo: Institute of Financial Studies, Bank of Japan.

Kokusho, I. (1928) *Hoken shakai no tosei to toso* [Controls and protests in feudal society], Tokyo: Kaizosha.

Maruyama, M. (1994) '*Hansatsu*: local currencies in pre-industrial Japan', in C. Duncan and D. Tandy, eds., *From Political Economy to Anthropology*, Montreal: Black Rose Books.

Maruyama, M. (1996) 'Hansatsu no chiiki tsuka toshite no igi' [The significance of *hansatsu* as local currency], in *Shakai kagaku kiyo* [The proceedings of social sciences], 46, Tokyo:

The Department of Advanced Social and International Studies, University of Tokyo.
Misaka, K. (1977) *Hagi han no zaisei to buiku seido* [The budget of Choshu-*han* and Buiku-system], Tokuyama: Matsuno Shoten.
Miwa, T. (1938) 'Choshu hagi no hansatsu' [*Hansatsu* of Choshu-*han*], *Shakai keizai shigaku* [Journal of socio-economic history] 8(6): 657–87.
National Archives (1993) *Edojidai no shihei* [Paper currencies in the Edo period], Tokyo: University of Tokyo Press.
Okayama-City (1966) *Okayama shishi* [The history of Okayama-City], Okayama: Okayama-City.
Shimbo, H. (1976) 'Kinsei koki niokeru bukka, kinsoba, kawase uchigin soba' [Prices, gold and silver exchange markets in the latter half of the Tokugawa period], in M. Umemura *et al*, eds, *Nihon keizai no hatten* [The development of Japan's economy], Tokyo: Nihon Keizai Shinbunsha.
Taniguchi, S (1964) *Okayamahan*, Tokyo: Yoshikawa Kobun Kan.
Tsuchiya, T. and Yamaguchi, K. eds, (1975) *Nihon no kahei* [Monies in Japan], vol. 6, Tokyo: Toyokeizai Shimposha.
Yamaguchi, K. (1966) 'Hansatsu kenkyushi josetsu' [An introduction to the study of the history of *hansatsu*], in *Tsuka kenkyu shiryo* [Materials for currency studies], vol. 15, Tokyo: Bank of Japan.
Yano Kota Commemorative Society ed. (1997) *Nihon kokusei zue CDROM* [The chart of Japan]. Tokyo: Kokuseisha.

5 Official standardisation vs. social differentiation in Americans' uses of money[1]

Viviana Zelizer

In the days of electronic money, many observers of economic change suppose that a century-old nightmare of depersonalisation is finally imprinting itself on everyday life. Georg Simmel stated the view strongly at the turn of the twentieth century: money's 'colorlessness', he declared, repainted the modern world into an 'evenly flat and gray tone' (Simmel [1908] 1950: 414). All meaningful nuances were stamped out by the new quantitative logic that asked only 'how much' but not 'what and how' (Simmel [1900] 1978: 259). Although analysts have repeatedly conceded that the process remains incomplete – thus legal theorist Margaret Radin (1996) speaks of 'incomplete commodification' – they have just as regularly worried out loud that unchecked rationalisation of currency would produce general desiccation of social relations. Jürgen Habermas, for instance, argues that money is the medium by which the economic system 'colonizes' the 'lifeworld' – the arena of routine social life – irrepressibly and systematically undermining 'domains of action dependent upon social integration' (Habermas 1989: 327). Social observers thus still accept with a remarkable lack of scepticism the notion that once money enters the realm of personal relations it inevitably bends those relations in the direction of instrumental rationality.[2]

For a century, therefore, the prevailing interpretation of money has shaped an absolute model of market money, based on the following five assumptions:

1 The functions and characteristics of money are defined strictly in economic terms. As an entirely homogenous, infinitely divisible, liquid object, lacking in quality, money is a matchless tool for market exchange. Even when the symbolic meaning of money is recognised, it either remains restricted to the economic sphere or is treated as a largely inconsequential feature.
2 All monies are the same in modern society. What Simmel called 'money's qualitatively communistic character' denies any distinctions between types of money (Simmel [1900] 1978: 440). Only differences in quantity are possible. Thus, there is only one kind of money – market money.
3 A sharp dichotomy is established between money and nonpecuniary values. Money in modern society is defined as essentially profane and utilitarian in contrast to non-instrumental values. Money is qualitatively neutral; personal,

social, and sacred values are qualitatively distinct, unexchangeable, and indivisible.

4 Monetary concerns are seen as constantly enlarging, quantifying, and often corrupting all areas of life. As an abstract medium of exchange, money has not only the freedom but also the power to draw an increasing number of goods and services into the web of the market. Money is thus the vehicle for an inevitable commodification of society.

5 The power of money to transform nonpecuniary values is unquestioned, while the reciprocal transformation of money by values or social relations is seldom conceptualised or else is explicitly rejected.

It is not utterly foolish to suppose that the monetisation of social life spreads uniformity, precision, and calculation. After all, a money economy made a significant difference to social organisation. For example, it facilitated the multiplication of economic partners and promoted a rational division of labour. In the years between 1860 and the early 1930s, the United States saw – among other financial innovations – the creation of postal money orders (1864), travellers' checks (1891), fixed prices (1860s), fixed-price stores, such as Woolworth's nickel or dime stores, (1870), mail-order catalogues (1870s), credit cards (1914) the first electronic funds transfer system (1918) as well as the intensified use of time-payment plans, such as instalment buying and the credit system (Beniger 1986: 329, 331; Schlereth 1989: 364; Mandell, 1990). The question then is not whether money made a difference but whether its effects worked as standard theories suggest.

In the face of strong assertions that commodification and monetisation depersonalise and standardise social life, I argue that people are smarter than commodities and money. This paper shows how at each step in money's advance, people have reshaped their commercial transactions, introduced new distinctions, invented their own special forms of currency, earmarked money in ways that baffle market theorists, incorporated money into personalised webs of friendship, family relations, interactions with authorities, and forays through shops and businesses.

Creating a national currency

Starting in the nineteenth century, the American state worked vigorously to create the Simmelian 'colorless' currency; a standardised national money. How did it do so? It taxed thousands of state-issued paper currencies out of existence, excluded foreign currencies from circulation, suppressed the private issue of tokens, paper notes or coins by stores, businesses, churches, and other organisations; and stamped out the personalisation of money by individuals. Consider for instance the 5,000 or more distinct varieties of state banknotes – not including additional thousands of counterfeit issues – circulating in the nineteenth century. Merchants and bankers had to rely on banknote directories to keep track of the unwieldy varieties of monies, as the value (as well as the size and style) of banknotes differed from bank to bank and in different states. In fact, it was common for bank customers to specify 'in what sort of money deposits were to be withdrawn and with what sort promissory notes were to be repaid' (Hammond [1957] 1967: 702–3).[3] As Eric Helleiner (1996: 3) has pointed out, foreign currencies also circulated widely within the United States:

> ... foreign coins in fact made up the dominant portion of the money supply before the 1850s. By far the most common coins in circulation were Mexican coins. Also prominent were the silver fractional coins of many European countries, including Britain, France, and Holland. (Helleiner 1996: 3)[4]

The government set out to eliminate distinctions among currencies. In 1863 the National Banking Act allowed newly chartered national banks to create a uniform national currency. A few years later, the federal government taxed multiple state banknotes out of existence. Earlier, prompted by the financial crisis of the Civil War, Congress in 1862 authorised the Treasury to print millions of 'greenbacks', the country's first paper currency without gold backing which circulated nationally as legal tender (Friedman and Schwartz 1971: 15–25). But even after the National Banking Act, the stock of American money remained highly diversified. The new national banknotes circulated alongside other Civil War currency inventions; not only greenbacks, but interest-bearing legal tender notes, government demand notes, postage and fractional currency as well as silver and gold certificates ('yellowbacks'), not to mention the more traditional gold coins and subsidiary silver. These multiple official monies were in many cases earmarked for specified purposes. Greenbacks, for instance, were receivable in most payments, but not for duties on imports nor for interest on bonds and notes. Gold on the other hand although designated largely for foreign transactions was also reserved for certain domestic payments such as custom duties. Limited regional variation persisted as the West Coast remained mostly on a specie basis. Yet on the whole, after the Civil War, the American state moved towards a more uniform legal tender.[5]

Standardisation of money, however, was not a smooth, consensual process. In fact, defining American currency became one of the most explosive political and social issues of the late nineteenth century. Significantly, despite a dramatic post-Civil War increase in people's use of deposits rather than cash, the debates centred on currencies. Were greenbacks 'real' money, or did only 'hard' metallic money serve as authentic currency? Should gold, as monometallists argued, be the only 'true' standard? Or, could silver, as 'free silver' proponents maintained, serve as equally sound money? Were national banknotes legitimate? Or, as Greenbackers insisted, was only government-issued money acceptable? (James 1978: 22–7; Nugent, 1968; Carruthers and Babb, 1996). These were not merely word games or strictly technical distinctions; the 'money question' became a fiercely contested public debate, polarising social groups and shaping the political process of late nineteenth-century American society. *Money* magazine, established in 1897 'specially designed to simplify the present currency question in the United States', noted that voters were being 'suddenly called upon to digest arguments and technical essays which would puzzle any man who had not previously investigated the subject' (*Money* 1897: 9). Indeed, as one historian points out, only in the United States 'the argument about the form and function of money became public' (Nugent 1968: 167).

By the turn of the century the controversy waned, after free-silver proponents lost the 1896 election and the 1900 Gold Standard Act established the gold dollar as the national monetary standard. In short, within some four decades, the American state had achieved a significant degree of monetary standardisation although not until 1933 did Congress formally declare all United States coins and currencies as equal legal tender (Nussbaum 1964: 181).[6]

Creating currencies, however, was not entirely state business. At times, stores, businesses, and other organisations – including brothels – privately issued tokens, paper notes, or coins. In fact, Americans often responded to the periodic scarcity of small change by the resourceful production of substitute currency. There are even instances of 'church money', such as the 4-pence notes issued in 1792 by a church in Schenectady, New York or the tokens distributed by the First Presbyterian Church of Albany in that same period.[7] Most notably, merchants' copper cents – the 'hard time tokens' of the 1830s – successfully served as both commercial advertising and small change. Other tokens bearing patriotic emblems or political slogans animated economic exchange with timely debates, often satirising President Jackson's policies. Again in the Civil War, when subsidiary silver became more valuable as metal than coin, privately issued 'shinplasters' – paper money in small denominations – along with thousands of tradesmen's and political tokens were used as substitute currency in everyday transactions. Transportation companies, hotels, saloons, and retail stores reports one historian, 'that could not carry on business without change proceeded to manufacture their own currency'. Gold coins were also privately issued; between 1830 and 1860 thousands of coins were produced by individuals in California, Georgia, and other states. Indeed, from 1849 to 1855, private gold coins were the main circulating currency in California (Carothers [1930] 1988: 166).[8]

The government stepped in to make this private production of monies illegal. Until the 1860s, private coinage had been tolerated or ignored; the Constitution, for instance, contained no relevant prohibition, while early nineteenth-century counterfeiting laws referred only to fraudulent duplications or imitations of United States coins, not to their private issue. But in 1862 state forbearance ended; the postage currency law of that year criminalised shinplasters declaring that no 'private corporation, banking association, firm, or individual' could issue or circulate any 'note, check, memorandum, token, or other obligation, for a sum less than one dollar, intended to circulate as money'. To meet the critical demand for fractional currency – small change – Congress converted postage stamps into money (Carothers 1930: 195, 171, 341).[9] Legal restrictions against private monies increased in 1864 and then most forcefully in 1909 with a broad prohibition not only against the private issue of currency 'in the resemblance of coins of the United States', but also of 'original design'. Violators were threatened with a fine of no more than three thousand dollars, imprisonment for no more than five years, or both. Privately issued scrip wages also came under attack. In the late 1800s and early 1900s a number of constitutional and legislative 'store orders' or 'truck acts' upheld the right of workers to be paid in 'lawful money' rather than the scrip, coupons, punchouts, tokens, or trade checks dispensed by 'persons, firms, corporations, and companies' often redeemable only at the local company store (Carothers 1930: 195, 343).[10]

Endorsing and enforcing a single homogenous national currency was declared an urgent task; the government, stated one Indiana court case, 'should unyieldingly maintain the right to protect the money which it makes the standard of value throughout the country'. Even new immigrants were promptly instructed that in America, 'the right to *coin money* belongs to Congress alone'. When people 'manufacture metal or paper money', warned the United States Department of Labor's *Federal Textbook on Citizenship Training*, 'they must pay a heavy fine and are sent to prison for a number of years'.[11] The state moved as well against the personalisation of money by individuals; it broadened definitions of counterfeiting and mutilation, pursuing for instance the popular late nineteenth-century *trompe-l'œil* paintings of dollar bills. The government even forbade the common late nineteenth-century practice of inscribing coins with sentimental messages, calling that practice 'mutilation'. After 1909, a law forbidding the mutilation of coins turned the popular 'love token' gifts into an illegal currency. As the Supreme Court of Indiana declared in November of 1889, the government 'has a right to provide a currency for the whole nation, and to drive out all other circulating mediums by taxation or otherwise'.[12]

It was a losing battle. Although the American state achieved a significant degree of standardisation and monopolisation of legal tender, people continually disrupted monetary uniformity, actively creating all sorts of monetary distinctions. Even Congress resisted when the government's efforts to homogenise currency went too far. Consider for instance the intense debate provoked in 1908 by the proposal to restore the inscription 'In God we Trust', from United States gold coins, which had been removed by a Presidential order. While a few Congressmen applauded President Roosevelt's sensible decision, insisting that 'our coin . . . is a medium of secular, and not sacred, transactions', their more successful opponents argued eloquently in favour of the ritual marker, insisting that while 'the removal of [the motto] did not depreciate [money's] monetary value . . . it depreciated its sentimental value'. America, warned the representative of Georgia, should not coin an 'infidel money'.[13]

Thus, as Simmel's *Philosophy of Money* went to press in 1900, the real world of money in the United States belied his claims concerning its homogeneity and qualitative neutrality. Indeed, as the consumer society was being established, new forms of earmarking money emerged in a number of different settings. Monies multiplied both within households and in public settings. Even prisons debated the right kind of money for inmates, while some orphan asylums and foster-care supervisors proposed a separate currency for dependent children. Legislatures debated whether tips were an acceptable kind of money or a punishable misdemeanour, while businesses defended in court the legitimacy of coupons, trading stamps, and premiums to promote their products.[14]

Thus, paradoxically, the forms of monetary earmarking multiplied just as official money became *more* uniform and generalised. At least, public discussions of these issues became much more active in this period. That is precisely the irony; while the state and the law worked to obtain a single national currency, people continually disrupted monetary uniformity, actively creating all sorts of monetary distinctions. Outside the world of printing and minting, however, people spent less energy on the adoption of different objects as currencies than on creating distinctions among the uses and meanings of existing currencies – that is, on earmarking.

Clearly, a link is missing from the traditional approach to money. Impressed by the fungible, impersonal characteristics of money, classic theorists emphasised its instrumental rationality and apparently unlimited capacity to transform products, relationships, and sometimes even emotions into an abstract and objective numerical equivalent. But money is neither culturally neutral nor socially anonymous. It may well 'corrupt' values and social ties into numbers, but values and social relations reciprocally transmute money by investing it with meaning and social patterns.

Social differentiation of money

Despite its transferability, people make every effort to embed money in particular times, places, and social relations. Thus, I propose an alternative differentiated model of money as continually shaped and reshaped by particular networks of social relations and varying systems of meanings:

1. While money serves as a key rational tool of the modern economic market, it also exists outside the sphere of the market and is profoundly marked by varying cultural and social structures.
2. There is no single, uniform, generalised money, but multiple monies; people earmark different currencies for many or perhaps all types of social interactions, much as they create distinctive languages for different social contexts. And people will in fact respond with anger, shock, or ridicule to the 'misuse' of monies for the wrong circumstances or social relations, such as offering a $500 bill to pay for a newspaper or tipping a restaurant's owner. Money used for rational instrumental exchanges is not 'free' from social constraints but is another type of socially created currency, subject to particular networks of social relations and its own set of values and norms.
3. The classic economic inventory of money's functions and attributes, based on the assumption of a single general-purpose type of money, is unsuitably narrow. By focusing exclusively on money as a market phenomenon, it fails to capture the very complex range of characteristics of money as a social medium. A different, more inclusive coding is necessary, for certain monies can be indivisible (or divisible but not in mathematically predictable

portions), nonfungible, nonportable, deeply subjective, and therefore qualitatively heterogeneous.

4 The assumed dichotomy between a utilitarian money and nonpecuniary values is false, for money under certain circumstances may be as singular and unexchangeable as the most personal or unique object.

5 Given these assumptions, the alleged freedom and unchecked power of money become improbable. Cultural and social structures set inevitable limits to the monetisation process by introducing profound controls and restrictions on the flow and liquidity of monies.

Even estimating the quantity of money requires a social accounting involving more than purely rational market calculations. For instance, Simmel posited that money in 'extraordinarily great quantities', can circumvent its 'empty quantitative nature'; it becomes 'imbued with that "super-additum", with fantastic possibilities that transcend the definiteness of numbers' (Simmel [1900] 1978: 273, 406). The apparent objectivity of numbers, however, is escaped not only by large fortunes. Ordinary or even small sums of money can attain similar distinction. For example, in civil law countries that permit monetary compensation for the grief of losing a child in an accident, legal scholars advocate the '*franc symbolique*'. A token sum of money is perceived as the only dignified equivalent for such a purely emotional loss. Or consider the symbolic calculation of certain charitable gifts; donors to the *New York Times* annual Neediest Cases Fund, for instance, often select the amount of their gift by a personalised sentimental economics; like the couple who took the number of years they had been married (51) and multiplied it by the cost of their marriage licence (2), or the parents whose $134 donation was reached by adding $1 for each of their daughter's 33 years, $1 for good luck and $100 to keep pace with inflation. During the 1890s Americans made the nickel a socially distinctive currency; a five-cent coin, as one historian puts it, not only 'bought anything and everything' but even shaped language ('a nickel's worth', a 'nickel nurser', 'not worth a plugged nickel', to 'nickel and dime' someone, nickelodeon).[15]

The concept of multiple currencies leads us into delicate terminological terrain. Some analysts will prefer to call an object money only when a government issues it and assigns it value. Even there, we have to recognise that, as we've seen, in the United States alone all sorts of governments have issued different bills, coins, and any number of other tender. So have businesses and other types of private or public organisations.[16] Outside the realm of governments, organisations, or business, moreover, people constantly do the following three things: they convert selected objects into the equivalent of currencies, as in the case of cigarettes, postage stamps, subway tokens, poker chips, or baseball cards; they create physically distinct markers, such as gift certificates or food stamps; and they adapt government-issued currencies so vigorously that it seems reasonable also to call these variations monies.[17] That is how I use the term. These objects have no common physical characteristics; they qualify as distinct monies because of the uses and meanings people assign to them, because of the distinctions they represent in everyday social life. Social monies certainly include officially issued coins and bills but they also include all objects that have recognised, regularised exchange value in one social setting or another. I argue that the earmarking of informal monies is a phenomenon as powerful as the official creation of legal tender.

How and when do people create currencies?

How, then, are differences among monies created? While every situation or social relation shapes money to a certain extent, when do people make particularly vehement, visible and sustained efforts to control monies? And how, specifically, do they mark differences among monies? People adopt especially elaborate controls over money and establish differential earmarks when and where they are engaged in delicate or difficult social interactions. Some prominent examples are given in Table 5.1. In each of these examples, people create distinct kinds of monies. Consider for instance a wife's 'pin-money'. American households often mark a housewife's funds as a very different kind of money than a child's allowance or a husband's personal money. It is used differently, allocated in special ways, and its amount set by calculations distinctive to gender as well as class.

These examples of differentiated social interactions and earmarked monies listed here belong outside the sphere of the market, but each one finds an equivalent among standard market transactions. Among other places, earmarking shows very clearly in wages. A 'woman's wage' for instance has historically been a very different sort of payment than a 'man's wage'. As Alice Kessler-Harris persuasively documents, a woman's wage in the early twentieth century was not set by her efficiency or productivity alone but also by custom or tradition, specifically by beliefs of what income women needed. Particularly as the ideal of the 'family wage' (income earned by the man sufficiently large to support his wife and children) spread, women's wages were defined as supplementary income or an earned version of the domestic 'pin-money'. Women's earnings, Kessler-Harris suggests, were 'not in the same sense as males a "wage"'.[18] Indeed, determining women's wages often involved subtle moral quandaries; for instance, while high wages might dangerously encourage women's independence from her family, overly low wages might push young women into prostitution. Wages, or market monies more generally, are thus not exempt from the process of earmarking. There is no 'free' wage economy determined only by demand and supply but instead a highly differentiated system of wages or salaries shaped not only by gender but by such other factors as age, race and ethnicity.

Even when the sums earned may be comparable, different systems of payments are not equivalent forms of income; wages, for instance, differ from commissions, as does a Christmas bonus from a merit or incentive raise. The forms and amount of payment, moreover, often have significant symbolic value as in the case of an insurance agent who receives a publicised bonus for the most sales, or contrariwise, the executive who sees the writing on the wall at year's end when he gets no bonus at all. Types of pay vary as well in the degree of control they exert

Table 5.1 Examples of correspondence between social interaction and monetary forms

Social interaction	**Earmarked monies**
Creating or dissolving social ties	Courtship expenses, child support payments, alimony
Making strong attempts to control others	Bribes, token currencies in penal or mental institutions, restricted bequests at death
Establishing or maintaining equality	Welfare payments for the poor, monies for children, women's 'pin-money'
Maintaining delicate status distinctions	Tips to mailmen or nurses
Dealing with risk and uncertainty	Contributions of money to secure divine or magical intervention
Managing intimacy	Loans or money gifts to friends or kin; payments to sexual partners, legal monetary compensation for moral or emotional damages
Establishing or managing individual or collective religious group identity	Contributions to causes or organisations based on race, ethnicity, gender, or social orientation, donations to organisations, donor-named bequests to universities
Marking rites of passage	Fees, gifts, donations at weddings, funerals, baptisms, Bar-Mitzvahs
Establishing or maintaining honour	'Blood-money'
Managing inadmissible conflicts of interests	Payments for birthing or parenting – surrogate mother's fees, black-market payments, adoption fees, board payments to foster parents; payments for organs or blood
Maintaining clandestine social relations	Blackmail, drug-dealing payments, pay-offs to spies, payments to concubines

over a worker's autonomy; payment by result is more restrictive for instance than payment by time. And timing itself matters; wage payment by the day or the week is a different sort of income from a monthly or biannual salary.[19] As with non-market currencies, each of these cases reflects distinct ways of marking money; for example, paying in certain ways, restricting uses, or determining proper amounts of payments for specified recipients.[20]

The process of earmarking monies – both market and non-market – is not only complex and constant but often highly contested. Disputes arise when parties to an interaction have contradictory understandings of the relationship, when their values clash or they are pursuing conflicting interests, or even when they have adopted different techniques for earmarking, especially when the preferred techniques of one party mean something different and undesirable to the other party.[21] For example, burial monies – money earmarked to pay for the dignified funeral of a loved one – illustrate how conflicts arise when money is earmarked to cope with difficult social situations. These monies have been persistently earmarked by the poor as a sacred expense, often put ahead of other necessities. Death money was, and still is, clearly distinct from rent money, food money, or clothing money. To the poor, a pauper's burial looms as the ultimate existential and social degradation. Which explains why since the late nineteenth century, industrial insurance agents have sometimes been paid ahead of the landlord. To middle-class observers, however, burial monies have typically seemed an irrational form of consumerism. But their attempts to shift poor people's cents or dollars from insurance to a more 'rational' expenditure or into savings banks have notoriously failed.

Does this mean that the affluent do not earmark death monies? Spared the spectre of a county burial, upper- and middle-class people may not set aside burial monies but they still differentiate death monies from other income or routine expenses. Surely, bargaining or comparison shopping for final expenses, such as funerals, however sensible, is deemed sacrilegious, and even negotiating the officiating clergyman's fee has typically involved delicate social work. Death monies are often earmarked to honour the deceased by making special donations to her or his preferred charitable cause. Monies gained by a loved one's death are also treated differently. In child wrongful death lawsuits, as one example, middle-class plaintiffs often tend to ritualise the monetary award by donating it to charity, safety organisations, or scholarships for poor children. Even life insurance proceeds are set apart from other income, such as Social Security payments. Widows are more likely to use Social Security income for routine living expenses while earmarking life insurance proceeds not only for final expenses but as a 'nest egg' to be preserved or else spent in larger non-routine purchases, such as home repair or a child's education.[22]

How are multiple monies distinguished? How, concretely, do people set death money apart from rent money, or investment money from gift money? There are a number of different techniques, such as restricting the uses of money, regulating modes of allocation, inventing rituals for its presentation, modifying its physical appearance, designating separate locations for particular monies; attaching special meanings to particular amounts, appointing proper users to handle specified monies; and earmarking appropriate sources of money for specified uses. Indeed, the standard practice of budgeting constitutes a special case of earmarking; the subdivision of the funds available to an organisation, government, individual, or household into distinct categories, each with its own rules of expenditure.[23]

This phenomenon of earmarking is not restricted to people's uses of state-issued money but applies also to other objects; from tokens and commercial paper to art objects, and even including kitchen recipes or jokes – anything, in fact, that is socially exchangeable. At issue here, however, is to show that precisely where interpreters of modernity see the utmost depersonalisation of life, in the circulation of state currency, people continually introduce distinctions, doubts, and directives that defy all instrumental calculation.

While contemporary social observers were right to predict that money would enter ever more social and commercial exchanges, they were wrong in their assessment of the consequences. Suffering from a sort of intellectual colour-blindness, Simmel's brilliant analysis of money, for instance, failed to capture the rich new social hues emerging in a monetary economy as people improvised different ways to personalise and differentiate monies. Where the colour blind see only shades of grey, people of normal vision see the whole rainbow. But money-marking people go one better; they create their own spectra in place of those provided by governments and banks.

Notes

1 Author's note: This chapter adapts sections of Chapter 1 from my book, *The Social Meaning of Money* (1994).

2 For further discussion, see Zelizer (1996).

3 The heterogeneity of state notes went beyond their diverse economic values; banks also frequently personalised notes with elaborate designs of individuals or scenes meaningful for their locality. For an excellent collection of banknote illustrations, see Christie's catalogue (1990). For evidence of the diversity of American currencies in the eighteenth century, see Alice Hanson Jones's thorough analysis of probate inventories in the thirteen colonies (Jones 1980: 8, 132–3). According to Jones, financial assets ranged from bonds and notes to gold and silver coins, the local paper money issued by each particular province, English pound sterling notes, and including the 'joe's or Johannes, a Portuguese gold coin, or the 'piece of eight' or Spanish dollar. People often used in-kind payments at accepted valuations in local money; in Maryland and Virginia for instance, taxes and other debts were settled in pounds of tobacco.

4 See also Helleiner (1997).

5 On the various circulating monies, see Friedman and Schwartz (1971: 20–9). For other cases of restricted receivability, see Breckinridge (1903: 124–6), Kemp (1956: 59–93). Richard F. Bensel (1990) sees the nationalisation of currency as further evidence of the general centralisation of state activities during and after the Civil War. Southern currency, however, remained in a state of 'unbelievable chaos,' as all sorts of paper currencies were being issued not only by the Confederacy but its states and municipalities as well as by state banks (Nussbaum 1964: 123).

6 Nussbaum points to the decrease in litigation over specific money as another measure of growing monetary uniformity (Nussbaum 1939: 59–60). Indeed, Bensel explains how 'by making the greenback a 'legal tender' for public and private debts, the Union in effect made the acceptance of paper currency mandatory in all contracts and transactions in which money changed hands if those obligations were to be enforceable in court' (Bensel 1990: 162n141). There were exceptions. As late as 1864 California and Nevada still upheld 'specie contracts' allowing for payment of a specific kind of currency (Breckinridge 1903: 126, 158–60; Mitchell 1903: 142–4).

7 On church money, see Nussbaum (1964: 42), *New York Times*, 10 September, 1989. On the brass check system used by brothels, The Pittsburgh Survey (1914: 36). For

other examples of eighteenth-century private coins and tokens, see Wilson (1992: 72–3), Crosby ([1873] 1974).

8 See also Low ([1900] 1935), Falkner (1901), Barnard (1917). On the private issue of gold coins, see Carothers (1930: 128), Wilson (1992: 124).

9 Mitchell notes that the postage currency lot did not prevent the circulation of town and city notes (Mitchell 1903: 162).

10 US Government (1909: Sec.167, 1120). On scrip wages, see e.g. Knoxville Iron Co. v. Harbison 183 US 13 (1901). While the courts did not suppress competing currencies, the law required that wages be paid in money if the wage earner so elected. There was opposition; some courts held that 'truck laws' violated the constitutional liberty of the labourer by interfering with his freedom of contract (Freund 1905: 307–8).

11 Hancock *et al.* v. Yaden, 366 Supreme Court of Indiana at 371 (1889); Clark (1926: 64).

12 Hancock *et al.* v. Yaden 366 Supreme Court of Indiana at 372. The Secret Service was founded in 1865 in great measure to control counterfeiting. For some general accounts of counterfeiting, see e.g. Smith (1944), Bloom (1957). In *After the Hunt: William Harnett And Other American Still Life Painters 1870–1900*, Alfred Frankenstein tells about Harnett's encounter with the Secret Service for his paintings of United States Treasury notes (Frankenstein 1969: 82–3). For specific legislation, see US Government (1909: ch.7, 1115–22). The Secret Service is still concerned with artistic representations of currency; as in the highly publicised case of J.S.G. Boggs who 'spent' over $250,000 of his hand-drawn bills by persuading merchants to accept his personalised renditions of legal tender in exchange for their goods or services. See Weschler (1993: 38–41); *New York Times*, 6 December, 1992, p. 42. On love tokens and other jewelry coins, see *New York Times*, 10 January, 1910; *American Journal of Numismatics* (1882: 88–9), Campbell (1972), McClure (1976: 14, 20, 22), Entenmann (1991).

13 US Congress (1908: 3387, 3389). The religious inscription had been authorised in 1864. Roosevelt argued that the motto came 'dangerously close to sacrilege.' *New York Times*, 14 November, 1907, p. 1. Some religious leaders agreed. See e.g. Emerson (1908). Emerson, a Methodist minister, sent copies of his pamphlet to Roosevelt ('the fearless President') and members of Congress strongly supporting the decision to remove the inscription from coins. Most religious organisations, however, passed resolutions condemning President Roosevelt's ruling; see the *New York Times*, 14–16 November, 1907. Even the government earmarked monies, authorising for instance commemorative coins – the first in 1892 for the Columbian Exposition in Chicago – or 'patriotic' currencies such as the extraordinarily successful Liberty Bonds during the First World War. Private issue of scrip was tolerated through the Great Depression as emergency substitutes for official money. About $1 billion in scrip were issued in the 1930s depression. See Wilson (1992: 218–21).

14 On prisons, see e.g. Barrows (1904: 186–7), Barrows (1912: 577), Harrison (1912: 1549–50), Randall (1915: 392–6); on tips, Zelizer (1994: ch.3). On orphanages and foster care policies, see e.g. Thomas (1926: 120), Zelizer (1985: 182–4). On coupons, trading stamps, and premiums, see Strasser (1989).

15 Rabinovitz (1991), Schlereth (1989: 79–85). On French compensation cases, see Mazeaud *et al.* (1957). For an example of the connection between quantity of money and its social and symbolic meaning, see Geertz (1973).

16 For instance, see Lea *et al.* on the introduction of therapeutic or behaviour-modifying token monies – metal or plastic chips, personalised stamps, printed paper – in mental hospitals, schools, and industry (Lea *et al.* 1987: 450–76). For examples of prison money, see Zara and Lemke (1981: 1–6), Kalinich (1980). At Club Med resorts where everything is pre-paid or can be charged, plastic bead necklaces are used as currency to purchase bar drinks (Biggart 1994: 687).

17 On the invention of new currencies, see R. A. Radford's (1945) classic case of the creation of the 'bully mark' paper currency at a prisoner-of-war camp. On cigarette currency within institutions, see Radford (1945), Goffman (1961: 270–3). *The Baltimore Sun*, 22 June, 1993, reports the circulation of dollar bills inscribed with the words 'gay money' or a pink triangle, apparently as an effort to dramatise gay economic power.

18 Kessler-Harris (1990: 17, 19–20).

19 On the link between modes of payment and systems of control over workers, see Granovetter and Tilly (1988: 201–7). Legislating the timing of payment has been the subject of considerable constitutional argument. See e.g. Freund (1905: 304–8).

20 For an excellent discussion of some of the social structural determinants of variation in market money, see Baker (1987). Max Weber (1968: 77) developed his own typology of legal tender, distinguishing 'free' or 'market' money, from 'limited' or 'administrative' money, and 'regulated money.'

21 Rodgers shows the controversial nineteenth-century construction of the wage (Rodgers 1979: 30–44). In a society where self-employment was a 'moral norm,' wage payment symbolised dependence and degradation.

22 On children's wrongful death settlements, see Zelizer (1985: 162–3); on widows' monies, Life Underwriter Training Council and Life Insurance Agency Management Association (1971).

23 See Padgett (1981).

Bibliography

American Journal of Numismatics (1882) 'Modern use of old coins', *American Journal of Numismatics* 16: 88–9.

Baker, Mayne (1987) 'What is money? A social structural interpretation', in M.S. Mizruchi and M. Schwartz (eds) *Intercorporate Relations*, Cambridge, Mass.: Cambridge University Press.

Barnard, B.W. (1917) 'The use of private tokens for money in the United States', *Quarterly Journal of Economics* 31: 600–34.

Barrows, I.C. (1912) 'When wardens differ who shall decide?' *The Survey* 28 (20 July): 575–7.

Barrows, S.J. (1904) 'Prisoner's earnings', *Charities* 13 (26 November): 186–7.

Beniger, J.R. (1986) *The Control Revolution*, Cambridge, Mass.: Harvard University Press.

Bensel, R.F. (1990) *Yankee Leviathan*, Cambridge, Mass.: Cambridge University Press.

Biggart, N.W. (1994) 'Labor and leisure', N. Smelser and R. Swedberg (eds) *Handbook of Economic Sociology*, Princeton, N.J.: Princeton University Press and New York: Russell Sage Foundation.

Bloom, M.T. (1957) *Money Of Their Own*, New York: Charles Scribner's Sons.

Breckinridge, S.P. (1903) *Legal Tender*, Chicago: University of Chicago Press.

Campbell, L.M. (1972) 'Love tokens', *Mana Journal* 16: 4–17;

Carothers, N. ([1930] 1988) *Fractional Money*, New York: John Wiley & Sons. Reprinted by

Bower and Merena Galleries, Wolfeboro, New Hampshire, 1988.

Carruthers, B.G. and Babb, S. (1996) 'The color of money and the nature of value: greenbacks and gold in postbellum America', *American Journal of Sociology* 101: 1556–91.

Charities (1905) 'Should not convict labor support the convict's innocent dependents?', *Charities* 14 (9 September): 1089–90.

Christie's catalogue (1990) *Important Early American Bank Notes, 1810–1874*, Christie's catalogue, New York.

Clark, L.P. (1926) *Federal Textbook on Citizenship Training* Part III, 'Our Nation' US Department of labor, Bureau of Naturalization, Washington: Government Printing Office.

Crosby, S.S. ([1873] 1974) *The Early Coins of America*, Lawrence, Mass.: Quarterman Publications, Inc.

Emerson, E (1908) *Money and Mottoes*, on file at the New York Public Library.

Entenmann, L.L. (1991) *Love Tokens as Engraved Coins*, Audubon, N.J.: Lloyd L. Entenmann.

Falkner, R.P. (1901) 'The private issue of token coins', *Political Science Quarterly* 16: 303–27.

Frankenstein, A. (1969). *After the Hunt: William Harnett And Other American Still Life Painters 1870–1900*, Berkeley: University of California Press.

Freund, E. (1905) *The Police Power*, Chicago: Callaghan & Company.

Friedman, M. and Schwartz, A.J. (1971) *A Monetary History of the United States, 1867–1960* Princeton, N.J.: Princeton University Press.

Geertz, C. (1973) 'Deep play: notes on the Balinese cockfight', in C. Geertz (ed.) *The Interpretation of Cultures*, New York: Basic Books.

Goffman, E. (1961) *Asylums*, Garden City, N.Y.: Anchor Books.

Granovetter, M. and Tilly, C. (1988) 'Inequality and labor processes', in N. Smelser (ed.) *Handbook of Sociology*, Newbury Park, California, SAGE Publications.

Habermas, J. (1989) *The Theory of Communicative Action*, Volume 2, Boston: Beacon Press.

Hammond, B ([1957] 1967) *Banks and Politics in America*, Princeton, N.J.: Princeton University Press.

Harrison, S.B. (1912) 'A cash-nexus for crime', *The Survey* 27 (6 January): 1541–56.

Helleiner, Eric (1996) 'Money and the nation-state in North America', unpublished paper, Department of Political Science, York University, Canada.

Helleiner, Eric (1997) 'One nation, one money: territorial currencies and the nation-state', ARENA Working Paper no. 17, Oslo: University of Oslo.

James, J.A. (1978) *Money and Capital Markets in Postbellum America*, Princeton, N.J.: Princeton University Press.

Jones, A.H. (1980) *Wealth Of A Nation To Be*, New York: Columbia University Press.

Kalinich, D.B. (1980) *The Inmate Economy*, Lexington, Mass.: Lexington Books.

Kemp, A (1956) *The Legal Qualities of Money*, New York: Pageant Press.

Kessler-Harris, A. (1990) *A Woman's Wage*, Lexington, Kentucky: The University Press of Kentucky.

Lea, S.E.G., Tarpy, R. and Webley, P. (1987) *The Individual in the Economy*, New York: Cambridge University Press.

Life Underwriter Training Council and Life Insurance Agency Management Association (1971) *The Widows Study*, Vol. II, 'Adjustment to widowhood', Hartford: Life Insurance Agency Management Association.

Low, L.H. ([1900] 1935) *Hard Time Tokens*, San Jose, California: Globe Printing Co.

McClure, D.L. (1976) 'Love token collecting offers romantic glimpse of history', *Numismatic News Weekly* (14 February).

Mandell, L. (1990) *The Credit Card Industry*, Boston: Twayne Publishers.

Mazeaud, H., Mazeaud, L. and Tunc, A. (1957) *Traité Théorique et pratique de la responsabilité civile délictuelle et contractuelle*, 5th edn, Paris: Editions Montchrestien.
Mitchell, W.C. (1903) *A History of the Greenbacks*, Chicago: University of Chicago Press.
Money (1897) 'The Field For "Money"', *Money* I (May): 9ff.
Nugent, W.T.K. (1968) *Money and American Society, 1865–1880*, New York: Free Press.
Nussbaum, A. (1939) *Money in the Law*, Chicago: Foundation Press.
Nussbaum, A. (1964) *A History of the Dollar*, New York: Columbia University Press.
Padgett, J. (1981) 'Hierarchy and ecological control in federal budgetary decision making', *American Journal of Sociology* 87 (July): 75–129.
Pittsburgh Survey, The (1914) 'Wage-earning Pittsburgh', *The Pittsburgh Survey*, New York: Russell Sage Foundation.
Rabinovitz, J. (1991) 'The math of giving: some use formulas to aid the neediest', *New York Times*, 5 February.
Radford, R.A. (1945) 'The economic organization of a P.O.W. camp', *Economica* 11: 189–201.
Radin, M. (1996) *Contested Commodities*, Cambridge: Harvard University Press.
Randall, F.L. (1915) 'Possible development of schemes for payment of prisoners on the basis of the services which they render', *Proceedings of the Forty-Second Annual National Conference of Charities And Correction*, May: 392–6.
Rodgers, D.T. (1979) *The Work Ethic in Industrial America, 1850–1920*, Chicago: University of Chicago Press.
Schlereth, T.J. (1989) 'Country stores, county fairs, and mail-order catalogues', in S.J. Bronner (ed.) *Consuming Visions*, New York: Norton.
Simmel, Georg ([1908] 1950) *The Sociology of Georg Simmel*, edited by Kurt H. Wolf, Glencoe, Ill.: Free Press.
Simmel, Georg ([1900] 1978) *The Philosophy of Money*, translated by Tom Bottomore and David Frisby, London: Routledge & Kegan Paul.
Smith, L.D. (1944) *Counterfeiting: Crime against the People*, New York: W.W. Norton & Company.
Strasser, S. (1989) *Satisfaction Guaranteed*, New York: Pantheon.
Thomas, F. (1926) 'The place of the institution in a child welfare program', *Twenty-Seventh New York State Conference of Charities.*
US Congress (1908) *Congressional Record*, Sixtieth Congress, First Session, volume 42, part 4 Washington, 16 March.
US Government (1909) *Statutes At Large*, vol. 35, Part 1, Washington: Government Printing Office.
Weber, M. (1968) *Economy and Society*, edited by Guenther Roth and Claus Wittich, New York: Bedminster Press.
Weschler, L. (1993) 'Money changes everything', *The New Yorker* (16 January): 38–41.
Wilson, T. (1992) *The Power 'To Coin' Money: The Exercise of Monetary Powers by the Congress*, New York: M. E. Sharpe, Inc.
Zara, J. and Lemke, B (1981) 'The media of exchange of our "penal institutions"', *TAMS Journal* 21 (April): 1–6.
Zelizer, Viviana A. (1985) *Pricing the Priceless Child: The Changing Social Value of Children*, New York: Basic Books.
Zelizer, Viviana A. (1994) *The Social Meaning of Money*, New York: Basic Books.
Zelizer, Viviana A. (1996) 'Payments and social ties', *Sociological Forum* 11 (September): 481–95.

6 A distant view

Imagery and imagination in the paper currency of the British Empire, 1800–1960

Virginia Hewitt

In 1996 the European Monetary Institute unveiled draft designs for the European single currency banknotes. With only a small space on the back of the notes left free for the national emblems of participating states, the designs are standard, based on architectural styles of bridges and gateways, to symbolise openness and communication within Europe and with the rest of the world. In Britain the popular response, as filtered through the media, was largely one of dismay at the projected loss of Britain's own Bank of England notes, proudly bearing a portrait of H.M. Queen Elizabeth II. Probably few people knew that the Bank had been issuing its own notes for over three hundred years, and fewer still that the monarch's portrait was introduced only in 1960; however, many perceived the proposed Euro note as undermining a national institution and as a threat to British sovereignty.

This reaction is an example of how closely paper currencies and the images they carry have become associated with national identity, not surprisingly since nowadays most nation-states have their own notes issued by a central bank or treasury and bearing designs chosen to represent national culture and prosperity. However, such an association is comparatively recent, becoming a global feature only in the second half of the twentieth century with the emergence of new independent states in the non-western world, and the increasingly centralised control of note issue. The present situation has in fact evolved from historical origins different in two key respects: firstly, early notes were often private commercial issues subject to little regulation; secondly, in the nineteenth and early twentieth centuries the spread of banking and paper money across the world was encouraged by European colonisation and imperial ambition. Thus, in many countries the first banknotes were evidence not of national status, but of foreign interests.

This chapter is concerned with the notes issued in British colonies, looking particularly at the designs they carried and how these attempted to symbolise both British authority and indigenous cultures. In the nineteenth century, designs were redolent of western mythology, combined with romantic western interpretations of subject lands – effects and evidence of a distant view indeed. During the twentieth century, greater realism in pictorial representation and new note-issuing institutions brought about a new style in which portraits of British monarchs presided over exotic foreign landscapes; hybrids still, but containing seeds of the independent note issues which were to come. Given the extent of the empire and the diversity of notes that were issued, it is only possible here to give a broad survey, focusing on dominant trends in design. Nonetheless, exploration of this curious iconography, how it was influenced, and the attitudes of bankers, printers, government officials and native peoples, may show how colonial note issues paved the way towards modern national currencies, and reveal how one nation pictured the identity of others.

It should be said at once that issues of paper money in the British colonies did not appear as the result of any deliberate or cohesive policy. Rather, they varied according to circumstances and expediency, growing in as haphazard a fashion as the empire itself. Sometimes notes were issued by colonial treasuries, but many were circulated by private commercial banks. Indeed, in an empire born of and nourished by commercial interests, banking skills were an important British export. At the time of the first colonial issues, in the late eighteenth and early nineteenth centuries, it would have been surprising had it been any different, for in Britain itself, banking and note issue were still experimental, volatile and the subject of much debate, but little system. Before turning to the colonial issues, it is therefore helpful to look briefly at the development of the British banknotes which were their models.

Early paper money in Britain

Various banking services, including promissory notes with a limited circulation, were offered by goldsmith and scrivener bankers[1] by the middle of the seventeenth century, but the beginnings of more formalised note issue may be dated from the foundation of the Bank of England in 1694 and the Bank of Scotland in 1695, each of which began issuing its own notes soon after opening (Clapham, 1944; Richards, 1958; Byatt, 1994; Saville, 1995; Cameron, 1995). Despite the implication of their names, and certain privileges, these were not national, central banks, and they did not have exclusive rights of note issue. During the eighteenth century the demands of trade, industrialisation, and shortage of coin during war encouraged the growth of local banks and the use of paper money. By the 1810s there were many hundreds of different banks operating in towns throughout Britain, issuing a myriad of notes which circulated locally (Presnell, 1956).

The localised nature of banking was an important influence on banknote designs. Printed in black and white, often on only one side, notes were dominated by text, usually in copperplate script but sometimes incorporating varying typefaces to discourage forgery by alteration of the value. On earlier issues, pictorial decoration was limited to small hand-engraved emblems or vignettes; from the 1820s production from steel plates encouraged more elaborate designs with finer detail in vignettes and abstract patterns of security printing. One function of ornamental devices on notes was to deter forgery, but they were also a means of identifying and advertising a bank; indeed, in some instances, such as the 'Ship' Bank in Glasgow, banking partnerships were named colloquially after the images they carried. The choice of illustration therefore tended to reflect local features or a banker's business background, as well as contemporary trends in graphic design. Custom-made designs ranged from the highly specific, such as local coats of arms, town views, or important local buildings, to broadly relevant images such as pastoral scenes of cattle or ploughing for an agricultural area, or ships at sea for a port. However, there was also a wide variety of all-purpose devices, symbolising appropriate concepts of flourishing commerce, wealth and economic growth. Most popular among these were female allegorical figures in classical style, recalling the deities of the ancient world. The Bank of England set an early example, adorning its notes with a seated figure of Britannia, bare-headed, holding an olive branch and looking at a pile of coins (over time the olive branch turned to honesty and the pile of coins became a beehive).[2] Many country banks followed this lead, some copying the Bank's style of Britannia very closely, others depicting her with helmet and spear, sometimes accompanied by the British lion. Frequently she appeared as the central figure in a graceful triumvirate, with Hibernia and Scotia, their identities revealed perhaps by devices on their shields, or by a harp for Hibernia and a feather bonnet for Scotia. These personifications were the most common form of national imagery on British notes in the nineteenth century. Monarchs were rarely depicted, and even then there was often a local connection; for example, Alfred the Great on a note of Wantage, where he was born c.848–49, or Victoria and Albert with a vignette of Balmoral for the Aberdeen Town and County Banking Company. Along with national allegories, country banks frequently chose to illustrate commercial and financial prosperity as represented by various permutations of goddesses of Fortune and Plenty; sailing ships and packages of goods for export; sheep and corn sheaves; ploughs and factory chimneys (Hewitt and Keyworth, 1987).

Britannia overseas

This then was the background against which paper money was introduced to British colonies. Much of the iconography on notes in the colonies drew heavily on European classical traditions and could just as easily have appeared on British notes. Pre-eminent both in frequency of incidence and in symbolic status was Britannia, who adorned commercial and government issues across the world from India and Ceylon to Canada, South Africa and Australia. Occasionally she was modelled on the Bank of England's emblem and was shown seated, bare-headed and framed in a foliated cartouche – for example, on Treasury notes of Ceylon or notes of the Colonial Bank of Mauritius, Bourbon and Dependencies in the early 1800s (Rey, 1996; 1997). Usually, however, she appeared in the warrior-like guise of Athena, with helmet, spear and shield, this latter sometimes bearing a gorgon's head (a feature of Athena's breastplate) but more often a Union Jack, in a clear statement of British authority. Quite often she was accompanied by the British lion, with its symbolic connotations of majesty, strength and guardianship. Other figures drawn from classical mythology, appearing singly or in combination, include Fortuna with her rudder, Mercury and his attributes of winged cap and staff, and Neptune in a sea-shell chariot. Thus a note of the Commercial Bank, Calcutta, featured a Britannia in Bank of England style and a vignette of an airborne Mercury greeting Fortuna, seated on parcels, with ships sailing in the background – all omens of propitious trade. It may be argued that these allegories in a European tradition carried overtones of the colonial relationship, at least as perceived from the mother country's point of view; Britain's power and protection in return for her possession's loyalty and produce. Figures of Britannia on notes, say, of India or Canada seem to proclaim 'Britishness' much more emphatically than they do on English country issues. Likewise vignettes of Neptune, which on British notes suggest the importance of the coast to an island race, but on notes of dependencies are a reminder of Britain's naval supremacy, itself a major factor in the creation of her empire, and a means to prosperity earned through overseas trade.

Printing firms and the classical tradition

Personifications and emblems of this sort were not indigenous to the countries in which the notes were issued, but they would have been familiar to British governors, traders and settlers from banknotes at home. Furthermore, they fitted comfortably into the repertoire of the London firms of printers and engravers who produced notes for British local banks and for overseas issues. Printer and customer alike were clearly influenced by the contemporary elevation of classical ideals. During the eighteenth century art schools and arbiters of taste promoted the imitation of art in antiquity, with results that permeated all branches of the arts, from Wedgwood vases and neo-classical architecture, even to the work of artists who travelled abroad with a specific remit to record accurately what they saw. It has been observed that the classical vision was so deeply embedded that 'the indigenous, semi-naked peoples of distant lands were invariably imagined in terms not just of the "noble savage" but also of the ancient Greeks and Romans' (Jacobs 1995: 12). William Hodges, a British artist in India in the 1780s, explained that 'to a painter's mind the fine antique figures never fail to present themselves, when he observes a beautiful female ascending these steps from the river, with wet drapery, which perfectly displays the whole person, and with vases on their heads, carrying water to the temples' (Jacobs 1995: 64). With the promulgation of such ideals and the prevalence of classical personifications on British notes, it is hardly surprising that they were exported by way of colonial issues. Indeed, if the view of Hodges was typical, many people may not have regarded this as the imposition of an alien iconography, though those who did might well have argued that they were disseminating a universally desirable standard.

Increasingly specialised skills in banknote manufacture developed alongside the growth of banking in Britain, with the main printing firms for notes in towns such as London, Edinburgh and Newcastle; it was to be expected, therefore, that colonial banks and treasuries would have their notes printed in Britain. This was a major factor in determining their style, encouraging similarities not just between individual British or colonial notes, but in banknotes across the British empire and, indeed, across the world. For example, allegorical figures and symbols of agriculture and commerce were standard features of paper money in Latin America, and commissioning the same printer could lead to similar or identical vignettes appearing on notes in the United States and Hungary, or Canada and Brazil. Homogeneity was enhanced by the fact that while bankers could commission their own special designs, it was cheaper to draw from a printer's standard range of vignettes, borders and so on. Examples of recurring images are readily found on notes of one of the most prolific firms, Perkins, Fairman and Heath (later Perkins, Bacon and Petch), who manufactured notes for many banks in Britain and overseas.[3] The firm of Perkins energetically solicited orders, sending out specimen designs and listing other customers as references; for example, writing to the agent for the colonial government of New Zealand in 1848 they asked 'to be pardoned for stating that we supply nearly all the Banks in Scotland and Ireland, a very high proportion of those in England, the East Indies, the private Banks in our Colonies & several Foreign Governments, & that for rapidity of working & Security from Forgery no-one can as yet compete with us'.[4] Such an approach, with the offer of sample designs, clearly made it easy for banks to choose from existing images. One example is found on designs for the Bank of Australia, which was founded as a local business in New South Wales in 1826, its shares being taken up mainly by government officials and British settlers. A historian of Australian banking history has described this and other banks set up in that period as operating on a localised basis similar to that of the country banks in England, a parallel that in this instance was clearly manifested in the note design (Butlin 1968: 8–9). A proof £20 note by Perkins and Heath uses the same lettering, wreath of oak leaves, and vignette of a beehive nestling in flowers as appeared on a design they produced for the Halifax Bank in Yorkshire. Images could also reappear across a divide of decades as well as continents. A vignette of Neptune seated in a clam-shell chariot drawn by sea-horses was engraved by William Finden from a drawing by Robert Smirke for a design Perkins offered to the Bank of England around 1821; in the 1870s it could be found on the back of a 100 rupee note for the Colombo branch of the Oriental Banking Corporation in Ceylon. The same figure of Neptune, with additional background of sea and sky but without the sea-horses, was used for the Commercial Bank of Sydney in the 1830s.[5]

Design negotiated by bankers

While some banks were apparently happy to follow the printer's suggestions, others had their own ideas as to what they wanted. Negotiations between Perkins and the Bank of Bengal over a new note issue illustrate the attention given to such matters, and the important influence of British prototypes in general, even if there were disagreements over detail. In the summer of 1848, the Secretary of the Bank wrote to Perkins requesting specimen designs for various items including a new banknote, 'as the one we have now in use is not much approved of, and the Directors are not indisposed to make a change, if a judicious one can be suggested.

Our present notes in my opinion are too small . . . The body of the Notes too, would be greatly improved if the border was left out, and there was less ink spread over the note generally. You can send however several specimens for inspection, and I should wish to have one of them as like the Bank of England Notes as you can make it.'[6] The printers must have found this rather galling, as they were responsible for the existing unpopular design. This included a conventional vignette of an allegorical female figure holding Mercury's wand, surrounded by borders and panels of machine engraving. Along the left-hand edge was a native script, contained within an unusual waved border of machine work, a device which was also used on Perkins's notes for the Leeds Union Bank in England. Indeed, the decorative design of the Bengal note – all that ink – was typical of Perkins's style, which was precisely intended to provide greater security than the Bank of England's simple note, highly susceptible to forgery.[7]

There had been much debate in Britain over the relative merits of simple or complex designs, with many country banks opting for the detailed steel-engravings offered by Perkins and other printers. But there were also those who followed the Bank of England's preference for a plainer note. In the case of the Bank of Bengal the Secretary seems to have argued on aesthetic grounds, but one wonders whether the Directors might not also have been attracted by the status of the Bank of England as a role model. In response to their request, Perkins Bacon sent two drawings. They explained that one was as close to the Bank of England note as possible, given the need for native scripts, and the Bank's monopoly over certain features. However, the printers urged strongly that this would give 'far too little security against either forgery or alteration more especially in such a country as India where your Notes have already many years back been altered and where the Natives are so noted for imitating almost every thing.'[8] They therefore offered a second design, which 'would make a good looking note with considerable white spaces about it', but nonetheless included such security features as a panel repeating the value of the note in tiny lettering, over twelve hundred times – another characteristic of Perkins's notes. Unfortunately the Perkins archives do not contain copies of the designs, but a new note issued by the bank in 1853 suggests that at least some of their advice prevailed. Indeed the note looks remarkably like the earlier issue, with the same vignette and a central panel of lathe-work. The borders round the whole note remained, but the waved line border round the native script had been removed, as had some scroll patterns and ornamental ribbons.[9]

Imagined views of distant lands

On most of the notes discussed so far, the pictorial elements of the design gave no clue that they did not circulate in Britain, but many notes combined overtly British symbolism with images representing the country in which they were issued. These touches of local colour ranged from token emblems of flora and fauna to specific buildings or landscapes. Palm trees and, sometimes, pagodas were among the standard repertoire for any colony in Asia, usually strategically

Figure 6.1 Design for a £2 note of the Treasury of Ceylon, *c.* 1849, showing Britannia with the British lion and Union Jack, and elephant and palms in the background. The printers had problems with the Singalese text on the left of the note. (Courtesy of the Chartered Institute of Bankers and the Trustees of the British Museum.)

placed in the background behind Britannia or some other allegorical figure. Animals were also popular. Elephants often stood underneath the palm trees, while tigers were suitable adornment for Indian notes. For example, around 1804 the London firm of Ashby engraved vignettes for the Asiatic Bank in Madras, depicting a sturdy figure of Fortuna with a powerful tiger stretched out at the foot of the rock on which she sits. A scrawnier beast, considerably less well-drawn, appeared on notes of Alexander and Company's Bank of Hindostan in the 1820s. Other indigenous creatures included a kangaroo (with Britannia and Queen Victoria) for the Union Bank of Australia, and a seal and codfish on notes of the Commercial Bank of Newfoundland.

Sometimes local emblems were used to customise otherwise standard designs. In the 1840s, Treasury notes in Ceylon and notes of the British Bank of North America carried identical figures of a seated Britannia with shield, lion and cornucopia, her outstretched hand graciously indicating her extended kingdom; however, the Ceylon note is distinguished by the addition of an elephant and a palm tree in the background (Figure 6.1). Attempts to characterise a note issue in this way could produce surprising results. A proof design by Silvester of London for a new Treasury issue authorised in Ceylon in 1826 shows a standing female figure with Mercury's wings and staff, holding the reigns of two camels kneeling docilely by her side: a striking image, not least because camels are not indigenous to Ceylon. Unhampered by this inconvenient fact, Perkins also produced a camel for the Bank of Ceylon in 1840, along with the ubiquitous Britannia, lion, elephant and palm. Only the forepart of the camel is visible, suggesting perhaps an unnecessary concern not to choose the wrong number of humps (Hewitt, 1998b).

The written word

It was not only wildlife that could confuse the printers. Most of the texts on colonial notes were in English, but an important distinguishing feature of paper currency in India and Ceylon was the use of native scripts, an indication that notes were not handled only by British residents and merchants. Evidently these scripts gave the printers considerable extra work. In 1838 Perkins Bacon wrote to the Bank of Bombay to say they were preparing drawings and quoting prices to produce notes. They explained that these were in line with their charges for other banks in India, and indeed for notes in England, but the cost of engraving the plates would be much higher than for the latter 'as we must not only have all the Native Characters engraved by our very best workman who is the only person we can safely trust with them from his long experience, but even he will be more than double the time about this part of the work than he would be in engraving an equal quantity of English characters.'[10] They went on to offer several contacts at other Indian banks as referees for their great and 'almost exclusive' experience in engraving these scripts. Despite this professed expertise, things could go wrong. Late in 1849, Perkins obtained the business of producing a new issue of Treasury notes in Ceylon. Discussing the design with George Baillie, the Agent for the Colonies, the firm promised that the 'Singhalese and Malabar Characters shall be carefully copied and engraved on each note.'[11] The Malabar, that is, Tamil, script was all correct, but the Sinhalese text contained a jumble of nonsensical words and invented characters. Unfortunately we do not know whether this was the fault of the engraver or of the source he copied, but it may be imagined that such errors would hardly inspire native people to have confidence in the notes.[12]

Further evidence that the use of native scripts did encourage wider circulation of notes is found in a later correspondence with the Bank of Bombay. Perkins Bacon had received a letter from the bank informing them 'that the Native Merchants object to receiving [the] new Notes, because the name of the Bank & the amount of the Notes are not printed in the Guzarattee [sic] language in the left hand lower part of the margin' and asking if this could be inserted.[13] The printers replied that they could supply this or any other language, but requested that the bank should send them 'the Native characters written with a pen either of the size you require them, or much larger if you prefer it, as you can do it with ease & it will save us much time and trouble & enable us to be more perfectly accurate in the shape & cut of the letters than we can otherwise be.'[14] Perhaps this is an implicit admission that earlier mistakes were due to the engraver's misinterpretation of examples he received.

Assumption of power

Local scenes or features helped to emphasise the country of issue, but were usually accompanied by British emblems. Occasionally these were also specific to the colony in question, such as statues of British governors on notes in Madras and Bombay, but more often they were images reflecting British sovereignty –

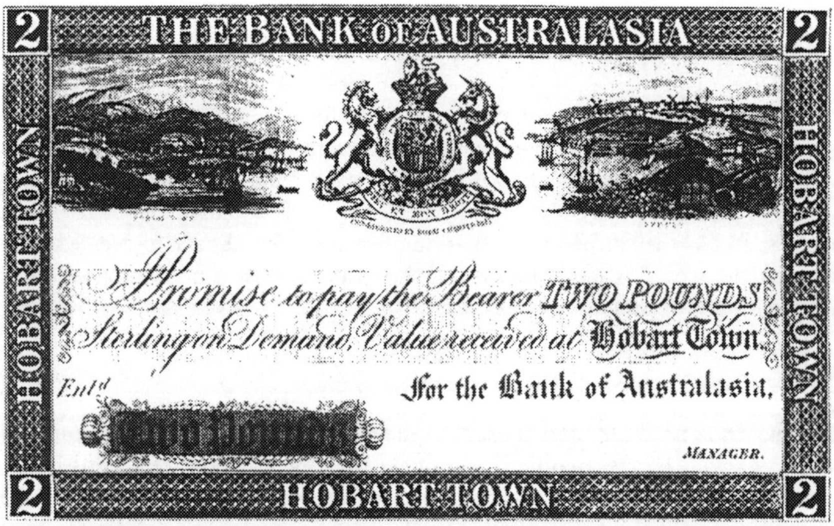

Figure 6.2 Design for a £2 note of the Bank of Australasia carrying the British Royal Arms and views of Hobart Town and Sydney. (Courtesy of the Chartered Institute of Bankers and the Trustees of the British Museum.)

Britannia, portraits of Victoria, or the Royal Arms. For example, the Bank of Australasia had designs with topographical views of Sydney and Hobart Town, but they were placed to either side of the Royal Arms, shown against a burst of sun-rays, a traditional symbol of glory, power and enlightenment (Figure 6.2). The choice of designs for notes used in Britain's colonies must have reflected the perceptions, conscious and unconscious, of the bankers and printers who produced them. The overriding impression is of the dominance of European symbolism stressing British authority. A striking example is seen in the dramatic new design introduced by the Bank of Bengal in 1857, engraved by the Edinburgh firm of W.H. Lizars.[15] In contrast to the bank's earlier request for a simple design like that of the Bank of England, the new notes were bedecked with ornamental panels, scrolls and floral decoration, and an elaborate vignette covered the full width of the top of the note. The background of the vignette is composed of an Indian landscape, with ships, temple, palm trees, an elephant and a less clearly identifiable animal which may be a rhinoceros. In the foreground is a seated Britannia, slightly elevated between two other allegorical female figures representing Justice and, perhaps, Commerce. Kneeling on the ground before them is a native Indian woman, gazing up at Britannia and offering a cornucopia of fruits. The relative positions of all these figures, with Britannia supreme over all, makes this one of the most obviously chauvinist images on colonial notes, but the same hierarchy of ruler and ruled may also be implied by the strategic placing of palms, pagodas and elephants in the background of vignettes. Even the first camels for a Ceylon design were secured by reins – though their non-existence in that country may have weakened the metaphor of control. The inclusion of native scripts was apparently a practical and unavoidable concession to indigenous culture. Judging by the correspondence in the Perkins archive, these printers, while boasting of their proficiency, regarded foreign scripts as at best secondary and at worst inimical to good design. They told the Bank of Bengal that 'the necessity of inserting the Native as well as the English characters interferes much with the beauty of the Note', and when the Bank of Bombay asked for Gujerati they were told that there was only room in the design for four native languages in the margin, and as they already had that number, they would have to decide which language to drop.[16] It seems likely that the bankers insisted on using the scripts because they encouraged native custom.

Contemporary responses and interpretations

Leaving aside native scripts, there is little evidence of how the designs on notes were regarded by the people who used them, but differing reactions to the activities of the banks are a warning against any tempting correlation between local imagery and popularity.[17] The Bank of Australasia, with its views of Australian towns, was founded in 1835 at a time of agricultural expansion and increasing foreign investment in Australia; it was promoted by London capitalists and used the advice of colonial residents to advance its success in earning profit for British shareholders. It was the first bank set up by Royal British Charter to operate in the colonies and was therefore subject to new banking regulations, which included limiting the liability of the shareholders in the event of the bank's failure. In the local press some writers welcomed greater competition among banks, but others protested against what they perceived as foreign exploitation: 'Why, we ask in the name of common sense and common justice, why is this new London piece of banking chicanery, to be enabled by law to put forth its notes and inveigle the people of this young and struggling colony to the amount of tens of thousands of pounds, and then not be liable to pay these notes 20s. in the £ . . .' (quoted in Butlin 1986: 264n). In the event there was no cause for alarm; the Bank of Australasia grew into a successful and long-lived business. But distrust of overseas interests was again evident in Victoria in the prosperous years after the Australian gold rush. In 1853 the Bank of Victoria was set up under the laws of the colony, and was explicitly promoted in the press on the grounds that 'the position and prospects of this colony imperatively demand that we should have a bank of our own, with its head office in our capital and its profits (instead of being enjoyed by a foreign proprietary) divided among our own inhabitants' (quoted in Butlin 1986: 9). The bank did indeed prove more popular than its 'Anglo' rivals, becoming the largest bank in Victoria within ten years of opening; yet there was little in the designs on its notes to advertise its localised character. A few buildings in the far background of the central vignette may have been based on a particular view, but the remainder of the emblems were the familiar non-specific symbols of trade and agriculture: a huge globe of the world, a plough, sheep, and ships under sail and steam and a portrait of a young Queen Victoria. Such images were engraved on paper money across the world, apart from Victoria who appeared only on notes of

Britain or the British Empire and, one would think, merely reinforced the colony's association with an overseas power.

In 1859 the British Bank of North America invited its managers in several Canadian towns to give their views on new note designs. Though differing in detail, the consensus was for a combination of images, the suggestions usually including the British Royal Arms, the local bank building, and the head of an Indian chief.[18] Such a compromise may be seen as typical of many British colonial note issues, recognising various relevant elements such as the monarchy, commerce, and ethnicity, but not necessarily according them equal status. It could also comply with differing ideologies of colonial rule, whether they favoured the assimilation of native institutions into the new European order, or the preservation of selected aspects of native life, which might nonetheless be segregated (see Thomas, 1994). Stereotypical and simplified symbols were consistent with existing traditions in note design and with the tendency in European visual art to synthesise romantic idealisation with naturalistic depiction of the exotic. A modern author writes of two artist brothers visiting Calcutta, who 'generally portrayed broad, variegated and grandiose views, framed these carefully with palms or banyan trees, and, on at least one occasion enhanced the beauty of a scene with the addition of a temple.'[19] It is only to be expected that nineteenth-century British bankers overseas, and their engravers, should come up with note designs that succinctly placed native cultures under British control and in a context which conformed to the accepted view.

The twentieth century: colonies and nations

In the first half of the twentieth century the appearance of paper money underwent considerable change. One major influence was more sophisticated printing technology, resulting in multi-coloured notes dominated by pictures rather than text, and with images covering both front and back. This did not necessarily involve a change in the content of designs; more elaborate engraving and colour printing were used on notes from the later nineteenth century, when allegorical and topographical vignettes were still in vogue. But the new style offered greater scope for more naturalistic imagery which was often used to depict national culture as colonies progressed towards independence. Two other factors were expansion of the scale of note issue, and change in its organisation, which progressively became restricted to centralised authorities. A contemporary survey of colonial currencies published in 1893 observed that 'a prominent feature in modern colonial currency is the circulation of Notes, by Governments or Banks' (Chalmers 1893: iii). In keeping with the eclectic character of British imperial organisation, there was no blanket policy for note issue in these disparate territories. In some areas private banks continued issuing their own notes, while dominions with a high degree of self-government, such as Canada, Australia and New Zealand, came to have national paper currencies authorised by their own parliaments. However, in many colonies notes were authorised by colonial governments and issued through a local currency board.

Types of note design also varied, but not necessarily according to the kind of issuer. For private banks, patriotism was a by-product of commercial success, and their notes were likely to retain traditional symbols of trade and industry. For example, in the 1870s and '80s, notes of the Oriental Banking Corporation issued in Ceylon and Australia carried allegorical scenes, mythical figures, and topographical vignettes of wagon trains and palms. The Hong Kong and Shanghai Banking Corporation combined architectural views of the bank with neo-classical allegories until well into the 1960s; one of the most charming examples personified the Bank's name in Chinese, 'Abundant Exchange', with an agile female figure in flowing robes, balancing on a winged wheel of communication while carrying cornucopiae filled with fruit and flowers (see Cribb, 1987). However, traditional imagery could also appear on centralised issues. Thus in 1910 the new Commonwealth of Australia avoided any delay in producing its own notes by the expedient of placing new validating stamps and the Australian coat of arms on unissued notes of the private banks, such as the Union Bank of Australia, the notes of which carried a charming portrait of the young Queen Victoria and a vignette of Britannia – albeit with a kangaroo in the background. Dominion of Canada notes from the 1890s featured important buildings and scenes of economic activity such as shipping or logging, but in 1935 the first notes of the Bank of Canada turned back to neo-classical figures such as Agriculture or Mercury.

Conversely, notes of private banks could carry national emblems, which might represent Britain or the country of issue. Thus the British Royal Arms appeared on notes of the Colonial Bank, which was founded by London merchants in the West Indies in 1836, and by 1917 hoped to become 'The Colonial Bank in fact as well as name, serving the Colonies and the Empire, and endeavouring by efficient banking facilities to cultivate trade between England and the Colonies and the Dominions'.[20] But the Bank of New Zealand (not a state bank) moved away from the British Arms towards vignettes of Maori figures, and a volcano with kiwi birds in the foreground, along with the New Zealand coat of arms. The kiwi vignette was the bank's seal, but it may also be noted that the Maori people and volcanoes were to be found in the North Island; whether or not it was deliberate, the juxtaposition of the two vignettes would seem to emphasise a non-European identity. Interestingly, this design was introduced in 1870, as the Maori Wars were coming to an end. In 1923 the bank introduced a portrait of the Maori chief Tawhaio; eleven years later this image was adopted by the new Reserve Bank of New Zealand, which specifically wanted distinctively national features.

The notes issued by currency boards developed into a consistent style. Unlike notes of private banks, they were clearly issued as part of the public administration of a colony and this may have encouraged more national imagery relating to the country concerned. At the same time, however, the notes still had to represent Britain, for the colonies were not yet nations. In a few cases, there were no pictorial images. Around the turn of the century, the colonial governments in India, Ceylon and East Africa issued notes of very similar appearance, printed on one side only with text and panels of machine engraving, and some colour. Only the country name and the inclusion of native scripts gave any clue as to the country of origin. But simple designs of this sort were prone to forgery, and a general shift towards highly pictorial notes occurred from the 1930s. Psychologically, too, more graphic imagery may have reflected a wish for sharper national distinctions amid the profound political and economic changes following the First World War. Certainly there were many more countries to be represented; with a shortage of precious metal coins and the abandonment of the gold standard, the use of paper money was increasing across the world, now reaching British possessions in Africa, Malaysia, the West Indies and the Caribbean. On these colonial note issues, Britannia and the ornamented views of the nineteenth century were superseded by portraits of the British king and naturalistic landscapes or other features of the colony.

Design through dialogue: security and authenticity

Designs for currency board notes were decided in discussions between the relevant colonial government, the printers, and an external consultant, Dr A.J. Bull of the London County Council School of Photo Engraving and Lithography. They were, therefore, bound to reflect a predominantly British perspective, but they were given detailed and serious consideration, as can be seen from correspondence between Bull and the Crown Agents, who liaised with the printers on behalf of the colonial governments.[21] The letters reveal the importance of security, attention to every detail and strong opinions on all sides, with the colonial governments' preference generally prevailing. Bull's overriding concern was with security against forgery and his comments should be understood in the light of his firm views as to how that could best be achieved. Thus his typical recommendation of a 'really good portrait head of His Majesty' was driven by practical rather than patriotic motives – though, of course, it does suggest an unconscious acceptance of the suitability of a royal British subject, since any well engraved portrait would have been just as difficult to forge. Bull was particularly interested in the technical benefits of good engravings, whether by hand or machine, and good watermarks, which he preferred not to be obscured by printing. Furthermore, he dismissed pictures as offering little deterrence against forgery, so it was not necessarily chauvinist or patronising when he wanted any views on Jamaican notes to be kept small, suggesting rather that 'perhaps a little foliage of Jamaica could be introduced?'[22]

Attempts to introduce local emblems were often instigated by the colonial government, but as long as security was maintained Bull could be even more assiduous in looking for authentic indigenous imagery. For example, in 1937 notes of the Straits Settlements, with a watermark of a roaring tiger, were to be replaced by new Malayan currency. Bull was informed that there was now to be a lion watermark and he appeared to concur, but after some months he wrote to the Crown Agents apologising that in previous correspondence he had typed lion when he meant tiger. He went on: 'The lion profile which has been sketched is very good and suitable for a watermark, but I think that when the printing of the note has been decided upon, a tiger profile (which I really had in mind) had better be substituted. The lion does not even occur in Malaya according to Lydekker, while the tiger is a well-known member of the local fauna.'[23] His concern was commendable, but ineffective; the lion remained in the watermark. The rest of the design consisted of the predictable portrait of George VI on the front and on the back, the arms and crests of the various constituent states – and these were to be accurate. The correspondence noted that the King's head had received Royal Sanction and that proofs were being sent to Malaya 'where the details of the arms and scripts will be checked', thus presumably avoiding such infelicities as had marred some earlier colonial issues.[24]

Symbols of sovereignty

A portrait of the British sovereign was a standard feature on currency board issues, usually placed in a dominant position on the front of the note. We have already seen that in the nineteenth century small portraits of Victoria were sometimes engraved on private bank issues in the colonies, particularly in Australia and Canada, but were not as common as the allegorical figure of Britannia. However, Victoria's first appearance on a government issue was a conscious move from imaginary being to living monarch. After the Indian Mutiny of 1857 control of India passed from the East India Company to the British Government, and in 1862 Government of India notes replaced the various issues of Indian banks. The new notes were produced through the agency of the Bank of England, and their design was closely modelled on Bank of England notes, but instead of Britannia in the top left corner, there was a crowned profile bust of Victoria, framed by a garland of olive branch and oak leaves (the latter requested by the Queen herself). The governor of the Bank of England recorded in his diary that the decision to replace Britannia with the monarch was made at a meeting with the Secretary of State for India, Sir Charles Wood, 'with a view to the strengthening of the note.'[25] In the same year new coinage was introduced, also bearing a portrait of Victoria, named as the sovereign ruler of India. Portraits of Victoria appeared on coinage in other colonies around this time, but the image of the British sovereign on currency issued by a new administration shortly after the Mutiny may well have had a rather more pointed significance in India. It is questionable, however, how much impact the message had. The notes proved unpopular with native merchants, who preferred their own exchange systems, and were used mainly by the British community (Bagchi 1987: 36). In 1874 they were replaced by the non-pictorial notes described above.

The vignette of Victoria on Government of India notes is an unusually early instance of a British monarch on a centralised issue, though from the 1870s royal figures and Governors-General drawn from the British nobility appeared on notes of the Dominion of Canada. However, widespread depiction of the British monarch on colonial government notes post-dated, and was perhaps inspired by, the British Treasury notes of the First World War, which carried an effigy of George V. This practice did not continue unbroken in Britain, for when the Bank of

England took over the issue of low-denomination notes from the Treasury in 1928, they opted for ornate machine-engraving, Britannia, and George and the dragon. In overseas territories, however, the monarch's portrait became a standard feature. A practical reason for this choice was to deter forgery, for the fine hand-engraving of a portrait has long been considered a major challenge to counterfeiters. But the choice of the British monarch for the portraits also sent a clear signal of British sovereignty over her vast and far-flung possessions; indeed, the notes may have been a useful vehicle for circulating an image of the monarch among foreign subjects.

Ambiguous emblems

Just as allegorical figures gave way to the living monarch, so too the earlier decorative scenes and topographical views were translated into naturalistic images of landscapes, flora and fauna, or important monuments of the colony, printed in colour and often covering most of one side of the note. There are, however, few instances of distinct cultural references, the Temple of the Tooth in Kandy for Ceylon being one exception. Romantic views of palm-fringed seas, waterfalls and mountains were particularly popular. For the Bahamas and Jamaica, there were scenes of workers in plantations. Similar subjects appeared on notes of the dominions, such as ploughing in India or sheep farming in New Zealand, and images of agricultural or industrial production are commonplace on modern, central bank issues all over the world. On colonial notes however, economic activity may have illustrated not only the wealth of the country, but also the benefit to be reaped in Britain's trade.

The colonies were also often represented by a seal or coat of arms. This followed a long tradition in British note design. On many country banknotes in Britain, civic coats of arms were symbols of local identity. From the later nineteenth century, the Royal Arms were often displayed on the notes of commercial banks incorporated by Royal Charter and trading overseas, such as the Bank of Australasia, the Oriental Bank Corporation, or the Chartered Bank of India, Australia and China. By the 1930s and '40s, colonial currency board notes sometimes showed the British arms, but also frequently bore the arms of the colony. These emblems were formal badges of identity, but because they were another imported European tradition, usually with Latin mottoes, and often granted to the country as a British colony, their significance in terms of nationality is ambivalent. The emblem for Barbados is a striking example, entirely based on British rule in the guise of European mythology. In 1663 the island was granted a public seal explicitly designed to symbolise British sovereignty over the seas by depicting Charles II 'representing Neptune in a Chariot drawn by two sea horses, and robed with his royal robes and crowned, with a trident in his left hand' (quoted in Shilstone 1933–34: 9).[26] From the late 1930s, notes of Barbados carried not only a conventional portrait of the king, but also the seal, now showing George VI in ermine robes, ruling the waves from a clam-shell chariot (Figure 6.3). On notes for Jamaica, the seal or coat of arms appeared to reflect a Jamaican, rather

Figure 6.3 Specimen $100 note of the Government of Barbados, *c.* 1944. The note carries a portrait of George VI and a vignette of the King in the guise of Neptune, in a chariot drawn by seahorses. (Courtesy of the Trustees of the British Museum.)

than British identity, but its origins suggest a rather different interpretation. The notes carried one side of the island's seal, granted as a coat of arms in 1957. This emblem included a shield with five pineapples on a cross, and one of the supporters was a West Indian woman holding a basket of pineapples. The motto read '*Indus uterque serviet uni*', that is, 'Let each India serve one master'. The other side of the seal, originally granted in 1661, showed Charles II enthroned, accepting pineapples proffered by a kneeling native woman, with the legend '*Duro de cortice fructus quam dulces*' – 'What sweet fruits from a hard rind'. Planning a new design in 1937, the colonial government suggested using the coat of arms for the watermark, but were advised by A.J. Bull that this was unsuitable, almost certainly on technical grounds.[27] He suggested a profile of George VI, but the government held out for a pineapple. Thus preference was given to a local emblem, but one which had been used to signify that indigenous fruits were also the fruits of empire.

This format of currency board designs continued into the 1950s and '60s, with portraits of Elizabeth II. (On notes of the British Caribbean States her effigy appeared on the seal of Barbados, her clam-shell flanked by dolphins.) It is possible to see an evolution from nineteenth-century notes, drawing parallels between Britannia and the monarch, small vignettes and naturalistic views, but it may be argued that the more lifelike images offered scope for more vital expression of nationality, particularly for the colonies. At the same time, portraits of the British monarch might seem to be a clear statement of British sovereignty, but what that signified is open to different interpretations. Firstly, the monarch was also depicted on the notes of countries such as Canada and Australia, which were largely self-governing in internal affairs, including the provision of currency. In such instances, therefore, it appears that membership of the Commonwealth was acknowledged as an aspect of national identity. Furthermore, both dominions and crown colonies continued to place the British sovereign on their paper money after they attained independence, reflecting the dual status of separate nations sharing one head of state. This raises questions as to how nationality is defined, and whether it is too simplistic to make an exclusive distinction between the Sovereign representing Britain, and other emblems and views representing the colony. The seal of Barbados offers an interesting sidelight here. The original seal granted in 1663 bore a motto, based on a line in Virgil's first Eclogue in which an Italian herdsman expresses his fear of being banished to Britain because it is so cut off from the world: '*et penitus toto divisos orbe Britannos*' – 'and the British, far removed from the rest of the world'. The Barbados seal altered one word to read '*et penitus toto regnantes orbe Britannos*', that is, 'and the British ruling throughout the whole world'. Quite apart from the explicit statement of power, the new phrasing is a significant shift from an isolated Britain to Britain connected to, indeed holding the reins of power in, countries across the globe. There is some sense here that colonisation did not involve merely the imposition of British control in other cultures, but also the drawing in of those cultures to the British world, and, therefore, that 'Britishness' now included something of these other identities.

Symbols of nationhood and depiction of the past

From the late 1950s, however, any notion of a common 'family' identity in the British empire was a rapidly receding ideal, if indeed it had ever approached being a reality, as the dominions which had already attained independence were joined by a growing number of former colonies in Africa, South East Asia, the Caribbean and the West Indies. But the rising tide of national consciousness of which this was both a symptom and a cause was not necessarily accompanied by sweeping changes in note design. In some cases new issuing authorities were set up as part of the planning for independence, and the retention of similar designs may well have been a deliberate policy to ease the transition and maintain public confidence; this can be seen in Nigeria, for instance, where notes of the new Central Bank in 1958 carried the same images as had been used by the West African Currency Board. Other countries moved further away from British influences, incorporating more overtly non-European cultural references in the designs. For example, the Central Bank of Ceylon illustrated important monuments, including sinuous bare-breasted maidens from the frescoes of the Lion Rock at Sigiriya, while in 1966 Australia adopted a decimal currency system based on dollars instead of pounds, and issued new notes still carrying a portrait of the Queen, but also showing figures and animals based on bark paintings by an Aboriginal artist.

As Britain's colonies turned into nations, their currencies reflected both change and continuity, for paper money had almost always been introduced by the British and bore designs evolving from European traditions, which now became a medium for redefining and proclaiming separate national identities. The ways in which independent countries have chosen to symbolise identity on their national currency is a study in itself, but there is one trend which gives this chapter a curiously appropriate coda. In the late twentieth century it is common for banknotes to illustrate national identity through historical themes. In 1971 the Clydesdale Bank in Scotland introduced a new series portraying famous Scots which included David Livingstone, his exploration of the Zambesi represented by a group of natives with a camel. More recently, he has been replaced by Mary Slessor, honoured for her missionary work in Nigeria – the contemporary trend to feature more women on currency here being counterbalanced by a traditional view of the civilising benefits of empire. In Australia, a special commemorative note was issued in 1988 precisely to mark the 200th anniversary of the first European settlers. One side of the note showed the ship *Supply*, from the fleet which landed at Botany Bay in January 1788, with a line of immigrants and the site of the first settlement at Sydney cove in the background. The other side celebrated Aboriginal culture with designs based on work commissioned from Aboriginal artists; the main features were an Aboriginal youth, ancient rock painting and hand stencils, and a ceremonial morning star pole. In such designs the colonial past may be absorbed into the national cultures of those who once were ruler and ruled, and the view, distant now in time as well as space, enters the imagery and imagination of history.

Notes

1 Scriveners performed a variety of legal and clerical work, such as writing out bonds and contracts; by the seventeenth century 'money-scriveners' were active in lending money and holding it on deposit.
2 The image was based on that of the Bank's Common Seal, which the new Directors decided should be 'Britania sitting and looking on a Bank of Mony'.
3 See Hewitt (1990) for more on the work of Perkins and Heath for British country banks in the 1820s and 1830s. The firm was founded by Jacob Perkins, an American inventor of diverse talents and interests (Bathe, 1943), and like many printers of the period he carried out a wide range of work, including production of Britain's first postage stamp, the Penny Black, in 1840.
4 Perkins Bacon to Herman Merrivale, 28 September 1848, Draft Letter Book February 1843–March 1851, p. 362. This, and all other Perkins letter books referred to, are in the Perkins Bacon Archive of the Royal Philatelic Society, London. I wish to thank the members and staff of the Society for their kindness in allowing me to consult this material.
5 The full vignette with seahorses reached beyond the British empire, also being used, for example, on notes of Buenos Aires in the 1850s and 1860s.
6 Quoted in Perkins Bacon's reply to Charles Hogg, Secretary and Treasurer of the Bank of Bengal, 14 November 1848, in Draft Letter Book February 1843–March 1851, p. 385.
7 Jacob Perkins came to London in 1819 hoping to get a contract from the Bank of England, which was considering ideas for an improved note design; see Hewitt (1998a).
8 Perkins Bacon to Charles Hogg, 14 Nov. 1848, loc. cit.
9 William Barrett has generously provided information regarding the note issues of this bank.

10 Perkins Bacon to the Bank of Bombay, 28 May 1838, Draft Letter Book May 1822 to February 1843, p. 262.

11 Perkins Bacon to George Baillie, 26 November 1849, Draft Letter Book February 1843 to March 1851.

12 I am grateful to Osmund Bopearachchi for identifying the faulty inscription.

13 Perkins Bacon to J. Stuart, Bank of Bombay, 2 October 1855, Draft Letter Book November 1854 to September 1864, p. 65.

14 Ibid., p. 66.

15 Lizars' engraving business was renowned for topographical views and natural history illustrations, but also produced notes for many banks, mainly in Scotland and the North of England. In this regard, Lizars' elegant steel engravings offered serious competition to Perkins. Correspondence of 1856 and 1859 shows that Perkins was submitting designs to the Bank of Bengal, and was disappointed not to get the business.

16 Perkins Bacon to Charles Hogg, Bank of Bengal, 14 November 1848, Draft Letter Book February 1843 to March 1851, p. 386; and to J. Stuart, Bank of Bombay, 2 October 1855, Draft Letter Book November 1854 to September 1864, p. 66.

17 It may be pointed out here that, irrespective of design, reactions to the introduction of paper currency varied from one country to another, and between different population groups within a country. Thus while banking and banknotes proliferated in Australasia, despite arguments over who should control them, in British West Africa the native population preferred coins to such an extent that the Currency Board did not issue notes until scarcity of coin in the First World War made them a necessity. Even then, some of the notes carried images of coins, perhaps to offer reassurance as to their value.

18 Perkins Bacon to Mr McNab, British Bank of North America, 20 October 1859, Draft Letter Book November 1854 to September 1864, pp. 334–8.

19 Jacobs, op. cit., p. 68.

20 This vision of international banking was set out in the chairman's speech to shareholders in 1917 (quoted in Anon 1938: 64).

21 All following references from this correspondence are taken from the Cartwright Papers in the paper money collection of the Chartered Institute of Bankers, placed on loan with the Department of Coins and Medals in the British Museum.

22 Bull to the Crown Agents, 18 November 1937.

23 Bull to the Crown Agents, 24 February 1938. Richard Lydekker (1849–1915) was a geologist and naturalist, known for his work on mammals.

24 Crown Agents to Bull, and Bull's reply, both dated 1 June 1939.

25 Bonamy Dobree, diary entry for 17 February 1860 (Bank of England M5/457). Sketches for the portrait were prepared by the engraver and medallist Leonard Wyon. This reference was kindly supplied by Philip Attwood, who is currently preparing Wyon's diary for publication.

26 I am most grateful to Clive Cheesman for information on this and the following references to arms, emblems and mottoes.

27 In this correspondence the emblem is referred to as 'the Arms', and Shilstone says that it was treated as the equivalent of the arms or the badge of the colony (Shilstone, 1933–34). Strictly speaking it was the Seal, arms only being granted to Barbados in 1965.

Bibliography

Anon. (1938) *A Banking Centenary. Barclays Bank (Dominion, Colonial and Overseas) 1836–1936* (published for private circulation).

Bagchi, A.K. (1987) *The Evolution of the State Bank of India. The Roots, 1806–1896. Part 2: Diversity and Regrouping, 1860–1876,* Bombay.

Bathe, G. and D. (1943) *Jacob Perkins. His Inventions, His Times, & His Contemporaries,* Philadelphia.

Butlin, S.J. (1968) *Foundations of the Australian Monetary System 1788–1851,* Sydney reprint.

Butlin, S.J. (1986) *The Australian Monetary System 1851–1914,* Australia, privately published.

Byatt, Derrick (1994) *Promises to Pay. The first three hundred years of Bank of England notes,* London: Spink.

Cameron, Alan (1995) *Bank of Scotland. A Very Singular Institution,* Edinburgh.

Chalmers, R. (1893) *A History of Currency in the British Colonies,* London.

Clapham, Sir J.H. (1944) *The Bank of England. A History,* Cambridge.

Cribb, Joe (1987) *Money in the Bank. An Illustrated Introduction to the Money Collection of the Hongkong and Shanghai Banking Corporation,* London.

Fry, Richard (1976) *Bankers in West Africa. The story of the Bank of British West Africa Limited,* London.

Henry, J.A. (1963) *The First Hundred Years of the Standard Bank,* London, New York, and Cape Town.

Hewitt, V.H. (1990) 'Secure and beautiful: the banknote designs of Perkins and Heath' *Bond and Banknote News* 38: 18–22.

Hewitt, V.H. (1998a) 'Beware of imitations: the campaign for a new Bank of England note, 1797–1821', *Numismatic Chronicle,* 158: 197–222.

Hewitt, V.H. (1998b) 'The camel that never was: British note issues in Ceylon 1800–1941' *British Numismatic Journal,* 67: 84–92.

Hewitt, V.H. and J.M. Keyworth (1987) *As Good as Gold. 300 Years of British Bank Note Design,* London: British Museum Publications.

Jacobs, Michael (1995) *The Painted Voyage. Art, Travel and Exploration 1564–1875,* London.

McCullough, A.B. (1984) *Money and Exchange in Canada to 1900* (Toronto and Charlottetown: Dundurn Press.

Mackenzie, Compton (1954) *Realms of Silver. One hundred years of banking in the East,* London.

Pressnell, L.S. (1956) *Country Banking in the Industrial Revolution,* Oxford.

Rey, C. (1996) 'A tentative review of Mauritius bank notes issued after 1810' *International Bank Note Society Journal* 35, 3: 10–18.

Rey, C. (1997) 'A tentative review of Mauritius bank notes issued after 1810' *International Bank Note Society Journal* 36, 2: 10–17.

Richards, R.D. (1958) *The Early History of Banking in England,* 2nd edn, London.

Saville, R. (1995) *Bank of Scotland. A History,* Edinburgh.

Shilstone, E.M. (1933–34) 'The Society's Corporate Seal' *The Journal of the Barbados Museum and Historical Society,* 1.

Singh, S. *et al.* (1976) *The Standard catalogue of coins and banknotes of Malaysia, Singapore and Brunei 1700–1976,* Kuala Lumpur.

Standard Catalog of World Paper Money, vols 1–3, published annually by Krause Publications, Iola, Wisconsin.

Thomas, N. (1994) *Colonialism's Culture. Anthropology, Travel and Government,* Cambridge.

Part II

Challenges to national currencies in the contemporary age

Introduction

The chapters in the second part of this volume examine various challenges to national currencies in the contemporary age. These challenges range from the supranational currency project in Europe and the growing use of currencies outside their country of origin, to the emergence of subnational local currencies in the last decade and the prospect of privately issued e-money in the future. Various aspects and issues associated with these challenges are addressed from a range of disciplinary standpoints.

Benjamin Cohen highlights the extent of the growing use of currencies – primarily the US dollar, but also currencies such as the DM and yen – outside their country of origin either for transactions between nations ('currency internationalisation') or within foreign states ('currency substitution'). Most existing literature that examines these developments has an economic focus, but Cohen breaks new ground in his analysis of the political significance of this new geography of money. Although states largely retain dominance over the supply of currencies (notwithstanding emerging local currencies and the prospect of privately issued e-cash in the future), Cohen points out that they no longer control demand for the currency they issue. Since market actors have increased access to alternative foreign currencies, governments must increasingly compete for the allegiance of these actors both inside and across borders. The resulting growth in authority of markets may help to check the arbitrary exercise of governmental authority, but Cohen emphasises that this shift in authority raises serious questions about equity and the legitimacy of governance in this new world of currency 'deterritorialisation'.

Eric Helleiner is also interested in the growing phenomenon of currency substitution, but his focus is less on its implications than on analysing the ideas of one of its leading proponents, Friedrich Hayek. He seeks to explain why Hayek and his liberal supporters are calling for a 'denationalised' monetary order (including even the private issue of currency) in the contemporary age when most of their liberal predecessors in the nineteenth and early twentieth centuries supported a monetary order – the gold standard – that helped to construct national currencies. Helleiner suggests that this reevaluation of the 'national question' in some liberal circles stems partly from the underlying individualism and cosmopolitanism of liberal thought and partly from a reaction against the uses to which national currencies were put when mass democratic politics replaced the narrow elite politics which had been characteristic of the era of the gold standard. He then evaluates the likelihood that Hayek's project of 'denationalising money' could be realised on a wide scale. Drawing on recent experiences with currency substitution in the developing world and ex-Eastern bloc, he argues that the denationalisation of money is much less likely to succeed than the previous liberal project of constructing the gold standard because whereas the latter was supported by nationalists, the former antagonises them. Helleiner explains briefly this source of resistance to the denationalisation of money.

Andrew Leyshon and Nigel Thrift focus their attention to two other ways that national currencies are challenged in the contemporary age. The first is the growth of eurocurrency activity in international financial centres. They focus their attention on the City of London which remains the world's leading eurocurrency centre and they explore the dominant moral ontologies of the actors in these powerful markets. As they underline, these actors are guided primarily by an instrumental moral calculus which is focused on institutional and personal accumulation. They then turn to examine groups that are trying to produce a different monetary morality, one based more on cooperation and association, and one which can include those excluded from the dominant morality of the market actors in global financial centres. They highlight local currency advocates as one of the more prominent of these groups. Drawing on Zelizer's work, they suggest that the supporters of local currencies and other alternative financial practices illustrate well how alternative moral stances towards money are possible today and how the making of money remains a socially constructed process which partly reflects the purpose and intent of individuals and groups.

Like Leyshon and Thrift, Nigel Dodd also turns his attention to 'offshore' currencies. But he is more concerned with evaluating those arguments that portray this new form of money not only as a major challenge to national sovereignty and somehow beyond the control of nation-states, but also as more inherently risky than money more closely associated with the nation-state. He suggests that these arguments should be viewed with caution. 'Offshore' currencies are not something floating above and outside national boundaries, and neither are they a form of money that exists beyond the control of nation-states. As he illustrates, the growth of the eurocurrency markets has been actively supported by nation-states themselves and states continue to cooperate with each other in regulating these markets. This regulation is often driven by a desire to reduce risks associated with the markets and these risks, he argues, are not necessarily greater than those associated with domestic financial activity. Indeed, much of the financial activity in eurocurrency markets is explicitly designed to help people manage risks. For these reasons, Dodd suggests that more research is needed before he will be convinced that this form of money poses a fundamentally new and distinctive threat to the nation-state or that it is inherently more risky than national currencies.

Amy Verdun draws our attention to the dramatic project to create a common currency in the European Union (EMU). As she illustrates, nowhere else in the world are countries so keen to replace their existing national currencies with a new supranational currency and she asks why this is the case with European governments. She argues that support for EMU reflects a complicated set of interests and circumstances. It partly needs to be understood in light of the broader support for European integration that has increased since the early 1980s. Equally important, the common currency project reflects the abandonment of more activist approaches to monetary management in the context of changing ideas and the constraints imposed by integrated financial markets. Verdun also points to the goal of many European governments to create a regional monetary order that is no longer so dominated by Germany as well as their desire to gain a degree of monetary power with regard to the outside world. In addition to explaining these diverse sources of support for EMU, Verdun also reminds us of the considerable opposition which exists, particularly in countries where the national currency has formed an important part of national identity or where citizens are especially concerned about the declining ability of national governments to look after their specific interests in the face of accelerating European integration.

In the Conclusion to the volume, Helleiner steps back to analyse the various challenges to national currencies from a broader perspective. Addressing the question of why national currencies are being challenged in such a widespread manner today, he argues that many of the causes of these challenges can be found in the reconfiguration of the historical processes and structures that produced national currencies in the first place (and which were examined in the first part of the volume). He also explores very briefly the consequences of these various challenges for the nation-state and suggests that the 'denationalisation' of money can undermine three key features of the nation-state: economic territoriality, the direct link between state and domestic society, and the collective identity that binds national citizens to each other. Moreover, while we might usefully examine the challenges to national currencies from a general vantage point, Helleiner emphasises that the enormous variation in the nature and intensity of these challenges ensures we must attend to the ways that these transformations can be expected to be very uneven and manifested in quite different ways around the world.

7 The new geography of money

Benjamin Cohen

When addressing issues of global finance, we are accustomed to thinking of money as effectively insular: each currency sovereign within the territorial frontiers of a single country or monetary union. In fact, nothing could be further from the truth.

For a currency to be truly 'territorial', its functional domain would have to coincide precisely with the political jurisdiction of its issuing state – a very special case. The currency would have to exercise an exclusive claim to all the traditional roles of money within the domestic economy. There could be no other money accepted for transaction purposes or used for the denomination of contracts or financial assets. And the government would have to be able to maintain sole control over the operation of the monetary system, dominating market agents. In matters of commerce, the equivalent would be described as 'autarky'; national self-sufficiency. In truth, however, autarky is no more commonly achieved in monetary matters than it is in trade.

As a practical matter, a surprising number of moneys today have come to be employed widely outside their country of origin for transactions either between nations or within foreign states. The former is usually referred to as 'international' currency use (or currency 'internationalisation'); the latter is typically described by the term 'currency substitution' and may be referred to as 'foreign-domestic use'.[1] Reciprocally, an even larger number of moneys now routinely face growing competition at home from currencies originating abroad. It is simply wrong to assert, as did one economist recently, that 'several currencies rarely circulate within the same state' (Hansson 1993: 165). In fact, the phenomenon is increasingly prevalent.

Both currency internationalisation (CI) and currency substitution (CS) are a product of intense market rivalry – a kind of Darwinian process of natural selection, driven by the force of demand, in which some moneys such as the US dollar or Deutschmark (DM) come to be viewed as more attractive than others for various commercial or financial purposes. As several of the essays in this volume demonstrate, cross-border circulation of currencies was once quite common prior to the emergence of the modern state system. More recently the practice has re-emerged, as declining barriers to monetary exchange have greatly expanded the array of effective currency choice. Competition between national moneys is accelerating rapidly. As a result, the domains within which individual currencies serve the standard functions of money now diverge more and more sharply from the legal jurisdictions of issuing governments. Money has become effectively 'deterritorialised'.

What is the political significance of this new geography of money? Most fundamentally, money's deterritorialisation alters the structure of governance in global currency relations. Where national governments once, in principle, reigned supreme – each claiming the right to an absolute monopoly within its own borders – practical authority in monetary matters has now become more diffuse, incorporating key market actors as well as agents of the state. The primary advantage of this accelerating transformation is that it provides more of a check on the arbitrary exercise of governmental authority. The main disadvantage lies in the fact that market actors are less accountable than politicians to the general electorate, raising serious questions about legitimacy and representation in this critical realm of decision-making.

The purpose of this chapter is to explore the changing nature of monetary governance in a world of growing cross-border currency competition. After briefly outlining some of the key dimensions of today's new monetary geography in the first section below, I address first the role of the state and then that of markets in the following two sections. Deterritorialisation, I argue, has not totally deprived states of their capacity to act on behalf of their citizens. But it does oblige states now to *share* authority with key market agents, each side playing a critical endogenous role in an ongoing dialectical process. Governance today is exercised not by political sovereignty but rather by the 'invisible hand' of competition, states *interacting with* private societal forces in the functional spaces created by the Darwinian rivalry among moneys.

Mapping the new geography

Regrettably, the full dimensions of today's new geography of money cannot be mapped precisely. Since comprehensive statistics on global currency circulation do not exist, neither CI nor CS can be accurately or consistently documented with any degree of refinement. Partial indicators, however, may be gleaned from a variety of reliable sources.[2] Though space limitations prevent their detailed reproduction here, some brief recapitulation can serve to underscore the impressive orders of magnitude involved.

The clearest signal of the accelerated pace of CI is sent by the global foreign-exchange market where, according to the Bank for International Settlements (1999), average daily turnover has accelerated from $620 million in 1989 (the first year for which such data are available) to close to $1.5 trillion nine years later – a rate of increase of nearly 30 per cent per annum. A parallel story also seems evident in international markets for other financial claims, including bank deposits and loans as well as bonds and stocks, all of which have grown at double-digit rates for years. Using data from a variety of sources, Thygesen *et al.* (1995) recently calculated what they call 'global financial wealth', the world's total portfolio of private international investments. From just over $1 trillion in 1981, aggregate cross-border holdings quadrupled to more than $4.5 trillion by 1993 – an expansion far faster than that of world output or trade in goods and services.

The clearest signal of the accelerated pace of CS is sent by the rapid increase in the physical circulation of several major currencies, including especially the US dollar, DM, and yen, outside their country of origin. For the dollar, an authoritative study by two Federal Reserve economists (Porter and Judson 1996) puts the value of US banknotes in circulation abroad at between 55 and 70 per cent of the total outstanding stock – equivalent to perhaps $250 billion in 1995. The same study also reckons that as much as three-quarters of the annual increase of notes in recent years has gone directly abroad, up from less than one-half in the 1980s and under one-third in the 1970s. Appetite for the greenback is obviously growing. Using a comparable approach, Germany's Bundesbank (1995) has estimated Deutschmark circulation outside Germany at about 30 to 40 per cent of total stock, equivalent to some DM 65–90 billion ($45–65 billion) at the end of 1994. In Asia, Bank of Japan officials are privately reported to believe that of the total supply of yen banknotes, amounting to some $370 billion in 1993, as much as 10 per cent may now be located outside Japan (Hale 1995: 164). Combining these diverse estimates suggests a minimum foreign circulation of the three big currencies of at least $300 billion in all – by no means an inconsiderable sum and, judging from available evidence, apparently growing rapidly.

The evidence also appears to suggest that a very wide range of countries is affected by the phenomenon, even if the precise numbers involved remain somewhat shrouded in mystery. According to one authoritative source, foreign banknotes account for 20 per cent or more of the local money stock in as many as three dozen nations inhabited by at least one-third of the world's population (Krueger and Ha 1996: 60–1). The same source also suggests that, in total, as much as one-quarter to one-third of the world's circulating currency is presently located outside its country of issue (Krueger and Ha 1996: 76).

These numbers clearly confirm the growing importance of both international and foreign-domestic use of money. Two main messages stand out. First, the scale of cross-border currency use is manifestly extensive, as well as growing rapidly, reflecting both the scope and intensity of market-driven competition. Monetary circulation really is no longer confined to the territories of issuing countries. Strict autarky in currency relations is indeed a special case.

Second, while the number of moneys actually employed for either international or foreign-domestic purposes tends to be rather small, the number of those routinely facing rivalry at home from currencies abroad appears to be remarkably large. Deterritorialisation also means that there is no longer a functional equivalence among national moneys. Even though all currencies of sovereign states enjoy nominally equal status as a matter of international law, some moneys – to paraphrase George Orwell – clearly are far more equal than others as a matter of practical reality. Many currencies, particularly in the developing world and so-called transition economies, face what amounts to a massive competitive invasion from abroad; others, especially those of the wealthiest industrial countries, are effectively immune from foreign rivalry at home. The population of the monetary universe is in fact distinctly stratified.

Topping the charts, quite obviously, is the dollar, which remains by far the world's most popular choice for both CI and CS. In effect, the dollar's functional domain spans the globe, from the Western Hemisphere (where the accepted synonym for currency substitution is 'dollarisation') to the former Soviet bloc and much of the Middle East (where dollars circulate widely as a *de facto* parallel currency). Next comes the DM, which clearly dominates currency relations within much of Europe, including East Central Europe and the Balkans. And not far behind are the yen and a handful of other elite international moneys, such as the pound sterling, Dutch guilder, and French and Swiss francs. Much lower ranked are the many currencies of poorer countries that are forced to struggle continuously for the loyalty of local users.

Add these two messages together and a picture emerges that is strikingly at variance with the conventional imagery of strictly territorial money – a universe of increasingly intense competition as well as distinct hierarchy among currencies. Individually, national moneys confront market forces that are increasingly indifferent to the barriers posed by political frontiers. Collectively, therefore, governments face a challenge to their monetary sovereignty that is unprecedented in modern times.

Role of the state

The tradition of monetary sovereignty is derived from the conventions of standard political geography which, ever since the seventeenth-century Peace of Westphalia, has celebrated the role of the nation-state, absolutely supreme within its own territory, as the basic unit of governance in world politics. Just as political space was conceived in terms of those fixed and mutually exclusive entities we call states, currency spaces came to be visualised in terms of the separate sovereign domains where each money originated. I label this the Westphalian model of monetary geography.

In the state-centric Westphalian model, national governments have been assumed to exercise monopoly control over the issue and management of their own money. As a result, power in monetary matters is conventionally thought to be concentrated decisively in the hands of the state. Not every government is expected always to be able to avail itself of all the advantages of a monetary monopoly. The need for frequent compromises is understood, leading often to either a subordination or a sharing of currency sovereignty among states. But even then, monetary governance is presumed to remain the privileged mandate of the government sector alone.

All that is now changed, however, by the deterritorialisation of money. In today's new monetary geography, the state is no longer automatically privileged in relation to societal actors. There can be little doubt, therefore, that governmental authority has been greatly eroded as a result. The only question is whether states retain any role at all in the governance of monetary affairs. The answer, I suggest, is that they do continue to play a vital role, but in a manner quite different from that assumed in the traditional Westphalian model.

The capital mobility hypothesis

That the monetary authority of governments is severely eroded today is hardly a novel proposition, of course. Students of international financial markets, noting the massive increase of cross-border capital flows in recent decades, have long stressed the resulting threat to national monetary sovereignty.[3] The conventional view, labelled by David Andrews (1994) the Capital Mobility Hypothesis, is that the growing world-wide integration of financial markets – financial globalisation, in the jargon – has effectively cost states their traditional monetary autonomy. As Andrews summarises the proposition:

> The degree of international capital mobility systematically constrains state behavior by rewarding some actions and punishing others . . . Consequently, the nature of the choice set available to states . . . becomes more constricted. (Andrews 1994: 193, 204)

But as Andrews himself cautions, this is only the beginning of the story, not the end.[4] In fact the Capital Mobility Hypothesis, for all its insight, borders on caricature, seriously misrepresenting both the scope and the severity of the challenge to contemporary government.

To be sure, there is nothing wrong with the logic of the proposition. Unless governments are willing to tolerate a virtually unlimited degree of currency instability, they must indeed tailor their policies to what is needed to avoid provoking massive or sudden capital movements. The challenge to state authority is real, neither easy to withstand nor, typically, amenable to formal negotiation. The constraint imposed by the globalised financial markets is not just a matter of individual constituencies with a self-interested axe to grind. Particularist pressures, exercised directly on government through lobbying or other 'rent-seeking activities', have always been an integral part of the policy process in every national capital. What is different about financial globalisation is the more indirect role that markets can now play in inhibiting public policy – a discipline at once both less tractable and more impersonal.

The key is the wider range of options that comes to more privileged elements of the private sector with the globalisation of financial activity. For societal actors in a position to take advantage of the opportunities afforded by market integration, capital mobility means more degrees of freedom – more room for manoeuvre in response to the actual or potential decisions of government. Higher taxes or regulation may be evaded by moving investment funds offshore; tighter monetary policies may be circumvented by accessing foreign sources of finance. And this broader latitude, in turn, means a significant increase of leverage in relation to political authority. Recalling the language of Albert Hirschman (1970), influence in the policy process may be thought to depend on the relative availability of the options of Exit, Voice, and Loyalty. The greater the ability of market actors to evade the preferences of public officials (Exit), the less will government be able to count on or command submissive Loyalty. 'Investors vote with their feet', as sociologist Saskia Sassen (1996: 39) puts it. As a result, more Voice is gained to promote private priorities and objectives.

In effect, therefore, financial globalisation gives selected societal actors a measure of *de facto* veto power over state behaviour, elusive but effective. It is elusive because it is exercised indirectly, through market processes rather than formal lobbying. Policy autonomy is threatened, but not from intent that is purposive or hostile. The leverage is effective because it involves a menace, the risk of exit, that may never be implemented but is forever present. The pressure on government officials is without end. The imperative for governments is to avoid provoking exercise of the Exit option. This means, above all, maintaining insofar as possible the confidence and good will of the private sector. The full implications of this new veto power have been aptly summarised, albeit with approval, by a former finance minister of France:

> The world economy is increasingly dominated by financial markets, and we have to get used to accepting their verdicts, whether favorable to us or not. I think I understand their mind-set. They've become watchdogs who will promptly punish any country that lets inflation or public debt get out of control. But they reward good economic policies. A champion of free markets like me thinks that they provide good discipline.[5]

The Capital Mobility Hypothesis thus does correctly identify the nature of the challenge to governments. Its logic is impeccable. Public policy, more and more, is indeed pressured to conform to what markets appear to desire, whether or not this coincides with the preferences of elected officials. Less and less can governments ignore the signals of the financial marketplace. Yet in pursuing that logic the proposition manages simultaneously both to *understate* and *overstate* the constraints presently imposed on state behaviour.

Constraints are understated because a focus on capital mobility, emphasising financial-market integration, highlights only one function of money; its use for store-of-value purposes. In fact, that is only part of the story. Cross-border competition is really far more extensive, involving all the standard functions of currency for both international and foreign–domestic use – not just money's role as a private investment medium – and penetrating to the very core of what is meant by national political sovereignty. Much more is involved here than just financial markets alone. It is, indeed, a matter of the basic effectiveness and legitimacy of government itself.

At the same time, constraints are overstated because a focus on capital mobility, stressing the preferences of currency users, highlights only one side of the market: the demand side. That too ignores an important part of the story – namely *supply*, which even in a deterritorialised world remains largely the privilege of the state. We must not forget that governments are still the principal source of the currencies that now compete so vigorously across political frontiers. The Darwinian struggle may be intense, but it is a struggle that remains, for now at least, limited almost exclusively to national moneys. Thus, though challenged, governments still retain a considerable influence of their own in relation to the private sector. The era of territorial money may be over, but that does not mean that states have become an anachronism in the governance of currency relations.

Competition on the supply side

Government dominance of the supply side is not absolute, of course. Even that remaining privilege could be eroded in time by competition from non-state sources. A variety of private moneys already exist, both domestically and internationally, to rival the official issue of central banks. Until now, however, none has had an impact on the Darwinian struggle that might be described as anything more than marginal – though that too could change significantly in the future.

At the domestic level, private moneys circulate in some countries in fairly sizeable numbers. In the United States alone there are as many as 85 local currencies in 26 states, the best known being the system of 'Ithaca Hours' based in Ithaca, New York (Frick 1996). In 1993, *The Economist* (1993) reported the existence of some 45 local currencies in Britain – many with exotic, not to say eccentric, names like beaks, bobbins, cockles, and kreds – and perhaps 300 world-wide. Such currencies, however, really are little different from institutionalised systems of multilateral barter and remain self-consciously local, circulating on a very restricted scale.[6] None trades across national frontiers.

At the international level, private substitutes for national moneys have long existed in the form of what economists call 'artificial currency units' (ACUs) – non-state alternatives designed to perform one or more of the conventional roles of money. Traditionally, though, most ACUs have functioned mainly as a unit of account or store of value, rather than as a medium of exchange, thus posing little direct threat to government dominance of supply. Currently the only non-state form of money used to any substantial degree internationally is a pool of privately issued assets denominated in ECUs, the European Union's old European Currency Unit that came into existence with the European Monetary System in 1979.[7] But despite having attained limited success in global bond markets, the ECU has never been widely accepted for private transactional purposes.

In fact, the only real threat of competition on the supply side would appear to lie still in the future – in the developing realm of cyberspace, the 'virtual' geography of the internet and World Wide Web. Clearly, present-day physical money is bound to become decreasingly important over time once digital entries in a computer can substitute effectively for everyday cash and checking accounts. Around the world, as communications and information technologies continue to develop, entrepreneurs are racing to develop effective electronic means of payment; electronic cash or e-cash, as it is sometimes called. If and when they succeed, governments will face a competitive challenge like none they have experienced in living memory – full-bodied ACUs beyond their individual or even collective control. Then dominance of supply, not just demand, truly would be lost.[8]

That future, however, could be rather distant, if it arrives at all, given the difficulties of introducing any credible new form of money into the market. The key issue, as it is for all moneys, is trust; how to command confidence in the general acceptability of any species of e-cash. Initially at least, value is likely to be assured only by promising full and unrestricted convertibility into more conventional legal tender. Later on, as *The Economist* has written, 'it is possible to imagine the development of e-cash reaching [a] final evolutionary stage . . . in which convertibility into legal tender ceases to be a condition for electronic money; and electronic money will thereby become indistinguishable from – because it will be the same as – other, more traditional sorts of money' (*The Economist* 1994: 23). But that day, surely, is still a long way off. Until then, officially sponsored moneys alone will continue to dominate the supply side for both international and foreign domestic purposes. Governments, therefore, will continue to play a role that is anything but insignificant.

The state as oligopolist

What, then, is the true nature of the relationship between states and societal actors in the governance of currency relations? In essence, the interaction has been transformed from monopoly to oligopoly. The monetary role of government has not so much been diminished as redefined. The status of states, once totally dominant in their own territories, has now become something like that of competing firms in an oligopolistic industry.

The point is simple. Markets have two sides: supply and demand. Hence not one but two sets of actors are involved – not just the users of money but also its principal producers, who happen still to be governments. With deterritorialisation states have lost the sole authority they once enjoyed over demand: their local monopolies. Since many transactors now have an alternative, the happy option of Exit, government can no longer easily enforce Loyalty, an exclusive role for their own currency within established political frontiers. But states do still dominate the supply side of the industry, largely retaining control over the issue of money. Thus they are still in a position, like oligopolistic firms, to exercise influence over demand insofar as they can successfully compete, inside or across borders, for the allegiance of market agents. Relevance, accordingly, is retained to the extent that user preferences can be swayed. Like oligopolists, governments find themselves driven to join the competitive fray; to do what they can, consciously or unconsciously, to preserve or promote market share for their product by shaping or managing demand. In this sense, producers of currency are essentially no different from producers of cars, chemicals, or computers.

Commercial rivalry between states is nothing new, of course. Governments have always competed with one another for markets and resources as part of the great game of world politics. Nor is the idea that states now vie to attract diverse market agents any longer particularly novel. More than a decade ago, Susan Strange had already noted how the spreading globalisation of world markets was pushing governments into a new kind of geopolitical rivalry, 'competing for world market shares as the surest means to greater wealth' (Strange 1987: 564).[9] More recently, Philip Cerny crystallised the idea in his notion of the 'competition state' – governments 'driven by the imperatives of global competition to expand transnationalization' (Cerny 1994: 225). The competition state, however, participates in markets only indirectly, mainly as a catalyst to alter incentives confronting agents on both the demand and supply sides. What is unique about cross-border currency competition is that the state participates directly, as the dominant actor on the supply side. It is the government's own creation, its money, that must be marketed and promoted.

Furthermore, all states (excluding those few scattered enclaves, like Monaco or San Marino, that have formally adopted another nation's money in lieu of one of their own) must be considered part of the oligopolistic struggle, no matter how competitive or uncompetitive their respective currencies may be. Rivalry is not limited merely to the small handful of moneys at the very top of the global hierarchy, as is sometimes suggested.[10] That would be so only if cross-border competition were restricted to international use alone; a few key currencies vying for shares of global investment portfolios or for use in trade invoicing. But deterritorialisation extends to foreign–domestic use as well – CS as well as CI – hence involving all national currencies, to some degree, in direct competition with one another, the weak as well as the strong. Money's oligopoly is truly global.[11]

Role of the market

In this altered environment, we are entitled to ask: Who now governs currency relations? Governments have clearly lost much of their privileged status in relation to societal actors. Yet private agents too remain subject to enormous influence through state efforts to manage the demand side of the market. How, therefore, is monetary authority actually exercised? Who makes the rules, how are they enforced, and where are outcomes determined?

Authority or anarchy?

For some observers, the answer to these crucial questions is simple: When power shifts to markets, *no one* governs.[12] Authority is replaced by anarchy. In fact, nothing could be more mistaken.

Representative is the view of Susan Strange, as expressed in a recent commentary aptly entitled *The Retreat of the State* (1996). Like many other scholars, Strange focuses on the challenge posed by economic globalisation to the traditional Westphalian model of state sovereignty. Her starting point is conventional, as she readily concedes: 'There is no great originality in the underlying assumption of this book – which is that the territorial boundaries of states no longer coincide with the extent or the limits of political authority over economy and society' (Strange 1996: ix). Nor is there anything particularly unusual in her observations about the increased 'hollowness of state authority' caused by the growing influence of 'impersonal forces of world markets' (Strange 1996: 4, 6). In her words:

> The authority of the governments of all states, large and small, strong and weak, has been weakened as a result of technological and financial change and of the accelerated integration of national economies into one single global market economy. (Strange 1996: 13–14)

More dramatic, however, is the conclusion that she draws from her analysis, which is that the system of governance itself is weakened in the process. The erosion of state authority, she argues, has left no one in charge. Again in her words:

> Some of the fundamental responsibilities of the state in a market economy – responsibilities first recognised, described and discussed at considerable length by Adam Smith over 200 years ago – are not now being adequately discharged by anyone. At the heart of the international political economy, there is *a vacuum*.... What some have lost, others have not gained. The diffusion of authority away from national governments has left *a yawning hole of non-authority*, ungovernance it might be called. (Strange 1996: 14, italics added)

In a formal sense, of course, Strange is absolutely right. Aspects of governance that we all take for granted at the national level – what Adam Smith called the 'magistracy' of the state, including protection of property rights, standardisation of weights and measures, and provision of a general framework of law, order, and justice – are obviously diluted or absent at the global level, where no legal government exists. To that extent, ungovernance is not an unfair characterisation. True, a wide range of substitutes for a single supranational authority, systematically institutionalised in multilateral organisations or in regularised procedures for inter-governmental cooperation, have been established over time to take on at least some of the responsibilities traditionally assumed by states. But without the powers that go with the notion of absolute sovereignty, such proxies are bound to remain pale imitations at best; less effective in providing outcomes that may be regarded as efficient, stable, or equitable. There can be little doubt that in today's increasingly globalised marketplace, many functions of governance are indeed no longer being discharged in a way that might be described as adequate.

But does this mean that no one remains in charge – that we are left with nothing but a vacuum? In fact such a bold claim, though widely shared, is based on a serious misconception of the meaning of authority in social relations. In politics and law, authority is commonly understood to embody a capacity to enforce compliance.[13] Like its synonym, the concept of governance, it represents an ability to exert influence over the behaviour and decisions of actors. Authority is inseparable from power, which in its many guises is the *sine qua non* for effective control of outcomes. But it is indeed separable from the state, which is by no means the only agent capable of making and enforcing rules. Authority may be exercised under the banner of sovereignty – the Westphalian model – but it can also originate in a wide variety of other social institutions, some of which may be far less visible to the naked eye than the formal offices and explicit rules of governments or multilateral agencies. In other words, governance can also take more informal or implicit forms.

As a mode of organising political space, authority falls somewhere between the contrasting modalities of coercion and persuasion. In the words of philosopher Hannah Arendt: 'If authority is to be defined at all, it must be in contradistinction to both coercion by force and persuasion by argument' (Arendt 1968: 93). Hints of each approach may be implicit in the notion of authority, but by presumption only. Persuasion, for example, works its will through systematic argument and appeal – what is generally termed a 'capacity for reasoned elaboration'. Coercion, at the opposite extreme, rests on the naked use of force – a capacity for repressive violence. Both alternatives may lurk in the background of governance, as possibilities to be brought forward should deviant behaviour occur. In certain circumstances, compliance may in fact be promoted by a belief that a capacity for either persuasion or coercion exists. But neither argument nor violence is a necessary condition for the effective exercise of authority.

The core issue is: Where does authority originate and how is it conveyed? For most scholars the usual starting point for analysis is Max Weber's familiar typology, which lists no fewer than three distinct foundations for authority: law, tradition, and charisma. In Weber's own words:

> There are three pure types of legitimate authority. The validity of their claims to legitimacy may be based on:
>
> 1. Rational grounds – resting on a belief in the 'legality' of patterns of normative rules and the right of those elevated to authority under such rules to issue commands (legal authority);
> 2. Traditional grounds – resting on an established belief in the sanctity of immemorial traditions and the legitimacy of the status of those exercising authority under them (traditional authority); or finally
> 3. Charismatic grounds – resting on devotion to the specific and exceptional sanctity, heroism or exemplary character of an individual person, and of the normative patterns or order revealed or ordained by him (charismatic authority). (Weber 1947: 328)

From this perspective, it is easy to see that much more may be involved here than governance by government alone. For Weber, of course, authority was directly associated with the state. His concern was with the sources of legitimacy for the traditional Westphalian model of governance. In fact, however, only one of his three categories, the *de jure* 'rational-legal' mode of authority, is truly exclusive to the notion of formal government. Authority may indeed derive from juridical supremacy as embodied in the familiar institutions of the sovereign state. But if Weber's two remaining categories are to be believed, that is clearly not authority's only possible provenance. Neither tradition nor charisma may be regarded as a monopoly of the state.

In fact, authority may be manifested through any number of *de facto* channels of control. Tradition and charisma are two of them; others include opinion, ideology, or even mere intellectual convention. It is by no means true, therefore, that we are left with a 'yawning hole of non-authority' just because power in the world economy has shifted away from national governments. Market forces may be 'impersonal', but that does not make them any less capable of governance.

The key point is simple. Authority, ultimately, is socially constructed – a product of intersubjective understandings built up from our own ideas and experiences. John Ruggie captures the point in his notion of 'social epistemes', which he defines as 'the mental equipment that people draw upon in imagining and symbolizing forms of political community' (Ruggie 1993: 157). As political philosopher R.B. Friedman writes, following Weber's logic, the effectiveness of authority is derived from 'some mutually recognized normative relationship' (Friedman 1990: 71). Its legitimacy is based on historically and culturally conditioned expectations about what constitutes appropriate conduct. A practical distinction between societal orders based on formal design and organisation (e.g., the state) and more spontaneous orders that emerge naturally from the mutual accommodations of many diverse and autonomous actors has long been a staple feature of Western social philosophy, going back to Bernard Mandeville's justly famous 'Fable of the Bees', first published in 1714. The unplanned spontaneous model may be regarded as no less legitimate – no less authoritative – than the deliberately devised variety.

Governance, therefore, does not necessarily demand the tangible institutions of government. It may not even call for the presence of explicit actors, whether state-sponsored or private, to take responsibility for rule-making and enforcement. To suffice, all that is really needed is a valid social consensus on relevant rights and values. As summarised by James Rosenau:

> Governance refers to activities backed by shared goals that may or may not derive from legal and formally prescribed responsibilities and that do not necessarily rely on police powers to overcome defiance and attain compliance. Governance, in other words, is a more encompassing phenomenon than government. It embraces governmental institutions, but it also subsumes informal, non-governmental mechanisms. . . . Governance is thus a system of rule that is as dependent on inter-subjective meanings as on formally sanctioned constitutions and charters. (Rosenau 1992: 4)

Authority may be formally articulated in explicit rules outlining specific prescriptions or proscriptions for action. But it may also express itself more informally as implicit norms defining standards of behaviour in terms of understood rights and obligations. Rules are normally enforced by 'rightful' rulers, which since the Peace of Westphalia have been most closely identified with the territorial state. Norms, by contrast, tend to exercise their influence more through the power of social institutions, including such familiar arrangements as the family, religion, and, of course, the market. Both explicit rules and implicit norms are part of what we mean by governance. We do not face a vacuum whenever influence is redistributed from the former to the latter.

Admittedly, governance may not be as tidy when it is effectuated through social institutions rather than national governments. The greater ambiguity of norms, as compared with rules, leaves actors more room for strategic manoeuvre; lack of overt compliance mechanisms (police, judiciary, etc.) heightens the temptation to renege on commitments when convenient. Outcomes, therefore, may be neither as stable nor as equitable as we might prefer. As indicated, Susan Strange is undoubtedly right when she suggests that many functions of governance are no longer being discharged as adequately as they could be. The certitude of formal government is replaced by the less predictable force of social convention. But that is not the same as 'ungovernance'. We must not confuse the *form* of authority with its *consequences*.

Hence it is not at all accurate to conclude, as Strange's argument suggests, that no one now governs money's new deterritorialised landscape. The monopoly power of states has been replaced not by anarchy but by the 'invisible hand' of competition. The authority that once derived solely from legal-tender laws and other political interventions has come to be embodied more in the norms and expectations that rule the Darwinian struggle among currencies. The power of governance, in short, now resides in that social institution we call the market.

Supply or demand?

But that still leaves us with our underlying question: Who in the market governs? The market is not a unitary actor, after all; we must avoid the social-science sin of reification. At least two sets of actors are involved here – the producers of money on the supply side, the users of money on the demand side. Who really is in charge?

In fact, both sides govern – producers of money as well as users. As in any market setting it is supply and demand together, interacting synergistically, that determine the organisation of currency space. The basic point was made many years ago by the renowned English economist Alfred Marshall, commenting on whether it is demand ('utility') or supply ('cost of production') that governs market outcomes ('value'): 'We might as reasonably dispute whether it is the upper or the under blade of a pair of scissors that cuts a piece of paper, as whether value is governed by utility or cost of production' (Marshall 1948: 348).

Likewise, in our own time, we might as reasonably dispute whether it is the state or society that shapes the new geography of money. In reality, as with Marshall's scissors, it is both, each playing a critical reciprocal role in an ongoing dialectical process. What links the two sides in their synergy are the transactional networks that define the functional domains of individual currencies. And what lies at the heart of these social spaces is, once again, the issue of trust; the collective faith of a group of like-minded transactors in a money's general usefulness and future acceptability. Governance is provided by whatever may influence market confidence in individual currencies.

In short, if money is accurately comprehended as a social institution derived from self-reinforcing patterns of historical practice, it becomes clear that neither formal organisation nor explicit rules are required for the effective exercise of monetary authority. The system of governance is the collectivity of actors, public as well as private, that comprise both sides of the market. Through their ongoing interaction, it is these agents together who jointly, if uneasily, make the rules and shape the contours of today's monetary geography.

A crisis of legitimacy

In the end, then, we find that the traditional Westphalian model has become little more than a convenient fiction – a 'territorial trap' for the unwary, to borrow from the language of geographer John Agnew (1994). In fact, today's monetary geography is governed by a hybrid patchwork of authority that is both diffuse and contingent. Where the sovereign state once ruled, market forces now prevail.

Does it matter? Given money's central role in modern economies, the answer is most certainly yes. Money affects us all, every day of our lives; its impacts are manifold and direct. The real issue is the *legitimacy* of decision-making in this new deterritorialised system of governance – a decidedly normative question. Should we be content with this dramatically new geography of money?

Many, particularly partisans of a more libertarian political persuasion, might well respond in the affirmative, since liberty would appear to be promoted. Ever distrustful of excessive governmental authority, libertarians celebrate all limitations on political behaviour imposed by the decentralised decision-making of the marketplace. For them, the market serves two valuable functions, dispersing power in society and also providing a potent counterweight to the awesome power of the state. Hence many would undoubtedly applaud such a passing of privilege from the public to the private sector – from despised politicians to competitive market forces. The monopoly appropriated by governments during the era of territorial money was frequently mismanaged or abused, as we well know, often resulting in corrosive inflation or macroeconomic instability. Are we not all better off if states must now act as oligopolists, competing keenly with one another for the allegiance of market actors? In lieu of compulsory Loyalty, we now have the option of voluntary Exit. Hence instead of the arbitrary actions of public officials, we may now enjoy the fruits of market rationality.

Moreover, libertarians continue, markets are inherently democratic because they reflect the attitudes and decisions of millions of individual transactors, functioning in effect as a sort of perpetual opinion poll – a kind of 'automatic, nonpolitical system for grading [policy] performance', as one economist has approvingly put it (Meigs 1993: 717). Why should we not be content with a governance structure that yields more power to the people?

The libertarian response, however, is seriously deficient in two respects, neglecting issues of both equity and accountability. It is true, for example, that cross-border competition gives many societal actors more voice in relation to governmental authority; the right to 'vote with their feet' if they disapprove of official policy. But votes are distributed not by person, the traditional 'One Person, One Vote', but by wealth. The constitutional notion of equality before the law is thus effectively violated, if not fatally compromised. In the words of economist Arthur Okun, writing of the 'big tradeoff' between the principles of democracy and capitalism, 'money transgresses equal political rights' (Okun 1975: 29). Those with the most money have the most votes. Such a skewed franchise seems greatly inconsistent with contemporary views of political legitimacy.

Worse, there is less accountability in a system of governance that gives as much voice to a privileged class of market agents as it does to elected officials. As an approach to political rule, such a transformation may be regarded as regressive or even pernicious, insofar as it subverts the will of the general electorate. Politicians may be ineffectual or unsavoury, but in many countries – certainly in representative democracies – they are supposed to govern with the consent of the governed. In other words they can, at least to some degree, be held accountable for their actions. Market actors, by contrast, are neither elected nor politically accountable, and may not even be citizens. If the will of the majority, however poorly refracted through the lens of representative government, can be thwarted by the economic power of an anonymous minority, democracy itself is threatened. This too would seem at odds with contemporary views of legitimacy.

That economic globalisation may threaten a crisis of legitimacy in political rule – what one source calls a 'legitimacy deficit' (Underhill 1996: 6) – has only recently begun to attract the attention of students of world politics.[14] The growing concern is well captured by the title of a recent book by Louis Pauly: *Who Elected the Bankers?* (1997). As Saskia Sassen puts the point:

> Central banks and governments appear now to be increasingly concerned about pleasing the financial markets rather than setting goals for social and economic well-being. ... Do we want the global capital market to exercise this discipline over our governments? And to do so at all costs – jobs, wages, safety, health – and without a public debate? While it is true that these markets are the result of multiple decisions by multiple investors and thus have a certain democratic aura, all the 'voters' have to own capital. ... This leaves the vast majority of a country's citizens without any say. (Sassen 1996: 50–1)

No one who believes in either equity or accountability in politics should be content with such a structure of authority. Currency deterritorialisation *does* matter.

Conclusion

The issue, therefore, is not that states have lost all role in the management of currency relations. They are still part of money's implicit system of governance.

But in the new deterritorialised geography that has supplanted the old Westphalian model, governments must consciously adapt to a dramatic transformation of their status, from monopolists to oligopolists, if they are adequately to represent the interests of all their citizens in monetary affairs. Whether governments are up to coping with this new challenge to their traditional sovereignty is not at all clear.

Notes

1 Useful sources on currency internationalisation include Krugman (1992), Black (1993). General introductions to currency substitution include Giovannini and Turtelboom (1994), Mizen and Pentecost (1996).

2 Representative samples can be found in Thygesen *et al.* (1995), Eichengreen and Frankel (1996), Tavlas (1997), Cohen (1998).

3 For two recent surveys, see Cohen (1996), Andrews and Willett (1997).

4 In fact, much of Andrews' analysis is appropriately directed to qualifications and limits of the proposition. In his words: 'Caution is warranted when generalizing about the effects of heightened capital mobility on individual states' monetary autonomy' (1994: 193). Andrews does not concur unreservedly with the Capital Mobility Hypothesis, as I regrettably implied in my 1996 survey (Cohen 1996: 281).

5 Alain Madelin, a political conservative, quoted in the *International Herald Tribune*, 16 October, 1995, two months after he resigned from the government of Prime Minister Alain Juppé.

6 For some discussion, see Morehouse (1989), Solomon (1996).

7 Other examples include the IMF's Special Drawing Right (SDR) and an early predecessor of the ECU labelled the European Unit of Account (EUA). For more discussion, see Aschheim and Park (1976).

8 For some discussion, see Dorn (1997), Kobrin (1997).

9 Strange contrasts this with the older, more traditional rivalry between states for such things as territory and the wealth-creating resources that might be located within territory.

10 See e.g., De Boissieu (1988). De Boissieu, a French economist, writes of an 'oligopolistic monetary equilibrium' consisting of the dollar, DM (or EU common currency), and the yen. Such a perspective is common among mainstream international economists.

11 For further discussion of state responses to money's new oligopoly, see Cohen (1998).

12 Hirst and Thompson (1995) label such observers 'extreme globalisation theorists'. See this source for further references.

13 The literature on authority is voluminous, involving specialists from several disciplines. Intense debate is attracted by the relationship of the concept of authority to notions of duty or obligation, on the one hand, and to issues of liberty, rights, and the autonomy of the individual on the other. For a useful survey, see Miller (1987).

14 See e.g., Hirst and Thompson (1995), Pauly (1995), Sassen (1996).

Bibliography

Agnew, J.A. (1994) 'The territorial trap: the geographical assumptions of international relations theory', *Review of International Political Economy* 1, 1: 53–80.

Andrews, D.M. (1994) 'Capital mobility and state autonomy: toward a structural theory of international monetary relations', *International Studies Quarterly* 38, 2: 193–218.

Andrews, D.M. and Willett, T. (1997) 'Financial interdependence and the state: international monetary relations at century's end', *International Organisation* 51, 3: 479–511.

Arendt, H. (1968) 'What is authority?', in H. Arendt, *Between Past and Future*, New York: Viking Press.

Aschheim, J. and Park, Y.S. (1976) *Artificial Currency Units: The Formation of Functional Currency Areas*, Essays in International Finance No. 114, Princeton: International Finance Section.

Bank for International Settlements (1999) *Central Bank Survey of Foreign Exchange and Derivatives Market Activity*, Basle: Bank for International Settlements.

Black, S.W. (1993) 'The international use of currencies', in D.K. Das (ed.) *International Finance*, London: Routledge.

Cerny, P.G. (1994) 'The infrastructure of the infrastructure? Toward "embedded financial orthodoxy" in the international political economy', in R.P. Palan and B. Gills (eds) *Transcending the State–Global Divide: A Neostructuralist Agenda in International Relations*, Boulder: Lynne Rienner.

Cohen, B.J. (1996) 'Phoenix risen: the resurrection of global finance', *World Politics* 48, 2: 268–96.

Cohen, B.J. (1998) *The Geography of Money*, Ithaca, NY: Cornell University Press.

De Boissieu, C. (1988) 'Concurrence entre monnaies et polycentrisme monétaire', in D.E. Fair and C. De Boissieu (eds) *International Monetary and Financial Integration – The European Dimension*, Boston: Kluwer Academic Publishers.

Deutsche Bundesbank (1995) 'The circulation of Deutsche Mark abroad', *Monthly Report*, 47, 7: 65–71.

Dorn, J.A. (ed.) (1997) *The Future of Money in the Information Age*, Washington: Cato Institute.

Eichengreen, B. and Frankel, J.A. (1996) 'The SDR, reserve currencies, and the future of the international monetary system', in Michael Mussa, James M. Boughton, and Peter Isard (eds) *The Future of the SDR in the light of Changes in the International Financial System*, Washington: International Monetary Fund.

Frick, R.L. (1996) 'Alternative monetary systems: the Ithaca HOUR', *Durell Journal of Money and Banking*, 8, 2: 29–35.

Friedman, R.B. (1990) 'On the concept of authority in political philosophy', in J. Raz (ed.) *Authority*, Oxford: Basil Blackwell.

Giovannini, A. and Turtleboom, B. (1994) 'Currency substitution', in F. Van Der Ploeg (ed.) *The Handbook of International Macroeconomics*, Oxford: Basil Blackwell.

Hale, D.D. (1995) 'Is it a Yen or a Dollar crisis in the currency market?', *Washington Quarterly*, 18, 4: 145–71.

Hansson, A.H. (1993) 'The trouble with the ruble: monetary reform in the former Soviet Union', in A. Aslund and R. Layard (eds) *Changing the Economic System in Russia*, London: Pinter.

Hirschman, A.O. (1970) *Exit, Voice and Loyalty: Responses to Decline in Firms, Organizations, and States*, Cambridge: Harvard University Press.

Hirst, P. and Thompson, G. (1995) 'Globalisation and the future of the nation state', *Economy and Society*, 24, 3: 408–42.

Kobrin, S.J. (1997) 'Electronic cash and the end of national markets', *Foreign Policy*, 107: 65–77.

Krueger, R. and Ha, J. (1996) 'Measurement of cocirculation of currencies,' in P.D. Mizen and E.J. Pentecost (eds) *The Macroeconomics of International Currencies: Theory, Policy and Evidence*, Brookfield, VT: Edward Elgar.

Krugman, P.R. (1992) 'The international role of the dollar', in P.R. Krugman, *Currencies and Crises*, Cambridge and London: MIT Press.

Marshall, A. [1920] (1948) *Principles of Economics*, eighth edition, New York: Macmillan.

Meigs, A.J. (1993) 'Eurodollars: a transition currency,' *Cato Journal* 12, 3: 711–27.

Miller, D. (ed.) (1987) 'Authority', *The Blackwell Encyclopedia of Political Thought*, Oxford: Basil Blackwell.

Mizen, P.D. and Pentecost, E.J. (eds) (1996) *The Macroeconomics of International Currencies: Theory, Policy and Evidence*, Brookfield, VT: Edward Elgar.

Morehouse, W. (ed.) (1989) *Building Sustainable Communities: Tools and Concepts for Self-Reliant Economic Change*, New York: Bootstrap Press.

Okun, A.M. (1975) *Equality and Efficiency: The Big Tradeoff*, Washington: Brookings Institution.

Pauly, L.W. (1995) 'Capital mobility, state autonomy and political legitimacy', *Journal of International Affairs*, 48, 2: 369–88.

Pauly, L.W. (1997) *Who Elected the Bankers? Surveillance and Control in the World Economy*, Ithaca, NY: Cornell University Press.

Porter, R.D. and Judson, R.A. (1996) 'The location of U.S. currency: how much is abroad?', *Federal Reserve Bulletin*, 82, 10: 883–903.

Rosenau, J.N. (1992) 'Governance, order, and change in world politics', in J.N. Rosenau and E.-O. Czempiel (eds) *Governance Without Government: Order and Change in World Politics*, New York: Cambridge University Press.

Ruggie, J.G. (1993) 'Territoriality and beyond: problematizing modernity in international relations', *International Organisation*, 47, 1: 139–74.

Sassen, S. (1996) *Losing Control?: Sovereignty in an Age of Globalisation*, New York: Columbia University Press.

Solomon, L.D. (1996) *Rethinking Our Centralized Monetary System: The Case for a System of Local Currencies*, Westport, CN: Praeger.

Strange, S. (1987) 'The persistent myth of lost hegemony', *International Organisation*, 41, 4: 551–74.

Strange, S. (1996) *The Retreat of the State: The Diffusion of Power in the World Economy*, Cambridge: Cambridge University Press.

Tavlas, G.S. (1997) 'The international use of the US dollar: an optimum currency area perspective', *The World Economy*, 20, 6: 709–47.

The Economist (1993) 'Slip me a beak', (24 April), 60.

The Economist (1994) 'Electronic money: so much for the cashless society', (26 November), 21–3.

Thygesen, N. *et al.* (1995) *International Currency Competition and the Future Role of the Single European Currency*, Final Report of a Working Group on European Monetary Union – International Monetary System, London: Kluwer Law International.

Underhill, G.R.D. (1996) 'Financial market integration, global capital mobility, and the ERM Crisis 1992–1995', paper prepared for the 1996 annual meeting of the International Studies Association (manuscript).

Weber, M. [1925] (1947) *The Theory of Social and Economic Organisation*, Glencoe, IL: Free Press.

8 Denationalising money?

Economic liberalism and the 'national question' in currency affairs

Eric Helleiner

We live in an age when the ideology of economic liberalism is embraced by governments in almost all parts of the world. Not since the early years of this century has this ideology dominated the global economic order to such an extent.[1] One of the most important thinkers behind the 'neo-liberal' economic revolution of recent years was Friedrich Hayek. Among the more interesting of Hayek's ideas was his advocacy in 1976 of a world monetary system no longer centred around exclusive government-issued national currencies. In its limited form, this proposal would allow the co-circulation of foreign currencies alongside domestic currencies in each country's territory. In its more radical form, Hayek's reforms would do away with central banks and encourage private issuers of money to challenge the government's monopoly over currency. Hayek's (1976, 1990[1976]) advocacy of the 'denationalisation of money' – in both its limited and more radical approach – has attracted considerable attention in academic circles. Among policymakers, his proposal to allow co-circulation of currencies has also generated substantial interest, especially among those concerned with countries in the South and ex-Eastern bloc where 'currency substitution' is widespread.[2]

Most of the existing literature analysing Hayek's monetary ideas focuses on their economic costs and benefits. In this chapter, I aim to place Hayek's ideas in a more historical and political context. I begin by highlighting how different his proposals are from the international gold standard that existed in the last age when economic liberalism dominated policymaking. Although the gold standard is often seen as a very cosmopolitan monetary order, I call attention to the fact that its establishment in the nineteenth and early twentieth centuries was usually associated with the consolidation of the very state-managed 'national currencies' that Hayek now suggests we eliminate.[3] Indeed, I argue in the first section of the chapter that this link between 'nationalisation of money' and the creation of the gold standard – often neglected in existing literature – helps to explain why the latter was able to garner political support in that age of nation-building and nationalism. In the second section, I seek to explain why Hayek advocated the dismantling of the national currencies that his liberal predecessors helped to build. I suggest that his re-evaluation of the 'national question' in liberal thought stems partly from an underlying individualism and cosmopolitanism in liberal thought. At the same time, it also derives from his reaction against the uses to which national currencies were put when mass democratic politics replaced the narrow elite politics which had been characteristic of the era of the gold standard. In the final section, I examine the likelihood of his proposal gaining widespread political support in the contemporary age.

Gold standard and the 'nationalisation of money'

Economic liberals traditionally supported the gold standard for a simple reason; it was the monetary order that seemed most closely associated with their cosmopolitan *laissez-faire* principles. In its ideal form, the gold standard would maintain international equilibrium, discipline government policy, foster international trade and finance by providing fixed exchange rates and a common monetary standard. Moreover, it would accomplish these goals in an automatic fashion via the activity of self-regulating markets with a minimum of discretionary government involvement in the monetary sector.

The political prominence of liberal goals – as well as of the various domestic sectoral groups who would benefit from them (De Cecco 1984) – undoubtedly played a key role in explaining why countries joined the gold standard in the nineteenth and early twentieth centuries. But the fact that the gold standard triumphed in an era of nation-building suggests that it satisfied not just liberal objectives but also more nationalist ones. Some historians, for example, have noted how countries saw joining the gold standard as a source of national prestige and a way to emulate the monetary system of the world's leading economic power, the United Kingdom. For 'late developers', adopting the gold standard was also a way to attract international investment by creating a more credible and stable standard of value (Milward 1996; Gallarotti 1995).

Equally significant was the goal of consolidating the national monetary system under state control. Before the introduction of the gold standard, countries usually had rather heterogeneous and often quite chaotic monetary systems over which the state exercised only partial control. Moving onto the gold standard was often seen as the key monetary reform that could lead to a more unified and homogenous monetary order controlled by the state, a project that appealed to nationalists for a variety of reasons outlined below. This feature of the gold standard has often attracted less attention in existing literature, perhaps because of the influence of the liberal ideal of the gold standard. But it deserves scrutiny in order to highlight a key contrast between most economic liberals during the era of the gold standard and Hayek; while the latter called for the denationalisation of money, the former helped to 'nationalise' money through their support of the gold standard. This aspect of the gold standard also calls attention to the tacit acceptance by most liberals of the nation-building aspirations and nationalism of that age, an approach that Hayek and his supporters do not emulate.

The gold standard consolidated national monetary systems and brought them under greater state control in several ways. To begin with, before adopting the gold standard, the dominant forms of money in domestic circulation were usually 'full weight' silver and gold coins whose assigned value was equivalent to the value of the metals they were made of. Under this kind of coinage system, changes in the official gold–silver exchange rate or changes in world market prices of these metals could cause considerable disruption to the domestic monetary system as one or other of the dominant coins quickly disappeared from circulation. The gold standard eliminated this age-old problem of traditional monetary systems overnight. The central significance of the introduction of the gold standard in this respect was the creation of a subsidiary 'token' coinage; that is, a coinage where the face value of lower denomination coins no longer derived from their metallic content but from a value assigned by the state *vis-à-vis* gold. To maintain their value, the supply of the token coins became closely managed by the state. In most countries (and of course particularly those who joined the gold-exchange standard), these token coins quickly came to comprise most of the coinage and few 'full-weight' gold coins were actually used in domestic payments. This transformation of the coinage did much to reduce monetary chaos since it ended the risk of a sudden disappearance of a large portion of the coinage.

The fact that the gold standard brought the domestic coinage under this more homogenous and managed order often acted as the central reason for countries to join the gold standard. In his important though often neglected study, Neil Carothers pointed out that the United Kingdom (UK), the United States and many continental European countries introduced the gold standard during the nineteenth century 'primarily due to the impelling need for a stable and convenient small change currency' (Carothers 1930: 137). Faced with sudden shortages of low-denomination silver coins when the gold–silver price ratio changed dramatically, countries joined the gold standard and created a token silver currency as a way of preventing low-denomination money from disappearing from circulation.

Angela Redish (1990, 1995) points out that governments were unable to contemplate this coinage reform until industrial minting technology enabled such coins to be produced in a fashion that was difficult to counterfeit during the nineteenth century. If this supply-side innovation was a precondition for monetary reform, the move to the gold standard was also encouraged by a demand-side change. The need for a solution to the problem of small change only became particularly pressing when more and more of the population came to depend on monetary transactions for their livelihood. The rapid spread of the money economy and its penetration into daily life took place at different speeds in different countries during the nineteenth century under the pressures of industrialisation and the emergence of national scale markets. But everywhere that this process took place, the poor became more vulnerable to the sudden disappearance of small change (on which they relied heavily) that was a constant risk associated with the old 'full-weight' coinage systems. And as this vulnerability increased, shortages of small change triggered waves of popular protest and domestic petitions calling for a more adequate and reliable low-denomination money. In the age of the nation-state, these protests and petitions met with a more receptive audience than they would have before the nineteenth century. They were, after all, made by people who were now considered 'citizens' with a voice in the affairs of the nation. It was in response to these demands that the gold standard was frequently introduced (Carothers 1930; Reis 1996: 172–3). In these contexts, the creation of the gold standard can be seen as an effort to find a monetary order more appropriate to an emerging market-based national economy and national polity.

The introduction of state-managed token subsidiary coins via the gold standard also enhanced the orderly nature of the monetary order in a second way. Under a coinage system with 'full-weight' coins, an internal exchange rate existed between the value of gold and silver money. When the relative value of the two fluctuated frequently, considerable accounting difficulties and transaction costs were experienced. Indeed, to cope with changing relative values of coins – often further complicated by the presence of foreign coins (see below), widespread counterfeiting and the failure to withdraw old and worn coins – abstract units of account were often used to value the various forms of money in circulation. The introduction of the gold standard ended this confusion by creating a single standard that ensured all coins now existed in a fixed relationship to each other over time. Supporters of the gold standard often called attention to this benefit of the new monetary structure. For example, in his 1805 *Treatise on the Coins of the Realm* that paved the way for the introduction of the gold standard in the UK, Charles Jenkinson ([1805]: 1880 136–8) noted that a monometallic standard was essential for this reason in a country such as UK which had a such rapidly expanding commercial activity. Commercial cities such as Amsterdam, he noted, had also encountered the transactions costs associated with multiple standards in the past and had them addressed through the creation of 'bank-money' for leading merchants. But as the first economy with commercial activity spread out evenly across the entire nation, the UK, he argued, required a single homogenous standard available to all. The gold standard, in other words, was seen by Jenkinson as a necessary feature of the new 'national-scale' commercial economies emerging in the nineteenth century.

A third way that the new state-managed token coins of the gold standard contributed to the consolidation of a homogenous monetary system was that they encouraged the disappearance of foreign coins from domestic circulation. In a monetary system dominated by full-weight coins, it was common for foreign coins to circulate alongside domestic ones and in some countries the majority of the currency in circulation was of foreign origin. But as coins everywhere increasingly assumed a 'token' form, they were less likely to be accepted abroad. Their value no longer depended on their intrinsic metallic content but rather on some knowledge of the trustworthiness of the government that issued them as well as the prospect that the holder could redeem these coins into gold with that government. The introduction of the gold standard also encouraged public authorities to make active efforts to remove foreign currencies from circulation since their circulation could complicate the governments' need to manage carefully the supply of token coins in domestic circulation. In addition, the role that foreign coins had often played in supplementing an inadequate domestic small denomination coinage also was less useful once a modern subsidiary silver coinage was produced under the gold standard (Martin 1977).

The introduction of the gold standard was thus often the key development that ended the circulation of foreign coins, including various famous 'cosmopolitan' coins such as the Mexican dollar (Andrew 1904).[4] While this development sometimes provoked complaints from international merchants and travellers (Knapp 1924[1905]), it appealed to policymakers seeking both to reduce the transactions costs associated with a heterogeneous domestic coinage and to enhance their control over the domestic monetary system. It also had some symbolic appeal. The circulation of foreign coins was often seen by nationalists as something that 'hurt national pride' (Reis 1996: 161) or that was 'humiliating' (Government of Canada 1975[1869]: 464) to the nation. Not only was the existence of foreign coins seen as infringing on the sovereignty of a country, but it also raised symbolic concerns as imagery on coins increasingly took on nationalist overtones in the nineteenth and early twentieth centuries (Helleiner 1998b).

Finally, while the discussion above focused on changes in the coinage, the introduction of the gold standard also came to be associated with a homogenisation of the banknote circulation. As paper money increasingly began to be issued during the nineteenth and twentieth centuries, it often initially contributed to the heterogeneity of the money in circulation as many institutions – from various levels of government to a multitude of private banks – began to issue notes. Not only did the denominations and appearance of these different forms of paper money often vary considerably, but so too did their 'quality' and thus the degree of their acceptance across the economic space of each country. The introduction of the gold standard was frequently the moment when states moved to consolidate the issuing of notes by granting monopoly note issue rights to a national central bank.

This link between the gold standard and note issue monopolies was not present in all cases during the nineteenth and early twentieth centuries; many countries on the gold standard in that era continued to have multiple note issues and other countries had a monopoly note issue without being on the gold standard. But the association between the gold standard and note issue consolidation became an increasingly common one after the UK's 1844 Bank Act granted the Bank of England monopoly note issue as part of an effort to make the gold standard operate more smoothly. The link between the gold standard and the consolidation of the national note issue grew particularly strong after the First World War. At the Brussels (1920) and Genoa (1922) international economic conferences, resolutions were passed calling for the creation of central banks with monopoly note issues in all countries who had not yet created them as part of the effort to restore the international gold standard in that era.

Some economic liberals in the nineteenth century opposed the monopolisation of the note issue, preferring to see a competitive system of note issue (although interestingly, few extended this argument to the issue of coinage). But the influence of this 'free banking' school dwindled in the years leading up to the First World War and then collapsed after 1918. The dominant position in economic liberal circles for most of the nineteenth century, and especially by the 1920s, was that countries on the gold standard should create a central bank with a monopoly note issue for a straightforward reason; it was necessary to ensure that the supply of notes was regulated in a manner in keeping with the automatic self-regulating principles of the gold standard. Whether this control was to be exercised along the rigid lines advocated by the Currency School in 1844 or along the more flexible lines suggested by the 1919 Cunliffe Committee, central banks with a monopoly note issue came to be seen as central to the smooth operation of the international gold standard. After the First World War, they were also seen as important in facilitating both a rapid restoration of currency stability as well as international co-operation in the monetary realm.

The link between the gold standard and a central bank with monopoly note issue held different appeal to those whose focus was less internationalist and more focused on the domestic task of national monetary consolidation. After all, it was not just liberals during the 1920s but also nationalists in Eastern Europe, Latin America, the British Dominions and parts of Asia who welcomed the Brussels and Genoa resolutions (De Cecco 1984: ii, 1995: 131; Plumptre 1940; Drake 1989; Fry 1979: 279–80; Minai 1961: 159). To them, the creation of a central bank with monopoly note issue represented simply one more way in which the move onto a gold standard was associated with the consolidation of the national monetary system under state control. A central bank with monopoly control over the note issue not only helped to reduce transaction costs within the nation (particularly for the poor and illiterate who had difficulty discriminating properly between 'good' and 'bad' private notes). It also gave the state a valuable source of seignorage revenue as well as a tool to influence more effectively the nation's internal economy and its economic relations with the outside world (since the gold reserves of the country came under centralised control). In Marcello De Cecco's words, adopting the gold standard thus 'was in most cases a giant step towards dirigisme' (De Cecco 1984: ii).

In addition, it should not be forgotten that the monopolisation of the banknote under state control often had symbolic value for nationalists. Eric Hobsbawm (1983) explains how governments across the world launched extensive initiatives to 'mass produce tradition' of a nationalist kind in the last third of the nineteenth century as a means of maintaining legitimacy in the face of domestic challenges to their rule. Elaborate images on state-issued bank notes played a major role in these initiatives. The images included national landscapes, important events and personalities in the history of the nation, and portrayals of the everyday life of citizens and the economic progress of the nation. Policymakers recognised that images on notes were particularly effective tools of propaganda – more so than flags or anthems – because they were encountered so regularly in the context of daily routines in an age when the use of money was becoming increasingly pervasive (Helleiner 1998b).

The introduction of the gold standard thus encouraged a more consolidated and rationalised national currency to emerge under state control. This feature of the gold standard helps us to understand why the gold standard had particular appeal in an era of nation-building and nationalism. Although economic liberals saw the gold standard in primarily economic and internationalist terms, nationalists saw it in a more domestic and political manner as useful for their goals of strengthening state power and its control over the economy, cultivating a sense of collective national identity, and consolidating the internal economic coherence of the nation. The latter goal was particularly significant for nation-builders during the nineteenth and early twentieth centuries. The transaction costs and uncertainties associated with heterogeneous monetary systems were usually very significant for public authorities in areas such as tax collection as well as for private economic actors seeking to operate in the emerging economic space of the nation (Helleiner 1997). The more consolidated monetary order associated with the gold standard reduced them, often in a dramatic manner, thus both creating a more efficient public sector more capable of mobilising national resources, and fostering the growth of a more smoothly functioning national market economy. For this reason, the gold standard was often seen as a particularly 'modern' monetary order well-suited to the age of nation-building.

Hayek's re-evaluation of the 'national question'

If economic liberals in the nineteenth and early twentieth centuries were able to find support for the construction of the gold standard among many nationalists of their era, proponents of Hayek's proposal seem unlikely to repeat this experience. In calling for the 'denationalisation' of money, they can expect to arouse the opposition of nationalists who see national currencies as an essential part of the political fabric of a nation. Why then would Hayek and his supporters advocate the dismantling of the very national currencies that his liberal predecessors helped to build? What explains this re-evaluation of the 'national question' in currency affairs?

In part, Hayek's proposal stems from a strong individualism and cosmopolitanism in his thought, and his hostility to nationalism and its consequences. Indeed, in *The Denationalisation of Money*, he made clear that it was not just national currencies he opposed but even national economies themselves: 'There is indeed little reason why territories that happen to be under the same government should form distinct national economic areas' (Hayek 1990: 114).

These individualistic and cosmopolitan sentiments are in fact not so different from those of his nineteenth-century predecessors. Such thinking was important, for example, in leading some economic liberals of that era to oppose monopoly note issue in favour of 'free banking' as we have already seen. Similarly, although other economic liberals in the pre-1931 era found themselves frequently allied with nationalists in supporting the gold standard, they showed only limited interest in the latter's objectives. To be sure, many liberals certainly welcomed the more orderly and 'scientific' domestic monetary order that was ushered in by the gold standard. But their interest in the relationship between the consolidation of national currencies and the broader political project of nation-building was usually limited. Indeed, whereas nationalists usually saw the goal of nation-building as an end in itself, most economic liberals hoped the construction of a coherent national economy was merely a temporary way station on the way to the construction of universal global community (Hobsbawm 1992: 43).

A key attraction of the international gold standard was that it seemed to help them begin to reach this cosmopolitan goal by maintaining international equilibrium and fostering the growth of international trade and investment. Indeed, to many liberals, the gold standard created a monetary order which had a *de facto* global currency; gold. Most economic liberals did not find much significance in the fact that the gold standard rested on the foundation of national currencies with their distinctive imagery, names and units of account. In Karl Polanyi's words, 'If the nation was deemed by them an anachronism, national currencies were reckoned not even worthy of attention. No self-respecting economist of the liberal age doubted the irrelevance of the fact that different pieces of paper were called differently on different sides of political frontiers' (Polanyi 1944: 202). They were, after all, simply 'different tokens representing the same commodity' (Polanyi 1944: 196).

In keeping with their cosmopolitan sentiments, various economic liberals called for the creation of a truly universal currency at different times during the nineteenth and early twentieth centuries. The most prominent initiative came at the high point of the influence of economic liberalism during the 1860s when a proposal was made for the introduction of a universal coin that could circulate in all nations. Not only would this coin reduce transaction costs associated with handling various distinct national currencies, but it would also help people to transcend national identities by making people, in Walter Bagehot's words, 'think they were of one blood' (quoted in Perlman 1993: 318). The initiative garnered a remarkable degree of support from liberals across the world from Europe to Asia and the Americas, but it ultimately failed to gain the support of key governments. A significant reason for its failure was that – in contrast to the gold standard – it worked against the nationalist aspirations of the age. In a number of leading countries, the proposal ran into opposition from nationalists who felt strongly that national currencies were a source of identification with the nation. The initiative was also torpedoed by Germany's decision after unification to consolidate its coinage system on a basis that was not easily reconcilable with that of other nations. This decision highlighted how the goal of domestic national monetary consolidation took precedence over that of global monetary integration (in addition to reflecting Bismarck's suspicions of French interest in the universal coin proposal) (Russell 1898: 117).

The whole universal currency episode thus highlighted to many liberals the practical political barriers in the way of their cosmopolitan ideals. Although they did not embrace nationalism enthusiastically, they came to accept its political influence, just as 'free bankers' were also forced to. This is not to say proposals for supranational forms of money did not continue to resurface in liberal circles (e.g. Kemmerer 1916, Van De Putte, 1920). But they were acknowledged by most to be politically unrealistic given nationalist sentiments of the age. It had become clear that any world monetary system had to be built on an 'inter-national' basis – that is, on the foundation of nations and national currencies, as the gold standard was – rather than on more 'cosmopolitan' principles.

If liberals in the pre-1931 era thus resigned themselves to national currencies and the power of nationalism despite their underlying individualistic and cosmopolitan ideals, Hayek was less inclined to do so. This partly reflected his fierce opposition to all forms of 'collectivism'. But it also stemmed from a second source: his reaction against a change in the nature of nationalism and its influence on how national currencies came to be managed in the interwar period and after.

The goals of nationalists posed little challenge to liberals when the former sought simply to enhance the state's control of the monetary system in order to provide a more efficient monetary order and stable currency by joining the gold standard. This was the dominant approach of nationalists in the pre-1931 period. But throughout the nineteenth century there had also been a strand of nationalist thinkers less enamoured of the gold standard. These were figures with a strong commitment to 'popular sovereignty', one of the principles of modern nationalism that had emerged from the French and American revolutions. In their mind, there was no particular reason why this principle should not extend to the monetary realm; that is, that 'the people' should be allowed to manage the national currency. For this management to be free from external constraints, the currency could not be tied to gold but rather would need to be inconvertible. Johann Fichte's *The Closed Commercial State,* written in 1800, provided the first developed example of this kind of thinking in nationalist circles. Inspired by the French experiment with assignats, he called for an inconvertible token money that would be actively managed by the state with the objective of promoting the welfare of its citizens (Hayes 1931: 263–5). Fichte's ideas were echoed throughout the nineteenth century by many other nationalists and found perhaps their most sophisticated expression in the English nationalist Thomas Attwood's proto-Keynesian ideas about how an inconvertible national currency could be printed in sufficient quantities to ensure full employment (Moss 1990).

These advocates of an inconvertible currency and an activist national monetary policy were seen in liberal economic circles in the nineteenth century as radical heretics. But liberals were also forced to recognise the potential power of the arguments in an age when the state had assumed greater control over the monetary system and new nationalist ideas of popular sovereignty were current in the political realm. When the British government refused to consider his proposals, for example, Attwood highlighted the connection between his ideas and the claims of popular sovereignty, leading the campaign in the 1830s to widen the electoral franchise out of a belief that the people would surely embrace his ideas even if elites did not. As Frank Fetter notes, fear among liberals of his potent combination of mass democratic politics and radical currency reform played a key role in garnering support for Peel's 1844 Bank Act and its effort to depoliticise the conduct of monetary policy (Fetter 1965: 177–80, 212–14).

Liberal fears intensified as the electoral franchise began to be extended dramatically during the late nineteenth and especially during and after the First World War, giving the poorer classes more power to express their views on the management of the national currency. As Barry Eichengreen (1992) has noted, political parties supporting labourers in this period frequently were attracted to monetary policies that would more actively manage the national currency to address problems of unemployment and economic growth, and their growing power posed an important challenge to supporters of the gold standard. In the 1920s, liberals attempted to counter their influence through the establishment of a network of independent national central banks and the promotion of orthodox financial policies. This project was, of course, ultimately unsuccessful. In the wake of the financial crisis in the early 1930s and world depression, the gold standard collapsed and liberal conceptions of orthodox monetary management were abandoned almost everywhere. The very structures that had been constructed under the gold standard – national central banks and homogenous national token currencies – came under the control of politicians and were used to serve more activist purposes. With the triumph of Keynesianism in the post-1945 period, this new approach became dominant across much of the world.

It is out of this experience that Hayek's call for the denationalisation of money needs to be understood. As politicians sought greater control over the management of national currencies during and after the interwar period, the dangers of the alliance between liberalism and nationalism became apparent. In promoting the gold standard, liberals had created structures such as central banks with a monopoly of the note issue and token coinages that could be used for more interventionist purposes. In an era of nationalism, this had turned out to be a risky strategy. Liberals had helped to construct monetary structures that could easily be used for goals that they opposed. Far from being a quaint but antiquated community on the way to a more cosmopolitan world, the nation had become a dangerous end point.

As a consequence, it is no surprise that at this time Hayek and other liberals began to write for the first time about the dangers of 'monetary nationalism' (Hayek 1937). They used this phrase to refer to the kind of activist monetary policies that became popular after the First World War (usually without acknowledging that the gold standard too had been a 'nationalist' monetary institution for many groups). It was also in this period that liberals – including Hayek's mentor Ludwig von Mises (1953[1924]: 396–9) – began to question whether the earlier liberal support for national currencies had been a mistake (Smith 1990[1936]).

During the Bretton Woods era, economic liberals who remained committed to orthodox monetary goals and the gold standard could take some comfort in the fact that the international monetary order still rested, at least via the dollar, on gold (even if countries used unorthodox adjustable pegs and capital controls to maintain this link). With the breakdown of the gold standard in the early 1970s, however, all currencies in the world became what Fichte, Attwood and other 'heretics' during the nineteenth century had dreamed of; pure fiat currencies. The breakdown of the gold standard highlighted to economic liberals how difficult it had become to 'protect money from politics' (Hayek 1990: 16) in the traditional way when the principal commitment of governments in an age of mass democracy had become activist monetary management aimed at domestic monetary objectives. The inflation of the following decade did little to calm their concerns about the dangers of the new world of universal fiat money.

These events of the 1970s – combined with discussions about European monetary integration at the time – appear to have triggered Hayek to re-evaluate his thinking about the merits of national currencies. If the gold standard could not be reintroduced as a means of preventing politicians from controlling national currencies, he was led to wonder whether monetary discipline could better be achieved by eliminating national currencies altogether. If people were given 'choice in currency' (either between government-issued currencies or between privately issued currencies), Hayek argued, they would choose the most stable currency. Currency competition would thus discipline governments, forcing them to maintain the value of money they issued and restrain spending.

Hayek's re-evaluation of the national question thus partly reflected an underlying individualism and cosmopolitanism in economic liberal thought. At the same time, however, it reflected his reaction to the monetary experience since the interwar period. In an age of mass democratic politics when politicians were beholden to what he called 'special interests', Hayek believed the nation was no longer a community which could be trusted to manage money according to his ideals.[5] Whereas many nineteenth-century liberals had seen their acceptance of nationalism as politically necessary and often even desirable as the first step *en route* to a more cosmopolitan order, Hayek thus saw the need to make more of a choice; embracing national currencies might preclude the realisation of his individualistic and cosmopolitan ideals.

Towards a denationalisation of money?

To what extent is Hayek's vision for the future of the world monetary system likely to be realised in the coming years? There is little evidence of his proposals being introduced in the near future in 'Northern' countries. Even those who support Hayek's limited proposal of co-circulation of national currencies, such as Toyoo Gyohten, concede that '[f]or the moment . . . this is sheer fantasy' (Volcker and Gyohten 1992: 310). To be sure, the British government's support for the 'hard ecu' proposal – which it advanced in the context of the discussions of monetary union in the European Union – drew on Hayek's ideas. But it has received little support beyond Britain. The prospect of the growth of 'e-money' has also generated some literature arguing that Hayek's vision of privately issued currencies is soon to become a reality in Northern countries because the new technologies will make it difficult for states to control the issuing of money. As I have argued elsewhere, however, this view underestimates the extent to which government authorities can, and most likely will, regulate the new 'e-money' (Helleiner, 1998a).

As many observers have noted, the strongest evidence that Hayek's vision may become a reality comes not from developments in Northern countries but rather from increasingly widespread 'currency substitution' within many countries in the 'South' and ex-Eastern bloc during the last two decades. In many of these countries, citizens have genuinely come to acquire 'choice in currency' within the domestic monetary system as foreign currencies – usually the dollar – have increasingly replaced the local currency as the dominant currency in use. Hayek's limited proposal for the denationalisation of money, thus, is not just of academic interest for people in these countries. It is in fact a reality that has been experienced to varying extents over the last two decades.

This currency substitution process has partly been what Hayek might approvingly call a 'spontaneous' market-led one. Individuals – particularly wealthy individuals – have been prompted to reduce their holdings and use of the domestic currency by high rates of inflation, overvalued currencies and/or political instability. In most cases, the national currency's role as a store of value has been replaced first, but the replacement process has often – particularly in situations of hyperinflation – also extended to money's role as a medium of exchange and unit of account. This market-driven process has frequently taken place without the state's consent and in countries with weak state capacity, policymakers have seemed powerless to stop it.

But the currency substitution phenomenon has also often been encouraged by governments through their decisions to legalise foreign currency deposits in banks or even the use of foreign currencies as legal tender in everyday transactions. For the most part, these policy decisions have not been driven by any great enthusiasm for Hayek's thinking. Instead, defensive motives were more important. As financial markets have become more liberal and globalised, wealthy asset holders had found increasingly easy opportunities to take their assets abroad in response to unfavourable economic and political circumstances. This has been particularly true in Latin America where the elite have long had what James Mahon calls 'cosmopolitan' asset preferences (Mahon 1996: 47). Permitting the domestic use of foreign currency has been a way of trying to encourage this elite to bring their capital back home (e.g. Brand 1993).

The lack of enthusiasm for Hayek's vision in policymaking circles is hardly surprising. Hayek and many of his supporters often argue that the central barrier to their project's realisation is the state's desire to maximise the revenue it derives from monopolising money. But equally significant is the fact that the trend undermines the political role that national currencies are seen by many to play in nation-building. Not only is the internal coherence of the national economy undermined by the prevalence of dollarisation as transaction costs increase but also threatened is the state's ability to manage money – either through discretionary monetary policy or exchange rate policy – in a manner that responds to the preferences of citizens. Even the ability of the national currency to foster a sense of collective identity may be undermined in situations where currency substitution is widespread. Although Hayek's supporters usually focus primarily on the economic benefits to arise from their proposal, these broader political consequences are often of central concern to policymakers. After all, although this is an era when economic liberalism has triumphed, it is also an age when nationalism remains alive and well in most parts of the world.

For this reason, many governments, particularly those with strong nationalist orientations, have responded to the rapid growth of currency substitution with 'de-dollarisation' initiatives involving regulatory changes and dramatic stabilisation plans designed to restore confidence in the national currency and reduce capital flight. Many of these initiatives have been quite successful; for example, Israel in 1985 (Bruno 1993), many ex-Eastern bloc countries in the early 1990s (Brand 1993). Others have been less successful or have been quickly reversed primarily because of the kinds of factors already mentioned. In weak states, policymakers have been forced to recognise their incapacity to influence citizens' behaviour in this area, particularly when stabilisation programmes have not been perceived as credible. In other cases, the de-dollarisation initiatives have promoted extensive capital flight which, in turn, has forced a re-evaluation of the strategy.[6] The denationalisation of money has, therefore, often persisted not because of any enthusiasm for the process but rather because of poor state capacity or the constraints imposed by capital flight in this age of financial globalisation.

It is interesting to note that the introduction of stabilisation plans to reduce currency substitution usually involve not just fiscal and monetary restraint, but also the creation of an independent central bank or even a currency board. In this way, these stabilisation plans in fact achieve the objective Hayek sought; that of disciplining government policy and 'removing money from the realm of politics'. But, unlike Hayek's proposal, they do so in a way that allows economic liberal goals to work hand-in-hand with the more nationalist objective of re-establishing a degree of control over the monetary system. The introduction of currency boards is perhaps the most dramatic example of this phenomenon. By reintroducing the kind of discipline associated with the classical gold standard, currency boards are usually seen as a dramatic example of a repudiation of nationalist approaches to economic policy. But frequently they have been introduced for quite nationalist reasons: to re-establish a degree of control over the monetary system, to expel foreign currencies, to re-cultivate 'pride' in the national currency and to attract international investment (e.g. Saavalainen 1995: 3). Politically astute economic liberals have in fact recognised the potential nationalist appeal of currency boards, as an alternative to currency substitution, in this respect (Hanke 1992: 18, 21).

The way that economic liberals have been able to work alongside nationalists in attempting to re-establish national currencies in situations such as this is reminiscent of the alliance between the two during the era of the gold standard. Supporters of Hayek might call attention to the dangers in this approach, arguing that these national currencies will ultimately be used for more interventionist purposes by democratic governments in an age when they are no longer disciplined by the gold standard. But the likelihood of governments pursuing monetary policies that liberals disapprove of in the contemporary era seems slim. During the last decade, there has been a dramatic convergence of views, particularly in the developing world, in favour of orthodox liberal monetary goals. One cause has been the fear of the discipline of international financial markets against governments who depart from these goals; the discipline of the new globalised financial markets, in other words, has to some extent replaced that of the gold standard. At the same time, this trend has also been caused by a disillusionment with the kinds of activist monetary policies pursued in the middle decades of this century in the context of both the rational expectations revolution in economics and the actual experiences of inflation that sometimes accompanied those policies (Maxfield 1997).

Democratic governments thus appear less of a threat to liberal goals in the contemporary age than Hayek suggested. In contrast to the experience earlier in this century, 'the people' appear to be expressing a preference for the same goals as economic liberals in the monetary realm today in many regions of the world. Importantly, however, this loss of interest in activist monetary policy has not usually translated into a loss of interest in national currencies. In addition to their roles of fostering national identities and internal economic coherence, national currencies are still linked closely to a sense of popular sovereignty; that is, even if money is not to be actively managed, the people would like to keep that choice in their own hands. Instead of abandoning national currencies, most governments have chosen to 'protect money from politics' through the establishment of independent central banks, or in some cases currency boards.

Ironically, this triumph of liberal approaches to monetary policy provides a further barrier in the way of Hayek's ideas gaining more political influence. Not only do nationalists oppose it, but so too do many economic liberals. This opposition stems in part from many detailed economic arguments about the pros and cons of free banking or currency substitution that I will not discuss here (except to say that they are often similar to arguments made by liberals in the nineteenth and early twentieth centuries in support of currency monopoly – e.g. Goodhart 1988, Mizen and Pentecost 1996). But equally important is the sentiment that, given the triumph of liberal goals in the monetary sector, those fighting for the denationalisation of money seem to be fighting an old battle. Two decades after Hayek first published his proposal, national currencies have ceased to pose the kind of threat that he perceived in many contexts. Consequently, it seems politically much simpler to embrace national currencies – rather than incur nationalist opposition – and ensure that they are managed in an orthodox fashion.

This is, for example, the approach adopted by liberal policymakers within the International Monetary Fund (IMF) in their advice to new nations in Eastern Europe and the former Soviet Union. Analyses by IMF staff suggest that they do not see much of a case for discouraging currency substitution on strictly economic grounds (Calvo and Vegh 1992). But closer to political realities than Hayek's academic supporters, IMF officials have been forced to recognise the power of nationalism in this region and the importance that nationalists attach to the creation of a national currency.[7] Like their predecessors in the League of Nations, IMF officials have not only recognised the need to embrace national currencies but even helped to create them in new nations through technical assistance programs that include such detailed advice as how best to design banknotes to reflect nationalist identities and ideas (Abrams 1995). As in the pre-1930s period, however, the price for their support of national currencies has been that these currencies must be run in an orthodox fashion.

Nationalists in these regions have often been willing to accept this price, not just because of the discipline of international financial markets and their commitment to orthodox goals. In contexts where the state is weak and the nation is being consolidated, the IMF's support for the project of maintaining a national currency has political value for them. This parallels the late nineteenth-/early twentieth-century experience when prominent liberal 'money doctors' introducing the gold exchange standard in peripheral regions were often welcomed by local nationalists who saw their missions as useful in helping to design and implement 'modern' national currencies as well as to signal 'credibility' to international investors (Drake 1989). It is not just liberals, therefore, who often recognise the worth of an alliance with nationalists. As they did before the 1930s, nationalists too often see advantages from a close association with powerful liberals.

In sum, while a considerable degree of interest has been generated by Hayek's proposals, supporters of them seem to underestimate the important political barriers that stand in the way of their widespread and enthusiastic adoption. Hayek himself often identified the prime obstacle as the state's desire to maximise revenue it derives from being the monopoly producer of currency. But this analysis neglects the way in which the creation of national currencies historically was linked not just to revenue goals, but also to the objectives of both Hayek's liberal predecessors and nationalists in the nineteenth and early twentieth centuries. Not only do many liberals today remain committed to the idea that states should retain this monopoly, but so too do nationalists. To nationalists, a national currency is much more than an economic instrument. It is also a political tool that is closely linked to the coherence and identity of the nation as well as the nature of national citizenship. This is often acknowledged in passing in much of the economic literature on currency substitution and monetary reform, but rarely analysed in depth. Indeed, it appears that only in contexts where the state is already weak or particularly vulnerable to capital flight that Hayek's proposal is being realised in a substantial way.

Conclusion

The triumph of economic liberal ideas today encourages parallels to be drawn with the era before the 1930s when they also dominated world economic affairs. I have attempted to highlight, however, how one of the key intellectual leaders of the recent resurgence of economic liberalism, Friedrich Hayek, recently called for a monetary order very different from the gold standard that his liberal predecessors had endorsed during the nineteenth and early twentieth centuries. Despite its cosmopolitan *laissez-faire* image in liberal circles, the gold standard was a monetary institution that helped to consolidate the very state-controlled national currencies that Hayek's followers now seek to dismantle. Indeed, it was this feature of the gold standard that often garnered support for it in that age of nation-building and nationalism. Although economic liberals in the nineteenth and early twentieth centuries were not terribly interested in this link between national currencies and the broader political project of nation-building, they were forced to recognise its political significance.

In calling for the dismantling of the very monetary structures that his liberal predecessors helped to build, Hayek's proposal would certainly usher in a different world from that which existed in the pre-1930s period. Hayek emphasised the similarities; the creation of a world of denationalised money was an alternative route to achieving the same low inflation objectives and lack of discretionary government control over money as existed during the era of the gold standard. But that earlier liberal world monetary system was built solidly on the base of national currencies, currencies which also helped to consolidate the economic coherence of nations, the link between state and citizen, and even national identities. By contrast, a world of 'denationalised money' would encourage a more deterritorialised sense of economic space, a different sense of citizenship, and even alternative identities. In regions already experiencing widespread currency substitution, these trends can in fact already be seen to some degree (Cohen 1998).

What are the sources of this new interest in the denationalisation of money in the contemporary era? In Hayek's case, I have suggested the source was both an underlying individualism and cosmopolitanism in liberal thought, and a reaction against the way national currencies came to be used when mass democratic politics replaced the 'oligarchic' (Johnson 1970: ch. 2) politics characteristic of the era of the gold standard. At the same time, I have also argued that the influence of Hayek's ideas in regions experiencing currency substitution should not be overstated. Currency substitution has become widespread in many countries during the last two decades not because of any great enthusiasm for Hayek's ideas in policy-making circles. Rather, the phenomenon has become extensive primarily in countries – particularly those characterised by persistently high inflation, overvalued exchange rates and/or political instability – where policymakers have only reluctantly accepted it either because they recognise their inability to prevent it given weak state capacity or because it appeared to be a way of reducing extensive capital flight.

Lack of enthusiasm for Hayek's ideas in policy-making circles is understandable. Although this is an age when economic liberal ideas are prevalent, it is also one in which nationalism remains a potent force throughout most parts of the world. Like many of his liberal predecessors, Hayek seemed not to recognise the enduring broader political significance of national currencies for nationalists. Moreover, with activist monetary management increasingly being abandoned around the world, many economic liberals – assuming they even agree with Hayek's ideas – also see little reason to challenge the widespread political commitment to national currencies (except in contexts such as the EU where a broader supra-national political project exists). The easier route is to endorse national currencies, while ensuring that they are managed in an orthodox fashion. Thus, while Hayek's proposal suggests that a very different kind of relationship between monetary and political space might emerge from that which existed during the pre-1930s period, in instances such as these the similarities between the two eras seem more apparent than the differences. Both then and now, economic liberals have often been forced to acknowledge both the political significance of nationalism as well as the fact that the 'national question' in currency affairs raises issues that go well beyond narrow economic concerns.

Acknowledgements

I thank the Social Sciences and Humanities Research Council of Canada for assisting this research. I am also grateful for helpful comments to: Knut Borchardt, William Branson, Jennifer Clapp, William Clark, Benjamin Cohen, Marc Flandreau, Harold James, Don Moggridge, Lou Pauly, Robert Skidelsky, and David Wolfe.

Notes

1 In referring to 'economic liberalism' in this chapter, I do not include what John Ruggie (1983) calls 'embedded liberalism'; that is, the more interventionist forms of liberalism that became popular in the Keynesian age. In monetary affairs, I consider the hallmarks of the economic liberal perspective to be a belief in stable money and a scepticism of discretionary monetary policy by governments.

2 The term 'currency substitution' is used differently by different authors. In this chapter, it refers to the use of foreign currency within the domestic territory of a country.

3 In this chapter, I use the term 'national currencies' to refer to currencies which are homogenous and exclusive within the territorial boundaries of a nation-state.

4 This is not to suggest that all countries who joined the gold standard eliminated foreign coins from domestic circulation. Some countries allowed the 'full-weight' gold coins of other nations to continue to circulate domestically, particularly if they did not produce such coins themselves. In most of these cases, however, few of these coins were actually in circulation. Some others also allowed foreign 'token' coins to circulate domestically up until the First World War, such as the member countries of the Latin Monetary Union (LMU) and the Scandinavian Monetary Union (SMU). They did so partly for reasons of convenience but also for broader political reasons associated with French imperial goals and influence in the case of the LMU and 'pan-Scandivanian' sentiments in the case of the SMU (e.g. Nielson, 1933). In these instances, however, it is important to note that foreign token coins now circulated domestically only under the terms of these international agreements which regulated their production and acceptance in each participating country.

5 For Hayek, the denationalisation of money also had particular appeal because of his scepticism about the value of any kind of government planning. Thus, he attacked not just Keynesians but also monetarists for believing that even conservative monetary planning was desirable.

6 See for example the cases of Mexico (1982), Peru (1985) and Bolivia (1982) analysed in Calvo and Vegh (1992). Also significant has been a kind of hysteresis where currency substitution becomes difficult to reverse even after a successful stabilisation.

7 As the IMF Managing Director Michel Camdessus (1992, p.4) acknowledged in discussing currency arrangements among the Soviet successor states, the decision of newly independent countries to create national currencies may have many economic drawbacks but it is a decision that 'lies at the heart of national sovereignty. For many countries, an independent currency is a potent symbol of nationhood, like the flag or the national anthem'. The IMF has also been supportive of efforts to create national currencies in many regions of the ex-Eastern bloc as a way to avoid the monetary instability associated with transitional common currency regimes.

Bibliography

Abrams, R. (1995) *The Design and Printing of Bank Notes: Considerations When Introducing a New Currency*, IMF Working Paper no.26. Washington: IMF.

Andrew, A.P. (1904) 'The end of the Mexican dollar', *Quarterly Journal of Economics* 18: 321–56.

Brand, D. (1993) *Currency Substitution in Developing Countries*, Munich: Weltforum Verlag.

Bruno, M. (1993) *Crisis, Stablisation and Economic Reform: Therapy by Consensus*, Oxford: Clarendon.

Calvo, G. and Vegh, C. (1992) *Currency Substitution in Developing Countries*, IMF Working Paper no. 40, Washington: IMF.

Camdessus, M. (1992) *Economic Transformation in the Fifteen Republics of the Former U.S.S.R.*, Washington: IMF.

Carothers, N. (1930) *Fractional Money*, New York: John Wiley and Sons.

Cohen, B. (1998) *The Geography of Money*, Ithaca: Cornell University Press.

De Cecco, M. (1984) *The International Gold Standard*, second edn, London: Frances Pinter.

De Cecco, M. (1995) 'Central bank cooperation in the interwar period: a view from the periphery' in J. Reis (ed.) *International Monetary Systems in Historical Perspective*, London: Macmillan.

Drake, P. (1989) *The Money Doctor in the Andes: the Kemmerer Missions, 1923–1933*, Durham: Duke University Press.

Eichengreen, B. (1992) *Golden Fetters*, Oxford: Oxford University Press.

Fetter, F. (1965) *Development of British Monetary Orthodoxy 1797–1875*, Cambridge: Harvard University Press.

Fry, M. (1979) *Money and Banking In Turkey*, Istanbul: Bogazici University Publications no. 171.

Gallarotti. G. (1995) *The Anatomy of an International Monetary Regime: The Classical Gold Standard 1880–1914*, Oxford: Oxford University Press.

Goodhart, C. (1988) *The Evolution of Central Banking*, Cambridge: MIT Press.

Government of Canada 1975[1869] *House of Commons Debates* 1st Parliament, 2nd Session, Ottawa: Information Canada.

Hanke, S. (1992) *Monetary Reform for a Free Estonia: A Currency Board Solution*, Stockholm: SNS Forlag.

Hayek, F. (1937) *Monetary Nationalism and International Stability*, London: Longmans, Green and Co.

Hayek, F. (1976) *Choice in Currency*, London: Institute of Economic Affairs, Occasional Paper no. 48

Hayek, F. (1990 [1976]). *Denationalisation of Money – The Argument Refined*, third edn, London: Institute of Economic Affairs.

Hayes, C. (1931) *The Historical Evolution of Modern Nationalism*, New York: Richard Smith Inc.

Helleiner, E. (1997) *One Nation, One Money: Territorial Currencies and the Nation State*. Oslo: ARENA Working Paper no. 17.

Helleiner, E. (1998a) 'Electronic money: a challenge to the sovereign state?' *Journal of International Affairs* 51, 2: 387–410.

Helleiner, E. (1998b) 'National currencies and national identities' *American Behavioral Scientist* 41, 10: 1409–36.

Hobsbawm, E. (1983) 'Mass-producing tradition: Europe, 1870–1914', in E. Hobsbawm and T. Ranger (eds) *The Invention of Tradition*, Cambridge: Cambridge University Press.

Hobsbawm, E. (1992) *Nations and Nationalism Since 1780*, second edn, Cambridge: Cambridge University Press.

Jenkinson, C. ([1805] 1880) *Treatise on the Coins of the Realm*, London: Effingham Wilson.

Johnson, B. (1970) *The Politics of Money*, London: John Murray.

Kemmerer, E. (1916) 'A proposal for Pan-American monetary unity' *Political Science Quarterly* 31: 66–80.

Knapp, G. (1924 [1905]) *The State Theory of Money*, translated by H. Lucas and J. Bonar, London: MacMillan.

Mahon, J. (1996). *Mobile Capital and Latin American Development*, University Park: Pennsylvania State University Press.

Martin, D. (1977) 'The changing role of foreign money in the United States, 1782–1857', *Journal of Economic History* 37, 4: 1009–27.

Maxfield, S. (1997) *Gatekeepers of Growth: The International Political Economy of Central Banking in Developing Countries*, Princeton: Princeton University Press.

Milward, A. (1996) 'The origins of the gold standard' in J.B. De Macedo, B. Eichengreen and J. Reis (eds) *Currency Convertibility*, London: Routledge.

Minai, A. (1961) 'Economic development of Iran: under the reign of Reza Shah 1926–1941', Ph.D., American University. Ann Arbor: University Microfilms.

Mizen, P. and Pentecost, E. (eds) (1996) *The Macroeconomics of International Currencies*, Cheltenham: Edward Elgar.

Moss, D. (1990) *Thomas Attwood: The Biography of a Radical*, Montreal: McGill-Queen's University Press.

Nielson, A. (1933) 'Monetary unions', *Encyclopedia of the Social Sciences* 10: 595–601.

Perlman, M. (1993) 'In search of monetary union', *Journal of European Economic History*, 22, 2: 313–32.

Plumptre. A. (1940) *Central Banking in the British Dominions*, Toronto: University of Toronto Press.

Polanyi, K. (1944) *The Great Transformation*, Boston: Beacon Press.

Redish, A. (1990) 'The evolution of the gold standard in England', *Journal of Economic History*, 50, 4: 789–805.

Redish, A. (1995) 'The persistence of bimetallism in nineteenth-century France', *Economic History Review*, 55, 4: 717–36.

Reis, J. (1996) 'First to join the gold standard, 1854', in J. B. De Macedo, B. Eichengreen and J. Reis (eds) *Currency Convertibility*, London: Routledge.

Ruggie, J. (1983) 'International regimes, transactions and change', *International Organization*. 36, 2: 379–405.

Russell, H. (1898) *International Monetary Conferences*, New York: Harper and Bros.
Saavalainen, T. (1995) *Stabilization in the Baltic Countries*, IMF Working Paper no. 44. Washington: IMF.
Smith, V. (1990[1936]) *The Rationale for Central Banking and the Free Banking Alternative*, Indianapolis: Liberty Press.
Van De Putte, J. (1920). *A World Currency*, London: Harrison and Sons.
Volcker, P. and Gyohten, T. (1992) *Changing Fortunes*, New York: Times Books.
von Mises, L. (1953[1924]) *The Theory of Money and Credit*, translated by H. Batson, New Haven: Yale University Press.

9 Moral geographies of money

Nigel Thrift and Andrew Leyshon

Introduction

Money is becoming less of a mystery to most people. At one time, the worlds of money were often represented through a series of clichés – the roguish, buccaneering financier; the barrow-boy foreign-exchange trader; the reliable but staid bank manager; and so on. But nowadays these representations are changing. The roguish buccaneering financier is being replaced by... us.[1] Increasingly, as pensions turn towards defined contribution retirement plans, on the US model, so each person will increasingly be in charge of their own investment strategy. Indeed, increasingly financially literate investors, wired up to telephone databases and internet sites, are already having major effects in the United States (*The Economist*, 1997). Meanwhile, the barrow-boy foreign-exchange trader is being replaced by... machines. So-called 'program-trading', involving computer software programmed to buy and sell financial instruments when they reach certain prices, is playing an increasingly important role within some international financial markets. And what of the reliable but staid bank manager? He – and it was a he – is also being replaced. Increasingly, banks are becoming like supermarkets (and, in some cases *are* supermarkets) selling a set of financial products. And the manager is often just an office manager, or even one of the salesforce (Halford, Savage and Witt, 1997), almost certain to be considered as a 'unit of resource' to be recovered by sales of financial products, and to be backed up by computer software and training programmes which emphasise personal interaction skills.

Until the beginning of the 1980s, geographers would have had little to say about these worlds. But in the last 15 years geographers have become more and more interested in money and finance. Why? Well, for one, because money and finance have become so visible. From the pink business and finance pages that have adorned so many newspapers since the mid-1980s through to all the investment magazines on sale in newsagents through to television programmes on 'You and your money', these are financial times (Leyshon, Thrift and Pratt, 1998). Second, because the effects of money and finance are now so great. From negative equity through property-crashes to high-cost inner-city insurance, money and finance clearly have the power to *hurt*. But, at the same time, more people are directly experiencing the power of the financial system to bring about 'passive enrichment' as in the 'windfall' profits that many British homeowners and investors have received in the 1990s from the demutualisation of building societies[2] of which they were members.[3] Third, because money and finance have very obvious geographies which are crucial elements of how the global financial system and national financial systems function. From European Monetary Union through the hierarchy of world financial centres to the closure of bank branches, money and finance is a geographical game. It is a geography. It uses geography. It makes geographies (Leyshon and Thrift, 1997).

In this chapter we consider two distinct worlds of money and finance: the first is the world of the international financial centre and eurocurrency market, while the second is the world of alternative local monetary and financial institutions. Both represent examples of an emerging new geography of money, in which an important feature is the creation of monetary forms that are distinct from the territorially homogenous and exclusive national currencies of the past.

Although both worlds are founded upon financial calculation, the modes of calculation within each are very different, and reflect differences in the moral ontologies of the actors who inhabit each world. By comparing these worlds, we hope to illustrate that the ways in which money is understood, and the ways in which it affects us, are in large part contextual and contingent, because the making of money is a socially constructed process which reflects purpose and intent on the part of actors and institutions, as well as reflecting happenstance, historical accident, and processes of path-dependent development.

Before we get to these different 'moral worlds' of money, we first set out the network approach we take to the study of money, and illustrate its efficacy by way of an analysis of the international financial system, which also serves as an introduction to the more detailed studies contained in the latter part of the chapter.

Worlds of money and networked worlds: the international financial system as a monetary network

One of the favourite motifs of much writing about the international financial system is the sheer speed with which vast amounts of money are moved around the world, courtesy of modern telecommunications. According to many commentators, modern telecommunications systems are bringing about, so far as the international financial system is concerned, the 'end of geography' (O'Brien, 1995), the 'death of distance' (Cairncross, 1997), or, to put it in the words of a recent British Telecom (BT) advertisement, 'geography is history'.

For all the apparent simplicity and speed of the movement of international money, that movement is, in fact, highly complex. From the blizzard of paper transactions which were the world of the fourteenth- and fifteenth-century merchant banker through to the vast amount of electronic information that is presented to the contemporary foreign-exchange dealer, no monetary exchange over distance is ever achieved with complete ease. What is remarkable about modern telecommunications systems, for example, which are at the heart of modern monetary networks to the point where certain forms of international money are effectively coincident with these systems, is the sheer amount of work needed merely to keep them going. They require software engineers, to ensure compatibility between systems, and other kinds of engineers to solve system crashes, and to carry out routine and emergency maintenance and servicing, and so on. All of these activities and more are needed *constantly* to produce monetary exchange. What is equally remarkable is just how rarely this support is ever, well, remarked upon. We seem to live in the frictionless telecommunicative world of the advertisements only because the friction is hidden from view. What maintains the telecommunicative world in existence does not exist.[4]

A more critical reading of the financial system, which takes into account the role of social action in time and space leads to the conclusion that the financial system does not exist as an overarching and seamless web. Rather it must be seen as a series of monetary networks; that is, networks of producers and consumers of particular forms of money which will include particular devices, particular monetary skills, and particular attitudes towards, and beliefs about, what money is (including, as we will stress later in this chapter, moral stances). In turn, these monetary networks construct their own times and spaces, sometime even using their own metrics to measure these times and spaces out. As Latour puts it:

> Time and space are not the Newtonian sensoria in which events occur and planets fall along ellipses. But neither are they forms of our perception, the universal *a prioris* that our mind has to use in order to frame or accommodate the multiplicity of beings and entities. Far from being primitive terms, they are, on the contrary, consequences of the ways in which bodies relate to one another. We must therefore link our meditation on time to a third tradition, the Leibnizian, which considers space and time as expressing some relation between the entities themselves. But instead of a single space–time we will generate as many spaces and times as there are types of relations. (Latour 1997: 174)

A conception of money which incorporates such a relational view of space, time and social action has four important consequences. First, it follows that money cannot be seen as a neutral instrument intended to ensure optimal efficiency, neither at the level of the individual rational maximiser nor at the level of the economic system as a whole. Nor can the monetary system be seen as a veil which masks the 'real' economy. Both these views fail to grasp the efficacy and relative autonomy of monetary networks in the process of economic growth. Luckily, a diverse set of authors from history, sociology and economics have tried to present an alternative non-functionalist view of money which chimes with geographical work (e.g. Dodd, 1994; Ingham, 1994; 1996; Zelizer, 1994; for a review, see Leyshon, 1997) on which we will draw in this chapter. Second, it follows that money is socially and culturally defined and used. A number of points need to be made here. To begin with, money is not a fully transportable commodity which can be casually transferred across diverse social situations. Rather it has multiple-use meanings, depending on different monetary forms and the different contexts in which these are deployed, because '[t]here is no single, uniform, generalized money, but multiple monies: people earmark different currencies for many or perhaps all types of social interactions, much as they create distinctive languages for different social contexts' (Zelizer 1994: 18–19). Then, following on from this point, money depends on reciprocity and trust. In part, trust in money depends upon money being constituted as a formal social institution, as money in general. But, trust in money also depends upon trust in the outcome of actual transactions which, in turn, depend upon a mixture of particular people, monetary forms, and regulations which will, often, of necessity, involve social ties. Following on again, money relies upon, indeed is, information:

> Information plays a substantive role in the constitution of monetary networks which cannot be reduced to the function of a lubricant within a processing monetary order. The role of information in the transaction of money is not confined merely to observation about an external and independent economic environment. Information is on the contrary the defining feature of money networks, for they are networks of, not just containers of, information. (Dodd, 1994: 26)

Thus, money cannot be deployed without information and obtaining this information requires social networks which rely, to a greater or lesser extent, on trust. And then, as Marx reminded us so often, money is social power. But this power cannot be reduced to just the possession of money. To deploy money to best advantage also requires communicative power which requires a credible social infrastructure which takes time and effort to construct. Money is clearly a part of the construction of these infrastructures, but it is only ever a part.

Third, it follows that money is a productive and creative medium. New financial practices, including new financial instruments, are constantly being brought into existence. Money is not one medium, but many media, each with their own conventions, and the generation of new monies is a constant feature of international finance (Leyshon and Thrift, 1997).

Fourth, it follows that money is a much more geographical phenomenon than is often depicted, a phenomenon which depends upon a history of the building of monetary spaces which is a long and complicated one, and which inevitably contains within that history sedimented spatial patterns which are formative of subsequent paths of development. For example, the current international financial system depends upon a spatial telecommunications infrastructure laid down many years ago. Thus, the telephone lines that American banks leased in the 1920s in order to make sure that they had privileged access to stock information are now fibre-optic cables transmitting a full range of monetary information; voice, data, images, and so on.

Therefore, the international financial system should be viewed as a series of intersecting monetary networks, some of which are closely correlated, some of which have remarkably little to do with each other. Then, what we see is a series of different geographies operating at different speeds and intensities. These networks are usually reckoned to be global in scope and fast, even instantaneous, in execution. But this is not necessarily so. There are networks like this and the classic example is the foreign-exchange market. Foreign-exchange dealing is usually taken as the typical international monetary network, for at least three reasons. First, there is the sheer amount of money 'moved' by the market each trading day; at the last survey in 1995 in excess of $1.2 trillion. Second, the fact that trading takes place on a 24-hour-a-day basis, around the world, at the near instantaneous speeds dictated by telecommunications technologies. Third, that Forex dealers are young, loud, male, single, under-educated, and over-competitive.

Yet, even here, care must be taken. First, money is rarely physically moved or circulated by this system; what is happening is that accounts in one computer and accounts in another change. Second, though the Forex monetary system spans the globe it does so only along narrow lines of communication and so covers some areas more intensely than other. Moreover, it is an inherently local market in operation; dealing is a matter of building a social network to which it is possible to market and from which it is possible to gain information and, though this network may be spread around the globe, at any point it is usually an interaction with only four or five people. Third, since dealing is a matter of timing and the 20,000 or so dealers around the world not only have to produce profits around the world for their organisations (chiefly banks) but have to do so quickly before passing on the book at the end of the trading day, dealers cannot afford to be shrinking violets. But one study of foreign dealers in London (Kahn and Cooper, 1993) found them otherwise not so very different from the general population; two-thirds of all dealers were married or co-habiting, more than half of dealers were aged 30 or above, about half of all dealers had a degree, and they were no more neurotic and no more likely to tell a lie than the population at large. Only 10 per cent of dealers were women but this was changing rapidly (McDowell, 1997).

However, not all international financial trading is like the Foreign Exchange Market. Take the case of trading in US Treasury Bonds. This market consists, firstly, of a primary market in treasury bills, notes, and bonds issued by the US Federal Government to finance its budget deficit and to meet its short-term cash management needs, and secondly, and significantly for this example, of a large secondary market in which already issued bills, notes and bonds are traded. This secondary market is one of the world's largest financial markets with an average trading volume of $125 billion a day. Trading takes place five days a week between three locations, New York, London and Tokyo. Positions are bought and sold in seconds in a highly competitive interdealer market, with trade sizes starting at $1 million for notes and bonds and $5 million for bills.

At first sight, this seems to be a global market place. After all, trading takes place 22 hours a day. The trading day begins at 8.30 a.m. local time in Tokyo (7.30 p.m. New York daylight saving time), closing at 4 p.m. (3 a.m. New York), pressing onto London, where it is 8 a.m. At about 12.30 p.m. local time trading passes to New York, where it is 7.30 a.m. Trading continues in New York until 5.30 p.m. But the geography of trading is not that simple. Not surprisingly, given these are US government securities, most of the trading takes place in New York. In 1994, for example, on average, 94 per cent of the trading volume of US securities occurred in New York, with less than 4 per cent in London and less than 2 per cent in Tokyo. Further, nearly all trading – even overseas – is a response to US events. For instance, market-relevant comments are often made by US government officials during 'overseas hours', as is central bank intervention in the market, to coincide with relatively quiet periods. In other words, what seems like a typical global monetary network actually turns out to have a very specific geography which is really quite narrow, and which is fast only in particular places at particular times.

If one cares to look for other kinds of 'global' monetary networks then these may be found, but here too they hardly conform to a world in which the friction of distance has been conquered by instantaneous communication. For example, consider the case of international monetary payments. The foreign exchange markets are the preserve of banks and other large players and they transfer currencies around the world between them in large volumes with relative efficiency. But so-called 'small-ticket' payments are an entirely different matter. This system is slow and determinedly national; there is no single international network for small value transfers:

> . . . when a bank wants to shift a surplus billion from Moscow to Mexico City the money moves instantaneously across its world-wide telecommunications network. But when a small customer wants to send money from Brussels to pay a bill in Bogota, the story is very different. (*The Economist*, 1997)

Indeed the small value payments systems is extraordinarily slow. Take the example of a customer at a small savings bank in Austria who wants to send money to a community bank in Tennessee. The paperwork has to be sent, first of all, to a big city bank in Vienna which can handle international dealings. This bank then uses the Austrian Central bank's clearing system to wire the money to a correspondent bank in New York. The New York bank then, in turn, uses the Federal Reserve's Clearing System to wire the money to a correspondent bank in Memphis which then sends it on to the community bank. So, by the time it reaches its destination, the money will have passed through two national clearing systems and five or six banks taking, on average, about six days. Given the complexity of the system, there are errors (messages sent by computer still have to be sent by hand and often have to be retyped the other end; transfer codes may contain different numbers of digits in different countries) and delays (in some countries, a payment received after early morning will not be processed until the next day; some banks only send batches of transfers to lower costs; some banks hold on to transfers in the hope of getting a better foreign exchange rate).

Therefore, there are multiple forms of monetary networks, varying in both intensity and durability through time and over space. Monetary networks differ in other ways too including, for example, in the kinds of moral frameworks upon which monetary calculation within the network is founded.

In the next two sections of the chapter we focus upon two separate monetary networks, each of which is founded upon a distinctive order of morality. First, we turn our attention to the moral world of the international financial centres and eurocurrency markets, before moving on to consider the moralities of alternative local monetary and financial institutions.

Moral worlds of money: the international financial centre and eurocurrency market

Let us now turn to the first moral world of money, the international financial centre and eurocurrency market. The bulk of the business of international finance is carried out in such centres – the so-called global cities of New York, Tokyo and London and, on another tier, Paris, Frankfurt, Singapore, Hong Kong, Toronto and Chicago – where many monetary networks connect and intersect. Much of the business in international financial centres – and particularly in London – is 'eurocurrency' activity; that is, activity in which the currency used is one other than the local one.

According to numerous commentators, international finance is not only a world of speed for speed's sake but also of greed for greed's sake. As one right-wing observer has noted, 'lefties of all sorts . . . have continued the long tradition of beating upon finance, demeaning it as a stinkpot of parasitism, irrelevance, malignancy and corruption, without providing more detail beyond that' (Henwood 1997: 2). The denizens of international finance are seen to be engaged in a Darwinian competitive struggle which is bent entirely to the accumulation of profits. But if such an impulse exists, then it is moderated and sometimes even negated by social and cultural factors. Nowhere is this clearer than in the social and cultural resources which contribute towards the construction of trust. Three of these resources are particularly relevant. First, there are formal knowledge systems, based on credentials like undergraduate degrees, masters courses, diploma courses, in-house courses and, increasingly, doctorates in mathematics. Then, there is knowledge gained from the media. International finance is awash with printed and screen-based information, ranging from specialist financial and economic analysis, which circulates among only a few subscribers, to the daily financial news, which appears on television, radio, newspapers, the internet, much of which originates with specialist financial 'wire services' like Reuters, Dow Jones and Bloomberg. Third, there is social knowledge about who knows whom, who knows what, who is important (and who is not), who is on the rise (and who is on the decline), and so on. This 'gossip', is, if anything, increasingly important. As markets speed up and market knowledge becomes more accessible, it is often only this knowledge that keeps the professionals ahead of the game (Henwood, 1997). Most of this knowledge can still only be obtained through face-to-face interaction, because:

> effective communication depends on non-verbal, possibly even non-visual, cues. The barely perceptible hesitation introduced by a satellite link invites

> misunderstanding when we are used to interpreting hesitation in other ways. Shared experiences and values are a central element in developing trust. The linking of social and commercial relationships increases the penalties for opportunistic behaviour. That is why the lunch room is a central facility of the City of London and extensive entertainment an integral part of Japanese business culture. (Kay 1995: 7)

It is this last resource – social knowledge – that we want to expand on here by reference to the case of the city through which much of the business of international finance is done, the City of London. This is an area of research that geographers have been particularly active in since Goddard's work on contact networks in London in the 1960s (Goddard, 1968a; 1968b).

Since the 1960s the City of London has, of course, changed; indeed, it has changed almost beyond recognition. The World has come to the City and the City has gone out into the World again, just as in its nineteenth-century heyday. What accounts for this transformation? There are, of course, many reasons, but four stand out. First, the floating of exchange rates and the growth of the eurodollar market in the 1960s were a signal that the rhythms of the world economy were increasingly being conducted to the beat of the world of money and finance. Since the 1960s large numbers of new financial instruments, frequently denominated in dollars and other foreign currencies, have been continually invented in places like London, often piggy-backing on other financial instruments and thereby creating a system of echoes which mean that money can be traded and capital borrowed and lent further than ever before. As a result, cities like London, New York and Tokyo can now call on vast reserves of money, and their markets are continuously liquid.

Second, and partly as a result of the first reason, London has become a vast conglomeration of technical expertise. Its 332,000 workers in financial services in the City include many experts on a full range of financial issues and, taken together with their compatriots in New York and Tokyo, it is they who, in a sense, embody the world financial system. This financial community is very different from that of the 1950s, both in terms of skills and social make-up. Most importantly of all, it is a more cosmopolitan community, because of the arrival, from the 1960s onwards, of large numbers of foreign banks – 257 of the world's largest 1,000 banks now have branches in the City, more even than in New York – and because, for many of the jobs in the City, the labour market is now international (Thrift, 1994; Leyshon and Thrift, 1997; McDowell, 1997).

Third, the City is a space where government regulation favours making money. The City is not a 'deregulated' space. Indeed parts of it are now strongly regulated, especially as a result of the discovery of financial fraud. But much regulation is still 'light touch' and, combined with the Bank of England's understanding of the City, this makes it a relatively easy place to do business (Moran, 1991). Particularly important has been the Bank of England's support since the 1960s for the emergence of eurocurrency activity.

Fourth, London has become reconnected to the rest of the world. It is connected physically through the large numbers of telecommunications networks which are centred on the City. And it is connected socially. The City is not a static place, rather it is a place through which many thousands of people flow every day – to do deals, to seek advice, to gain knowledge or to seek out new business opportunities. Similarly, people who work in the City spend much of their time travelling overseas doing precisely the same things. In other words, the City is a vast pool of formal and social information which is constantly being called upon and updated (Thrift and Leyshon, 1994). After all, in the world of money and finance victory goes to the most well-informed. In turn, that also makes the City a very sociable place; to obtain information you have to know people, and that means building relationships of trust and confidence. So cafés, restaurants, wine bars, meeting rooms, and the like, and the knowledge which circulates within such sites, are as much a part of the City's daily currency as money.

This last point is worth expanding on, since geographers have spent so much time researching it (e.g. Thrift, 1994). In the past, the social nature of international finance has chiefly been made apparent through tightly defined social networks based on a potent mixture of gender, ethnicity and class. Thus, in the old City of London, the chief networks were based on masculinity defined in terms of a particular British upper and upper middle-class background or, alternatively, various émigré origins, especially but not only a German refugee background. These networks were closely intertwined by dint of kinship and a series of common social arenas, including chophouses, freemasonry, London clubs, and so on (Thrift, 1994; Thrift and Leyshon, 1994) and allowed trust to be constructed with relative ease because of a shared moral stance to monetary practice. Michael Verey, former chairman of Schroders, provides an insight into this world (though one he himself hints is sugar-coated):

> The City has always been a place of very mixed blokes because a great many people, which includes one's self, were climbing up a fairly greasy ladder and the object of a great many of us was to get to the top if we could. It depended what means you used, whether you trod on people's hands or kicked them in the face to get there, or whether you decided you could only get there in a decent, well-behaved manner, something which other people would applaud. It's sort of how you were brought up as to which way you wished to go.
>
> As for Etonians in the City, it only makes a difference if they have maintained the Eton standards, which most of them have. During my time in the City, those who hadn't been to Eton were striving for Eton standards and the Eton ethos dominated from Kim Cobbold, Governor of the Bank of England downwards. Good Etonian standards means a total trust – if you say you'll do something, you'll do it . . .
>
> Within the Accepting Houses Committee, the standards were roughly the same. Those were the people one really came into contact with, or brokers of equivalent standard – the top half-dozen brokers. If you had gone to the bottom half-dozen brokers you could have found a very different life, but we never did. (Verey in Courtney and Thompson, 1996: 164–5)

But, since the breakdown of the Bretton Woods system, these close-knit homosocial networks have been subject to various forms of attrition. The marked growth of numbers employed in international finance has produced a dilution of their influence and has also broadened the social base upon which international finance is built. Most especially, it has involved more women, and more employees generally from diverse class backgrounds (McDowell, 1997). In other words, international finance has become more cosmopolitan and more multicultural. However, the need to obtain social knowledge in order to build up trust, a need rooted in the constitution of social networks does not seem to have dissolved in this more heterogeneous situation. Indeed, in some senses, the need has increased since trust has to be worked at more than in the past. Thus, social networking has become an even more important activity because of the increased amounts of knowledge of all kinds that now circulate, the need to interpret this knowledge, the need to keep certain kinds of knowledge exclusive and therefore the subject of competitive advantage, and the need to snap up unexpected business opportunities. The result has been the emergence of an 'interactional frenzy' (Thrift, 1994), in both London and New York. But this frenzy is based in more and more heterogeneous social networks which allow more and more heterogeneous experiences and values to be shaped. These experiences and values need to be stabilised to retain basic coherence. Thus a more structured space of mediated and face-to-face interaction/interpretation has been constructed in recent years, one which draws on the old social practices of the city, but which has extended and changed them. Trust is now being built in different ways. Specifically, five formalisations of social practice have been produced (Leyshon and Thrift, 1997). The first is the formalisation of the social encounter. In addition to pressures to conform to strict dress codes and idealised body shapes (McDowell, 1997), more and more people are trained in the arts of self-presentation (by the use of video, role play, and so on) and the whole business social encounter is now orchestrated by the use of devices like the business card, which have become endemic. The second formalisation has been the extension of old social arenas. Like the business card, the business lunch is now *de rigueur* and, as we suggested earlier, has become one of the main ways in which knowledge is exchanged and social contact maintained. The third formalisation is the construction of new social arenas. Of these, the most important has undoubtedly been the almost exponential growth of conferences and conventions. A fourth formalisation has been the technological supplement to face-to-face contacts. The telephone, the fax, pager, and other forms of telecommunications such as e-mail are all now used as ways of supplementing face-to-face contact, having become cheap and easy to use in this fashion. And, increasingly, computer software can be used to boost the social capacity of users. The fifth formalisation is the attempt to build up long-term networks without the benefit of gender, ethic and class homogeneity as in the past. This has been achieved in two ways; first, by the use of the relationship manager, and second, by the judicious use of two- or three-year secondments to other firms or 'overseas' offices (Beaverstock, 1994; 1996a; 1996b; Beaverstock and Smith, 1996).

However, at the same time, there is a general perception that, for all these new social devices, the level of trust to be found in the City is declining and with it ethical standards. There seem to be six reasons why this decline is apparent. First, old social conventions are being replaced by formal conventions based on legal frameworks; 'due diligence' is crucial. These legal frameworks tend to replace self-policing with legal sanction, which is a two-edged sword. Second, the often informal but still powerful influence of the Bank of England is much less pervasive than formerly and it is arguable if the new formal regulatory structures send the same ethical messages. Third, and relatedly, the influx of large foreign banks and of foreigners who are often on short-term contracts means that new conventions have been introduced to the City: 'different people have different views on what's right and proper' (Peter Spira, quoted in Courtney and Thompson 1996: 156). As Stanislas Yassukovich puts it:

> there is a huge turnover (of foreigners working in the City). They don't necessarily put down roots. In other words, individuals come to make a quick killing. They don't have time to participate in civic affairs or to serve on committees (which lay the ground rules to which all should adhere). They don't really much care. (Quoted in Scriven, 1998)

Fourth, there is a much greater degree of job turnover; more people are likely to change jobs and they are unlikely to have the same degree of allegiance to their firms. As Yassukovich, continues 'there are still some heavy hitters who have the old sense of commitment but they are far fewer than they used to be' (Scriven, 1998). They are, in a sense, overwhelmed by the greater mass movement and the bigger more complex, more bureaucratic houses. Fifth, the age structure of the City has changed. The City is now controlled by people in their thirties and forties, not fifties and sixties; According to Charles McVeigh III:

> We've bred a very mercenary type of young person who comes to make the most amount of money he can in a short a period of time as he can, who doesn't feel a great degree of loyalty to the organisation. He is grateful for the training he's had and for the opportunity to make a great deal of money, but he doesn't feel he really owes you anything. So there's a tremendous turnover today. (Quoted in Courtney and Thompson 1996: 158)

Sixth, there is the scale of rewards. Salaries and, more importantly, bonuses are now, in the late 1990s, in the midst of a boom that rivals that of the immediate post-Big Bang City. The average pay rise in intermediate financial services (which is effectively the City of London) was 9.6 per cent in 1997. And this is but the tip of the iceberg.

> The new stars are men like T J Limb, a Malaysian prised from Merrill Lynch to become head of fixed incomes at UBS (pending its merger with SBC Warburg) who is said to earn around $5 million a year, and Robin Nydes,

> an American at Daiwa Europe.'Nydes is a huge earner, on about two or three [million pounds] a year' says a rival. . . .
>
> At Saloman, there is Shigeru 'Sugar' Myojin who came to prominence last April when it became known that he had earned £19 million for his previous year's endeavours.
>
> The foreigners are, of course, capable of falling from grace (at least temporarily) like Jean-Francis Nguyen, a Frenchman in his mid-thirties, who was 'probably taking home $3 million to $5 million a year' until Natwest Markets dispensed with his services last spring.
>
> But for every casualty, there seem to be scores of successes, such as the Americans Tim Drinkall, head of research for emerging markets (Europe) at DMG and Mark Curtis, managing director of international markets at Nomura (only six per cent of that bank's London staff are Japanese; the remainder are drawn from 47 different nationalities). 'They're all over the place. In fact I can't think of any bloody English' reflects one English hedge fund manager 'all the pals of my old mates from University are box heads [Germans]'. (Scriven 1998: 8)

In other words, the Old City's practices of money have broken down to be replaced by new conventions which are based on active policing rather than internal control. We should not be too misty-eyed and nostalgic about this; there were major scandals and fraud cases in the Old City, after all. As Sir Martin Jacomb puts it 'there was plenty of questionable behaviour in the old days among the old guard, most of it smothered in a veneer of respectability so it never came to light' (quoted in Courtney and Thompson 1996: 133). But what seems to be happening now is a spread of more cynical attitudes encapsulated in a case we heard of where a bank employee was caught insider trading (by common consent, still hardly an uncommon practice), having made some £400,000. The overwhelming reaction of the rest of the bank's employees was one of amazement, not that the person had been caught out, but that they had been caught out for such a small sum of money; working on the adage that it is surely better to be hung for a sheep than a lamb, the person concerned was clearly inept!

Thus, through the linked monetary networks of the City is spreading a new moral calculus which is instrumental and which is bent to institutional and personal accumulation in ways which were much less obvious in the Old City. However, this is not an inevitable process. And in the next section of this chapter we want to illustrate some of the countervailing tendencies which are trying to re-moralise money (or rather produce a different monetary morality) which have been another area of endeavour by geographers.

Moral worlds of money: alternative local monetary and financial institutions

If morality is declining in the City of London, in other parts of Britain people are trying to construct monetary networks which can evince a moral stance, what Lee

(1996) has called 'moral money'. In setting out on this task, these networks are recognising two points. First, that hard issues of power and risk are involved in monetary networks, which arise particularly from the nature of the financial products themselves. For example:

> Floating rate instruments shift the risk of losing interest rates from lenders to borrowers. Adjustable rate notes protect bondholders against imprudent or capital-risky actions by management, like taking on gobs of new debt. Looser regulations on issuance like shelf registration, which allows corporations to file general prospectuses to be kept on file, rather than prepare custom prospectuses for a specific stock or bond issue, allow firms to sell their paper when the market looks friendly. (Henwood 1997: 52).

Second, that it *is* possible to have a moral stance to money. Money does not have to be seen as an inevitable corrosive which, once it 'invades the realm of personal relations . . . inevitably bends these relations in the direction of instrumental rationality' (Zelizer 1994: 11).

But to understand the impulse behind these new monetary networks it is necessary, first of all, to consider recent and related developments in British retail finance which have, to an extent, been the stimulus to their coming into existence. These developments have been threefold. First, the sector has seen much increased levels of competition as a result of new entrants (from building societies to supermarkets) and much wider product ranges. Second, the sector has seen massive technological innovation, including, for example, the telephone (Marshall and Richardson, 1996). Third, the sector has seen the rise of new organisational technologies, including new spatial templates and basic reorganisation of production and distribution based on notions like business process reengineering, all aimed at cutting costs and improving customer service (Leyshon, Thrift and Pratt, forthcoming). Increasingly these three developments have produced a mature industry which is in certain ways akin to the retail sector; that is, one that is highly sensitive to costs, obsessed by distribution channels, developing wide products ranges, and attempting to get ever closer to the consumer. Little wonder retail companies like Sainsbury's and Tesco are involved (Leyshon, Thrift and Pratt, 1998).

So far as many consumers are concerned, British retail finance is offering a good service at relatively low cost (though charging for accounts will come, chiefly through the back door via the growth of special account packages). But while many have greater access to the financial system than ever before, others face greater problems of gaining access to the financial system. A process of financial exclusion has taken hold of some parts of Britain and what is gradually being produced is the equivalent of the 'food deserts' that are being created by the supermarket chains as they concentrate their attentions on very specific sets of customers (Marsden *et al.* 1998). In an increasing number of areas there is no or very limited access to financial provision. Fuelled by public housing policies that increasingly concentrate poorer people in increasingly 'poor places' (Philo, 1995), lack of access has become more important as access to finance has become more important (for example, in the spread of discounts for direct debits, or benefits being paid directly into bank accounts). Indeed, some commentators have argued that access to finance – to a bank account, to small amounts of credit, to basic insurance, and so on – is now so important that it ought to be seen as a basic right; as financial 'citizenship rights' (Leyshon and Thrift, 1997).

In Britain, the problem of financial exclusion is usually reckoned to affect about 20 per cent of households in all, with exclusion resulting from a mix of causes according to the financial products concerned (Leyshon, Pratt and Thrift, forthcoming). For example, in their study of household contents insurance, Whyley, McCormick and Kempson (1998) found that one in four households were without household contents insurance in 1995 (6.2 million households in all), a similar proportion to that found in the mid-1980s but, due to the rate of household formation, an actual increase of 1.1 million households between 1985 and 1995. Lack of insurance was closely correlated with socio-economic group, age, housing tenure, and gender. The reasons for exclusion were found to be of three kinds; simple self-exclusion (often based on lack of knowledge), direct exclusion (usually based on insurance prices being too great for poorer households to afford or on conditions like annual premiums which poorer households could not meet) and market failure (usually resting on the lack of availability of appropriate products).

The process of financial exclusion has been exacerbated by the decline of bank and building society branch provision since the late 1980s. This process has been highly geographically concentrated. Bank closures have taken place across the country, but these closures have been very selective. Forced by GIS systems which are used to provide 'reverse location' models disproportionate closures have taken place in inner-city areas inhabited by poorer social groups.

Some commentators have argued that three factors will ameliorate this process of socio-spatial exclusion. One is that companies who have traditionally served poorer areas, such as weekly collection credit companies like Provident, and home collection insurance companies like Prudential, will make up the weight. But even these firms are retreating from some housing estates which, often for good reasons, are seen as 'no go' areas for collectors who are carrying cash. Another ameliorating factor is seen to be the spread of ATMs. But they are not being located in poorer areas; quite the reverse, in fact. Finally, it is sometimes argued that, if all else fails, telephone banking will come to the rescue. But, in fact, it is the inhabitants of the excluded areas which are least likely to have access to telephones. Access to telephones by households is strongly connected with socioeconomic status. And some areas of Britain have remarkably low rates of connection. For example, one 1992 study of a 'sink' Newcastle council estate found a household connection rate of only 26 per cent (Graham and Marvin, 1996).

This process of financial exclusion and isolation is mirrored by a process of exclusion and isolation from financial *information* exclusion and isolation which, in certain senses, is just as serious. Some financial consumers are becoming very well informed. Increasingly, there is a sophisticated financial 'audience' made up of consumers who are far more able to obtain information on what is happening in the financial sphere, to interpret that information and then to act upon it. This audience knows more about money and finance than formerly, mainly because of the explosive growth of financial media, and through their ability to act upon the information that comes from the media. This enhanced ability to act is the result of an increased range of products which allow more choice, the growth of financial intermediaries and the growth of new information technology which relays information, and allows a proactive stance to that information. Twenty-four-hour telephone banking is only the start of this process. Recent developments in information technologies, and the growing use of the internet by financial services firms, means that a person in possession of a personal computer is now able to assess their personal finances in real time.

But the other side of the growth of more sophisticated financial audiences is the information shadow which falls over those who do not have the money or the skills (the two being related) to obtain access to growing financial infrastructures. They are dependent upon fallback, alternative financial information infrastructures which may be effective – like family and friends or the Citizens Advice Bureau, for example – but cannot lift them out of their circumstances. The situation is all the more serious because so much of what is the formal financial system is now concerned with information that is processed, created even, through information technology. The widespread use of GIS, behavioural credit scoring, and the like, is evidence of the use of information to produce a world in which information asymmetries (the imbalance between what the borrower knows about the lender and the lender knows about the borrower) are tackled by the financial services industry 'at-a-distance' from the financial customer through database analysis (Leyshon, Thrift and Pratt, 1998). Indeed, because of new classificatory technologies one might argue the balance of power is shifting firmly in favour of the financial services industry. In these circumstances knowledge really is power, and the various campaigns for financial literacy which have now started seem increasingly important.

But what we can also see is that monetary networks are being constructed across the world which can combat this exclusion because they regard money as a moral issue; these are attempts to construct new spaces and times in which different moral metrics can survive and even flourish. Once money is no longer seen as a neutral veil, it can have all kinds of moral resonances heretofore lost to sight. There are, of course, many examples of monetary networks which have consciously attempted to act as moral forces; the building society movement, credit unions (now spreading in Britain and with plans well advanced to bundle them together so as to produce memberships with more financial clout and lower per capita administrative costs) and the like. What is remarkable is that over the last twenty-five years, a series of new models of these monetary networks with moral attitude have been invented and have begun to spread through western economies (Leyshon and Thrift, 1997). Here we will note just four of these networks.

The first, and most relevant to this volume's focus, is the rise of Local Exchange Trading Schemes (LETS). The idea of LETS can be traced back to Vancouver Island, again in 1983, when a self-employed Canadian, Michael Linton, was looking for a way of enabling local residents, who had been hit by an economic slump, and a consequent shortage of cash occasioned by the closure of a key externally-owned industry, to pay for his goods and services. He hit on an idea which had been tried before in North America and Europe, in the 1930s depression, a local currency system based on work time he called LETS.

> LETS are local systems of production, multilateral exchange, and consumption, articulated through a local currency – a single-purpose money – independent of, but often related to, the prevailing national currency. This currency is frequently named after some local association and so a geography of the LETS economy is central at the outset and is expressed in terms of its most profound expression – the means of exchange. Membership is open to all, usually on payment of a membership fee. Details of the offers and needs of members within the system, normally expressed in terms of products or labour power, are published in a regularly issued directory distributed to all members. Transactions are effected by agreement between transacting parties. They may occur either at a prepublished price or by negotiation and they are expressed in terms of the local currency or in terms of a mix between the local currency and the national currency unit. However, no money changes hands; transactions are recorded on cheques forwarded to and logged by the accountant or treasurer to the system. Details of all transactions are then published on a regular basis so that all members of the system have knowledge of the full transactional activity and trading balance (debit or credit) of all other members. (Lee 1996: 1378)

From Canada, Linton's idea has spread to the United States, Australia, New Zealand, and many of the countries of Europe including Denmark, Finland, France, Germany, The Netherlands, Norway, Spain, Sweden and Switzerland (Croall, 1998).

LETS provide a practical demonstration, however low key, that there are alternatives to competitive neo-liberal governmentalities based on cooperation and association:

> prospective members have to get involved in the active search for local information and direct contact with the co-ordinators of local groups, and membership is, by definition, active and participatory. Members cannot remain anonymous; their names, their telephone numbers, and the nature of their involvement – defined in terms of what services or products they can offer to the system and what needs they feel may be met through it – are published in the regularly published *Directory*. Even more significantly, the transactions . . . through which LETS operate are made known on a regular basis to all members as details of their trading accounts, including the nature of the transactions and the overall deficit or credit and are published throughout the system. (Lee 1996: 1379–80)

While LETS represents an example of an alternative network in the monetary realm, other alternative networks focus on the financial sphere. One of these is ethical investment. Started in the United States in the 1960s, often in response to Christian concerns, ethical investment is now reckoned to account for nearly one-tenth of total US investments. Ethical concerns include employment practices, tobacco and alcohol, political regimes, and environmental regimes.

The another financial model is the rise of micro-credit. The micro-credit movement is often seen as dating from 1983 when the Grameen Bank was set up in Bangladesh by Muhammad Yunus, an economics Professor from Chittagong University who pioneered lending to the rural poor. What Yunus could see was that the poor were bedevilled by the absence of cheap credit. Their only recourse was their family or loan sharks because they had no collateral. Experimenting initially on his own, acting as a guarantor for loans to impoverished village dwellers, Yunus then decided to start up his own bank. In its early years, the government owned 60 per cent of Grameen and the borrowers the rest. Today the 1.4 million borrowers, each with a mandatory share, own 88 per cent of the bank. Most of the loans to the Bank have come from aid agencies through the Bangladesh government.

> Grameen's average loan size is US $75, its maximum except for housing loans. It charges simple interest at a rate of 20% a year, compared with compound interest of 13 to 16% at Bangladesh's commercial banks. Principal is repaid first, so that a borrower of Taka 2500 would typically repay Taka 50 a week over 50 weeks. Interest, calculated weekly on the diminishing principal, is repaid only after the principal is paid off, making for an effective interest rate of 10 to 12%, Grameen sources say.
>
> Home loans are repayable over 10 years at the same weekly rates. The maximum home loan is Taka 12,000, which will build a tin-roofed house.
>
> Borrowers are formed into groups of five – the basic unit – and are indoctrinated in Grameen social values, known as the 'sixteen decisions'. . . .
>
> Graneen is effective partly because it is self-policing. Rather than bank officials it is the assetless themselves, meeting weekly, who approve the loans. Group members are residents of the same village, perhaps next door neighbours. It is this familiarity that provides transparency, guaranteeing that the recipients are truly those who need it most. A bank official attends the meeting, but group members decide who receives a loan, and they assume responsibility for ensuring its repayment. (Kamaluddin 1993: 38)

Not surprisingly, perhaps, Grameen Bank's costs are low and its default rate is minimal – 20 per cent. But the real key to Grameen's success is its target borrowers; 92 per cent of them are women. The Bank targets them because, quite simply, they are more reliable than men; their priorities are more likely to be ordered by their children and they are therefore unlikely to squander loans in the way men might do.

Of course, for all the rhetoric, there are problems. About one-third of borrowers never become any better off, and Grameen Bank loans are sometimes used – in defiance of the rules – as collateral for further loans from money lenders, producing a vicious circle of debt, or as contributions to dowries. But, still, the Grameen Bank has clearly brought about overall improvements in nutrition, has brought about structural changes in local economic relationships that have benefited women, and, in general, has 'effected change like termites, hollowing out structures quietly from within' (Todd 1996: 221). The Grameen model has become the iconic foundation of the micro-credit movement, spreading to more than 30 countries, and to many cities of the developed world. For example, Chicago's Full Circle Fund is modelled on Grameen (Counts, 1996).

The United States has also seen, quite independently, the rise of a series of different alternative micro-credit networks, and, in particular community development banks and community development loan funds, which accept money from socially minded investors and make loans to fund housing rehabilitation, non-profit housing development, and small businesses. Community Development Banks have grown rapidly in the United States, though their performance is mixed. For example, Estey (1995) found that the Chicago-based South Shore Bank, the first Community Development Bank founded in 1973, and in its own way as iconic as the Grameen Bank, had a suspect financial performance and its record of delivery on its social goals had been indifferent. Community Development Loan Funds are various non-bank forms of local lending dating from the mid-1980s. The industry is still quite small, but growing fast. At the end of 1995, the industry had $108 million in loans outstanding, and $204 million in capital, a third of the capital permanent, the rest borrowed. In the nine years from 1986 to 1995, members of the National Association of Community Development Loan Funds (NACDLF) financed 56,243 housing units, 73 per cent of them permanently affordable for low-income residents, and created or preserved 11,313 jobs, 59 per cent of them for 'low-income people', 51 per cent for women and 37 per cent for minorities. Their loan loss was only 0.92 per cent of loans made.

The final network is not-for-profit operations by private-sector financial institutions; operations which are run in tandem with government, not-for-profit operations, or operations which bundle particular segments of low-income populations together in such a way as to produce profit. For example, around the world household insurance schemes aimed at particular low-income communities have proved both successful and profitable.

In Britain, we can now see a genuine flowering of alternative monetary and financial networks which are attempting to produce moral monies, monies which will work for the excluded. Thus, ethical investment is growing in importance. Though the amount invested ethically is still small – about £1000 million of investments – it is growing, helped by an infrastructure of lobbying groups, specialist consultancies, and journals. Major high street names like the Cooperative Bank and Friends Provident have monitored environmental investment schemes, and there are a host of smaller funds. A number of pension funds are now regularly advised by ethical consultancies and a campaign is currently under way to persuade the trustees of the Universities Superannuation Scheme to take ethical criteria into account.

In addition, community development loan funds are beginning to be established. The first Community Development Loan Fund was launched in Birmingham in 1997 (the Aston Reinvestment Trust), modelled on the Philadelphia Community Development Loan Fund, and which is operating in four niche areas of the community (micro-credit for self-employment and small business, equitable utility payment and insurance schemes, housing repairs and energy self-sufficiency improvements, and mortgage resource for the over-indebted). LETS are also flourishing. The first LETS was established in Norwich in 1985 and there are now upwards of 400 LETS schemes in Britain, with a membership of about 40,000, most of them established since the early 1990s.

And this is to ignore private-sector financial schemes. For example, after a sticky start, local authority-sponsored household insurance schemes are now spreading. About 200,000 council and housing association tenants are now covered by these schemes, out of a potential 1.55 million. Another example, is the rise of schemes to promote financial literacy so as to give people more backup in their dealings with the world of money. Plans are advanced or in some cases under way to teach money skills in schools, for example.

Of course, moral monetary and financial networks are still fragile and many have difficulties. For example, they are small in scale and still comparatively few in number. Then again, they have sometimes proved to be middle-class redoubts. Croall reports this description of the West Glasgow LETS by one of its members:

> It's actually a very middle-class group; the directory has lots of word-processing on offer, but not much plumbing. And it's not that well known except among trendy lefties in the area; I hardly ever get phoned by anyone that doesn't already know me. There are a few working-class people, but they are not very typical, they've usually been to university'. (Croall 1998: 56)

And it is important that they are not seen as an excuse for lack of state intervention or pushed as vehicles of self-help which can allow the state to withdraw support from poor places.

What is important is not just the level of activity but the signals that such institutions send about money. These networks demonstrate that alternative moral stances are possible which can colour the practices of money in positive ways and show that money can be about more than harvesting profits.

Conclusions

This chapter has sought to give a sense, however fleeting, of the worlds of money which geographers are currently mapping out, worlds which are simultaneously economic, social and cultural. In turn, we have also tried to show that this is no passive academic contemplation. Geographers are becoming involved in these worlds in three ways. First, a large proportion of geography graduates now enter jobs in financial services and, increasingly, they are being taught about money and finance. Second, geographical work on money and finance is increasingly being used by business, government, unions, consumer associations, and the like. Third, geographers are becoming involved in campaigns to combat the more iniquitous efforts of financial systems and to provide meaningful morally acceptable alternatives. In other words, geographers are becoming seasoned travellers in the worlds of money.

And this is as it should be. For we are all getting going to get closer to money, whether we like it or not. As Hamish McRae has noted:

> For at least three generations the state has gradually taken on increasing responsibility for handling individual's finances. It has taken away more and more of their money and (after deducting expenses) given more and more back in services and other benefits. That whole process is now in reverse . . . even if taxes do not come down by very much, the benefits will, because there will be fewer earners and more dependants. It is therefore absolutely vital that the financial services industry takes on some of the responsibility shared by the state. This means creating products we can trust, making them cheaply, and selling them efficiently. It also means that all people . . . need to learn a modicum about money. (McRae 1995: 21)

In other words, if we have not done so already, most of us will embark upon a similar learning trajectory to that undertaken by Valerie Thompson when she started trading in the City of London; but in our case it will be learning about retail rather than wholesale financial services:

> All I ever knew was what I didn't know. I used to think, 'One day, they're going to wake up and I'm going to be completely exposed'. I used to get terrible indigestion pains in meetings because I thought 'If anyone asks me a question, I'm just going to die'. I didn't know the first thing about the basics of economics. I never looked at the *Financial Times* – I couldn't even read the *Daily Mirror*. But I learned it. I learned it and I made money. (Quoted in Courtney and Thompson 1996: 135)

Indeed, in one scenario this process will be taken to its extreme. As western financial consumers take an increasingly active interest in their financial portfolios – most obviously in shares, but also in various mutual funds and trusts, and even in their own pensions (through defined contribution plans and the like) – in time we might see a point at which the retail financial services industry becomes simply a warehousing and distribution operation; then the financial consumer really would become the financial king or queen. Just as Miller (1995) has argued that we live in the age of the vanguard consumer who searches out good value from goods and services with consequent and quite massive macro-economic effects, so we might come to live in the age of the vanguard financial consumer. As Miller points out, this places financial consumers in a powerful position – and one with real moral responsibilities they would not be able to shirk since it would be clear that what happened in the international financial system was increasingly not just the fault of shadowy banks and other financial institutions but of 'us'. In other words, as we interacted more with the future of our money so it would become increasingly clear that we were responsible for the future of the world. It wouldn't be 'them' doing sometimes terrible things, it would be us altogether. This would be a moral geography of money writ large.

Notes

1 Well, not quite all of us. As we shall illustrate later in this chapter, a significant minority of the population are excluded from the financial system, either because they are too poor, or because of where they live, or both (Leyshon, Thrift and Pratt, 1998; forthcoming).
2 Building Societies are the British version of North American Savings & Loans institutions, which were based upon mutual ownership, which consisted of all those who had money invested within the society, or who had a mortgage with them. Since the late 1980s building societies have been converting to public limited companies and/or been taken over my public limited companies, with the result that members have been rewarded with what would appear to be 'free money', in the form of shares, which former members can sell for instant profit. However, Tickell (1998) has argued the payment comes later, in higher than average rates for borrowers, and lower than average rates for savers.
3 Indeed, the search for such easy rewards have forced some of the remaining building societies to raise significantly the level of investment needed to qualify for membership so as to offset the growing number of so-called 'carpet baggers' making small-scale investments across a range of societies in anticipation of conversion, and clogging up business processes in so doing.
4 This deception is, at least in part, carefully constructed, because the 'seamlessness' of financial activity is used for rhetorical effect by the marketing divisions of financial services firms, and by the advertising agencies employed by them, in an effort to capture business from firms seeking 'global reach' (for example, see Roberts and Schein 1995).

Bibliography

Beaverstock, J. (1994) 'Rethinking skilled international labour migration: world cities and banking organisations' *GEOFORUM* 25: 323–38.

Beaverstock, J. (1996a) 'Revisiting high-waged labour market demand in the global cities: British professional and managerial workers in New York City' *International Journal of Urban and Regional Research* 20: 442–5.

Beaverstock, J. (1996b) 'Subcontract the accountant: professional labour-markets, migration, and organizational networks: the global accountancy industries' *Environment and Planning A* 28: 303–26.

Beaverstock, J. and Smith, R. (1996) 'Lending jobs to global cities: skilled international labour migration, investment banking and the City of London' *Urban Studies* 33: 1377–94.

Cairncross, F. (1997) *The Death of Distance*, London: Orion Books.
Counts, J. (1996) *Give us Credit. How Muhammad Yunus's Micro-Lending Revolution is Empowering Women from Bangladesh to Chicago*, New York: Times Books.
Courtney, C. and Thompson, P. (1996) *City Lives. The Changing Voices of British Finance*, London: Methuen.
Croall, J. (1998) *LETS Act locally: the growth of Local Exchange Trading Systems*, London: Gulbenkian Foundation.
Dodd, N. (1994) *The Sociology of Money*, Cambridge: Polity Press.
Estey, B.C. (1995) 'South Shore Bank: is it the model of success for community development banks?' *Harvard Business School Working Papers*: 95–1072.
Goddard, J.B. (1968a) 'Changing office location patterns in Central London' *Urban Studies* 4: 276–85.
Goddard, J.B. (1968b) 'Multivariate analysis of office location patterns in the city centre: a London example' *Regional Studies* 2.
Graham, S. and Marvin, S. (1996) *Telecommunications and the City*, London: Routledge.
Halford, S., Savage, M. and Witt, A. (1997) *Gender, Careers and Organisations: Current Development in Banking, Nursing and Local Government*, London: Macmillan.
Henwood, D. (1997) *Wall Street. How it Works and For Whom*, London: Verso.
Ingham, G. (1994) 'Staffs and Markets in the production of world money: sterling and the dollar' in S. Corbridge, N. Thrift, R. Martin, eds, *Money, Power and Space*, Oxford: Blackwell: 29–48.
Ingham, G. (1996) 'Money is a social relation' *Review of Social Economy* 54(4): 507–29.
Kahn, H., and Cooper, C. (1993) *Stress in the Dealing Room. High Performances under Pressure*, London: Routledge.
Kamaluddin, (1993) 'Lender with a mission' *Far Eastern Economic Review* 156, 11 (March 18): 38–40.
Kay, J. (1995) 'The foundations of national competitive advantage', ESRC Fifth Annual lecture, Economic and Social Research Council, Polaris House, North Star Avenue, Swindon SN2 1US
Latour, B. (1997) 'Trains of thought: Piaget, formalism, and the fifth dimension' *Common Knowledge* 6, 3: 170–91.
Lee, R. (1996) 'Moral money, LETS and the social construction of local economic geographies in Southeast England' *Environment and Planning A* 28: 1377–94.
Leyshon, A. (1997) 'Geographies of Money and Finance II' *Progress in Human Geography* 21: 278–9.
Leyshon, A., and Thrift N.J. (1997) *Money/Space: Geographies of Monetary Transformation*, London, Routledge.
Leyshon, A., Thrift, N.J. and Pratt J. (1998) 'Reading financial services: texts, consumers and financial literacy' *Environment and Planning D. Society and Space* 16: 29–55.
Leyshon, A., Thrift, N.J. and Pratt J. (forthcoming) 'Inside/Outside: geographies of financial inclusion and exclusion in Britain' *Urban Studies*.
McDowell, L. (1997) *Capital Culture*, Cambridge: Polity Press.
McRae, H. (1995) 'There's a bit of Sting in us all' *The Independent* 19 October: 21.
Marsden, J., Harrison, M. and Flynn, A. (1998) 'Creating competitive space: exploring the social and political maintenance of retail power' *Environment and Planning A* 30: 481–98.
Marshall, N. and R. Richardson (1996) 'The impact of 'telemediated' services on corporate structures: the example of 'branchless' retail banking in Britain' *Environmental Planning A* 28: 1843–58.
Miller, D. (1995) 'Consumption as the vanguard of history' in Miller, D., ed. *Acknowledging*

Consumption. A Review of New Studies, London: Routledge: 1–57.

Moran, M. (1991) *The Politics of the Financial Services Revolution: the USA, UK and Japan,* London: Macmillan.

O'Brien, R. (1995) *Global Financial Integration. The End of Geography,* London: Frances Pinter.

Philo, C., ed. (1995) *Off the Map. The Social Geography of Poverty in the UK,* London: Child Poverty Action Group.

Roberts, S. and Schein R. (1995) 'Earth shattering: global imagery and GIS' in J. Pickles, ed., *Ground Truth: the Social Implications and Geographic Information Systems,* New York: Guilford: 171–95.

Scriven, M. (1998) 'Why the City is now like Wimbledon' This is London: London Evening Standard Web Edition http://thisisLondon.com/html/new.html

The Economist (1997) 'Banking. Loose wiring' 6 September: 100.

The Economist (1998) 'Banking on the poor' 27 June 27: 58–9.

Thrift, N.J. (1994) 'On the social and cultural determinants of international financial centres' in Corbridge, S., Thrift, N.J. and Martin, R. L., eds *Money, Power and Space,* Oxford: Blackwell: 327–55.

Thrift, N.J. and Leyshon, A. (1994) 'A phantom state? The detraditionlisation of money, the international financial system and the international financial centre' *Political Geography* 13: 299–327.

Tickell, A. (1997) 'Restructuring the British financial sector into the twenty-first century' *Capital and Class* 62: 13–19.

Todd, J. (1996) *Women at the Center. Grameen Bank Borrowers After One Decade,* Boulder, Colorado: Westview Press.

Whyley, C., McCormick, J.J. and Kempson E. (1998) *Paying for Peace of Mind: Access to Home Contents Insurance,* London: Policy Studies Institute.

Zelizer, V. (1994) *The Social Meaning of Money,* New York: Basic Books.

10 Globalisation of money?

National sovereignty and the management of risk

Nigel Dodd

Introduction

Is there something fundamentally untenable, inherently risky, or even perverse about a form of money which is not linked to, dependent on or identified with a nation-state? Given the emerging markets crises of 1998 – an important trigger of which was excessive foreign-exchange debt – the answer might appear to be self-evident. Even George Soros – allegedly the freewheeling nemesis of Britain's participation within the European Exchange Rate Mechanism (ERM) in September 1992 – has recently added his voice to calls for much tighter international regulation of money and finance (see Soros, 1998). But the question cannot really be answered until we develop a more precise understanding of so-called international money. We have to grasp in a more exact way the different forms that international money might take before we can evaluate the nature of the threat it could pose to the ability of national governments to pursue their monetary policies. For example, we need to be able to distinguish between instances where states co-operate with each other in the issue and control of money, as against those where international or transnational institutions seem to be taking over or superseding the sovereign powers of individual states altogether. And we must decide how to characterise the problems posed by international money in a way which takes account of the fact that the emergence of such problems is the result of a process in which information is interpreted by and contested between experts and state representatives. In short, we cannot treat the risks of international money as given. We should therefore exercise caution before regarding them as particularly new or distinctive. This reservation underpins the four main questions I shall be addressing in this chapter:

- How important is the relationship between money and the nation-state?
- What, if anything, distinguishes international money from other forms?
- What is the nature of uncertainty and risk in relation to international money?
- What is regulation at international level? How does it work and who is responsible for it?

My overall objective is to outline and clarify some research questions that need to be addressed if we are to reach an understanding of international money and its implications for the nation-state that is neither alarmist nor complacent. I am concentrating on regulation because this is one important focus of my current research. The discussion at this stage is theoretical, but sensitive to the need to set out questions and concepts for ongoing research.

The nation-state and money

Is the control and issue of money an integral part of what a nation-state stands for? Or is it vital from the perspective of money? In historical terms, this is tantamount to asking whether the role of the nation-state in issuing and regulating money emerged because it was essential for the stability of money (particularly when the link with precious metal was severed); necessary for the viability of nation-states themselves (especially in connection with their ability to raise taxes); or some combination of both. This is the question I shall be addressing in this section of the chapter.

The argument that the state control of money is vital to the stability of money is usually advanced in materialist terms. One of the most striking examples of this can be found in Georg Knapp's *State Theory of Money*, first published in 1905. Knapp's argument is fairly straightforward. He maintains that paper money has no intrinsic value. It is 'degenerate' (Knapp [1905] 1924: 2). In effect, paper or token money is a spatially extensive form of credit, and must therefore be treated as a legal guarantee. Only the state can provide the necessary backing for such a guarantee (Knapp [1905] 1924: 45). The 'soul' of money is therefore legal and political, not economic (Knapp 1905: 1). A similar emphasis on the legality of money is contained in Frederick Mann's *The Legal Aspect of Money*. But unlike Knapp, he clearly separates the question as to what can be treated as money according to law on the one hand, from questions about the essence of money on the other (Mann [1938] 1992: 28). Historical analysis of the relationship between money and the nation-state tends to support this distinction.

One significant factor in the emergence of national currencies involved the fiscal measures undertaken by absolutist states in sixteenth-, seventeenth- and eighteenth-century Europe. Absolutism marked the beginning of a process of consolidating state boundaries, as the state came to refer to a distinctive geopolitical area which was coterminous with a linguistically and culturally homogenous subject population (Hintze 1975: 161; Wallerstein 1974: 137–8; Giddens 1985: 90). The measures in question were informed by a basic need to survive during an age in which military operations were increasingly technological, and correspondingly more expensive. A tax regime filtered through the traditional estates system was not conducive to survival in this sense (Kennedy 1988: 90–1). Neither was the fragmented and poorly co-ordinated monetary system which existed at that time. Not only military prowess, however, but economic expansion and cultural identity were at stake in the rationalisation of fiscal and financial affairs within the absolutist state (see Giddens 1985: 98–101; Poggi 1978: 73). Both as geopolitical entities and as markets, states were becoming more homogenous and more clearly demarcated (Hont 1990: 42; Pocock 1990: 138–9). They needed not only to fight and to trade, but to borrow in order to thrive (Mann 1986b: 483–90; Kindleberger 1984: 165). The establishment of the Bank of England in 1695 – within a constitutional monarchy much more conducive to the emergence of capitalism than the absolutist system – and of the Bank of France in 1791, can be understood against this background.

This is too complex a picture to portray in detail here, but the overall shape is clear enough (see also the Introduction to this volume). What appears to Knapp to be an essential feature of modern, token money – legal backing by the state – in fact emerged as a consequence of the centralisation of the state's administrative machine; the expansion of capitalism; a military-driven increase in state borrowing; and the rationalisation of fiscal accounting. All of these factors were essential to the emergence of the modern nation-state. And all went hand-in-hand with the gradual state monopolisation of money. To suggest, as Knapp does, that the state's role in issuing and administering money is largely a function of the worthlessness of paper is rather like saying that the state should control television because of a decline in the influence of the established church. In both instances, one is inclined to question not only the accuracy but the relevance of the connection. There is little to suggest that token money relies for its stability and value on relationships, processes and institutions that are different in any essential way from money that has been cast from precious metal. Not only historically, but also in the context of the present day, there are economists who suggest that nation-state governments have most to gain from the state monopoly over money (see for example Hayek, 1990). If we are to be alarmed by suggestions that this monopoly is being wrested away, we must look beyond the fallacy that the value of money would necessarily rest on precarious foundations without state backing. The real reason for our alarm, I would suggest, lies somewhere in the region of control, stability and risk. To discuss this, we must turn to the concept of globalisation and the historical origins of one of the predominant forms of international money, offshore currencies.

Globalisation and international money

Current definitions of globalisation do not seem entirely satisfying for research purposes (see Scott, 1997). In economic terms, globalisation is often referred to as a further stage in the development of the international division of labour (Wallerstein, 1990: 35–8). According to others, however, globalisation is part of a more fundamental, structural change in international political economy closely associated with post-industrialism (Harvey 1989: 121–97; Lash and Urry 1987: 196–209). In geopolitical terms, globalisation is sometimes taken to be synonymous with the erosion of national sovereignty, while others argue that it is a more complicated, uneven process in which national sovereignty is redefined but not essentially eroded (Cooper 1986; Held 1989: 237–9; Giddens 1990: 70–8). According to some commentators, globalisation necessarily entails a distancing between the individual and international political and economic processes (Lash and Urry 1987: 300–13). Others, however, contend that globalisation could signal a closer relationship in these terms (Archer, 1990; Giddens 1994: 47; Giddens 1991: 21–3; Friedman, 1990; Beck 1992: 223–35; Bauman, 1998).

At the very least, it is important to resist thinking about the process of globalisation merely as a process which goes on over our heads. Let me call this Caveat I:

> Globalisation should not be regarded as a process which is detached from the individual in his or her locale.

Giddens associates globalisation with a process he describes as time–space distanciation. He argues that globalisation is not only a process in which institutions take on an increasingly global shape, but signals increasing interdependence between local and global processes. Giddens characterises this as action at distance: on the one hand, 'day-to-day activities are increasingly influenced by events happening on the other side of the world', while on the other, 'local lifestyle habits have become globally consequential' (Giddens 1994: 4–5). One might therefore say that action at distance could include environmental pollution and many kinds of financial transaction, even those that appear to have no obvious international dimension.

In a literal, or state-centric, sense, the term globalisation is often taken to imply the withering away of the sovereignty of the nation-state. This, for example, is the approach taken by Held with regard to economic sovereignty, where he argues that 'the internationalisation of production, finance and other economic resources is unquestionably eroding the capacity of the state to control its own economic future' (Held 1989: 230). Even an approach as cautiously phrased as this, however, threatens to run important questions together regarding the precise sense in which national boundaries, and thereby the sovereignty of national governments to control their own economic affairs, are being eroded. For example, it might be more accurate to say that globalisation, while not exactly an erosion of state sovereignty, i.e. the right of state agencies and government to implement economic policy, does at least diminish the capacity of national governments to see their economic policies through (Keohane and Nye, 1977; Lash and Urry 1987: 280).

We should be able to conceptualise such complications. This, then, is Caveat II:

> The erosion of national economic boundaries may take several distinctive forms, with distinct causes and implications.

In a preliminary way, I would identify three such forms:

- *Openness* refers to the absence of barriers between two or more economies; in other words, an open economy has few legal, social, political, geographical or cultural obstacles to international trade and exchange (cf. Gilpin 1987: 145).

- *Identity* refers to similarity in economic characteristics between two or more countries: for example, between their key macroeconomic indicators, consumption patterns and material aspirations.
- *Integration* refers to economic interdependence between two or more countries, usually through international specialisation and the international division of labour (Panić 1988: 4).

Each in its own way, any one of these three concepts could provide the basis for a definition of globalisation which is quite plausible in its own terms. But on closer inspection, each definition might be taken to suggest causes of globalisation, and implications for the nation-state, which are actually quite different. For example, in the narrowest sense – taking inflation and public borrowing into account – economic identity has been set as the major precondition for European Monetary Union (EMU). Although of course, it is open to question whether this definition is too narrow, i.e. whether economic identity is genuinely achievable in such terms without much wider political and even cultural change. At this stage of the discussion, I want to propose that a useful working definition of globalisation – i.e. a definition which enables us more precisely to question the role of states in managing, controlling or regulating international money, and above all the risks generated by it – must refer to an increasing interdependence between local and global processes and institutions. I regard this definition as useful for research because the notion of interdependence between local and global processes and institutions suggests that, even if we acknowledge that globalisation is occurring in some form, this does not necessarily mean that we have to ignore regulatory institutions at a local, i.e. national, level.

This emphasis on local and global interdependence is vitally important in the context of international money. As long ago as 1985, Tsoukalis wrote that the international monetary and financial system represents 'a conscious, or unconscious, negation of the idea of a collectively managed system with a tight official control over markets' (Tsoukalis 1985: 289). This is intriguing because, according to Tsoukalis, the negation of official control has been conscious *or* unconscious. In other words, it may be *both* an unintended consequence of what states do *and* something they have themselves contrived. No doubt there is some truth in this, but already one fears that several questions are being run together. For example, one might look to the infamous Regulation Q instituted in the US during the late 1960s – limiting the rate of interest which banks could offer to domestic holders of dollars – as a regulation which unwittingly encouraged the development of the offshore market in dollars. Likewise, the US government's mistake over interest rate policy relative to the Deutschmark in the early 1970s gave another boost to the offshore market. But here we run into distinct areas of discussion; the first concerns the *regulation* of interest rates, the second, interest rate *policy*. Both involve the US government and Federal Reserve, but only the first involves actual regulation. They are therefore part of the same story – the role of government and state in unwittingly encouraging offshore growth – but not exactly of the same picture from the point of view of research. Much the same could be said for measures which consciously spurred the expansion of the international monetary and financial system, as I shall discuss in a moment (see also Dodd, 1995).

Reference to an international monetary system raises the question of borders or boundaries. By this, I mean national boundaries; boundaries which are vital when considering the problem of regulating or managing the system. A brief list of questions: Is the system without borders? Does it transcend existing borders? Or does it exploit them? Let me set about answering these questions by defining international money and placing it into historical perspective. It seems most reasonable to take international money to mean offshore money, that is, money lent and borrowed outside the country of issue. But even then, we should take account of the complex ways in which networks of offshore currencies overlap with more standard networks of currencies, say, in international money markets. This suggests that there are difficulties in thinking about one system at all. A broader and more satisfactory definition of international money would refer to international money and financial markets as networks which include cross-border transactions. According to this definition, these networks straddle, but do not necessarily supersede, national boundaries. Above all, the networks bring together national and international monetary and financial processes in ways that might continuously take on new forms but need not be essentially or fundamentally new.

Implicit in this picture is the poorly understood notion that nation-state governments and agencies such as central banks have less control over the transfer of money between countries, rendering them more vulnerable to crises which originate in other states. More alarmist analyses of this phenomenon draw on a rogue's gallery of incidents to reinforce the point, such as the BCCI banking collapse and the more recent Barings episode, or as a means of demonstrating the power of non-state institutions or individuals, the role of George Soros in the undignified withdrawal of sterling from the ERM in September 1992. One important problem with such examples is that they stem from a range of causes which are, in fact, seldom international in their own right, i.e. they often originate in processes or events which take place within, not across, national boundaries (see Dodd and Hutter, 1997). To put this another way, it is unclear whether anything much distinguishes these examples from other instances where a problem in one institution or sector of the economy has an impact on another. To suggest that the distinguishing factor is the inability of a state to manage or control what goes on outside its borders is obviously true (and has always been so) but begs more questions than it answers. In short, there is not much evidence to suggest that there is something about international monetary networks which is inherently risky or uncertain. Moreover, it is far from clear that international money actually presents quite the challenge to national sovereignty – and above all, to the nation-state monopoly over the issue and control of money – that some commentators would have us believe. Let me illustrate what I mean by considering briefly the emergence of offshore currencies. These are frequently cited as a primary source of danger to national currency systems. Yet their history reveals a combination of national, commercial and geopolitical forces which is of a similar level of complexity – and, from the point of view of the nation-state, ambiguity – to those which, as I suggested earlier, underpinned the emergence of national currencies themselves.

The very idea that a monetary form is offshore suggests that it represents an evasion of national sovereignty and therefore by extension, some kind of threat or challenge to it. I will turn to the second aspect of this later on, in the discussion of uncertainty and risk. But in what sense do offshore currencies and monetary transactions evade national borders? In a very basic sense, and as I have already said, offshore currencies are currencies transacted outside their country of issue, for example, dollars lent and borrowed in South Korea. The growth of these currencies, particularly of the so-called Eurodollar, can be traced back to the 1960s and 1970s, when – as I indicated above – a series of policy and regulatory measures by the US government unwittingly presented institutions with a strong incentive to place dollars outside the US (see Little 1985: 154; Clarke 1979: 203–4; Kindleberger 1987: 46).

In Britain, two crucial factors involved the imposition of credit controls during the 1960s which boosted parallel markets in sterling; and by the secondary banking crisis of 1973–4 (Ingham 1984: 51; Clarke 1979: 131). The growth-rate of offshore markets was increased by the US balance of payments deficit, and further enhanced by American companies' conversion of profits into dollars outside the US (Ingham 1984: 52; Clarke 1979: 203; Davis 1979: 21). But there are several other aspects to the history of offshore currencies which suggest that the role of national governments in stimulating their growth was more systematic; a deliberate, not unintended, consequence of policy. The Japanese government played a major role in this respect. Following the second major oil price rise in 1979, the Japanese Ministry of Finance instructed banks to offer the highest possible rates to attract surplus OPEC dollars, and engaged in diplomatic efforts to persuade Arab governments to place funds in Japan (Emery 1984: 110; Spindler 1984: 150–1). Restrictions that had been placed on the overseas operations of Japanese banks were relaxed. Not only did this present a significant boost to the growth of offshore markets. The OPEC funds actually strengthened the capacity of the Ministry of Finance in Japan to implement its own national economic policies, particularly with regard to its current account. This may not have been in the interest of the US government, but it was certainly consistent with the interests of Japan. To suggest that the growth of offshore markets represented an evasion of national sovereignty would therefore be to tell only part of the story. At the very least, it would be to ignore the fact that offshore markets have always consisted of a high proportion of sovereign funds (Gilpin, 1987: 310–11).

It is doubtful, moreover, whether the national interest even of the US was compromised by the growth of offshore currencies, at least in any straightforward way. To some extent, these currencies were part of a *de facto* privatisation of international aid, the surplus OPEC funds providing a conduit for grants and (mostly) loans to lesser-developed countries (LDCs) during the 1970s (see OECD, 1977; Gilpin 1987: 315). Yet as Spero has argued, a significant proportion of the OPEC funds were denominated in US Treasury Bills. And they went to middle, not low, income LDCs such as Venezuela and Nigeria. Some of these countries exported oil. In other words, this was in some sense a reinforcement of American hegemony, not simply a development which undermined the capacity of the Federal reserve to implement and see through its monetary policies. If anything, a complex series of interests and alliances was at stake in the growth of offshore markets, institutions and currencies: surplus OPEC dollars; commercially vigorous albeit sometimes naive private banks; capital-hungry sovereign states; and innovative multilateral aid organisations (Gilpin 1987: 317). To describe the offshore market as floating above national boundaries and threatening them from outside may be theoretically convenient from the perspective of globalisation, but it does not withstand close empirical scrutiny. Having placed offshore money into a slightly finer-grained historical context, we can now move on to ask what the risks are specifically associated with international money.

What is risk?

Recently, Nigel Thrift and Andrew Leyshon in the UK have explored the specific nature of risk in relation to international money. They refer to the international monetary system as 'an institutionally structured risk environment' (Thrift and Leyshon 1994: 302). Presumably, this is an environment where risk is not a mere side-effect of the system but is central to its organisation. This is suggestive because many financial instruments commodify risk. But the argument is inconclusive and possibly misleading. Yes, international money is structured around the commodification of risk. But a closer look at, say, the Futures Market in London raises the question as to whether this necessarily increases risk, or whether it is in fact designed to manage (and thereby reduce) risk. (And it is another question again whether the Futures Market actually succeeds in either direction.) The notion of commodified risk brings to mind the arguments of Giddens and Beck. Giddens (1990) writes of the 'globalisation of uncertainty', for example, and we begin to grasp what he means when we read Beck's argument (1992, but 1986 in its original German) that we live in a world where risk is both manufactured (we create it) and inclusive (none of us can escape from it).

In this latter context, Giddens makes much of the idea that the risks we now face are all of our own doing. They can be contrasted to the risk of living near a volcano, or of suffering an earthquake. Using the terminology of Johannes Berger, we might even say that volcanoes and earthquakes present dangers to us, i.e. 'circumstances an individual or collective actor . . . cannot control', whereas international money markets generate risks, i.e. 'the consequences of decisions, which could have turned out differently' (Berger 1994: 783). But Berger's distinction is more useful when broken down even further. In so far as all markets and systems have what Durkheim liked to call emergent properties, the sense in which specific risks are a consequence of specific decisions is open to serious doubt. Moreover, we might well want to ask; whose decisions? Berger refers to known probabilities when attempting to finesse his definition of risk. This raises more (and good) questions than it answers. One of the central themes in the analysis of risk in a financial context must be the role and interpretation of information, and I want to turn to this now.

I have already said that, when seeking to understand the specific nature of the risks associated with international money, it is important not only to think about forms of international money but about the series of systems, or networks, in which they appear. This is partly because such an approach enables us to address the question of borders or boundaries, but also because to conceptualise monetary relations in terms of a network is helpful in drawing out the importance of information on what money is, how it is used, and how it circulates. In a significant way, monetary networks are networks *of* information (Dodd, 1994) both in the sense that money transmits information (as economists and anthropologists have long argued when distinguishing monetary exchange from barter) and in so far as various forms of information – experience of the past, weak inductive knowledge about the future, and so on – play a role in shaping the way that money is used. I will not dwell on these questions here, but want instead to discuss the connection between information and uncertainty as it arises in relation to international money. This should help to clarify what we do and (more important) do not know about the risks of international money and further, has some bearing on how we might go about researching the problem of regulation and control in this context.

If Berger has a point when he refers to risk (as opposed to danger) as a consequence of our own actions and decisions, i.e. the product of an active stance towards the future (one might talk about trust in a similar way), it should be possible to define uncertainty in relation to a more passive stance towards the future (we might also mention faith, as opposed to trust, in this context). But for most people for most of the time, the concept of uncertainty arguably presents a more accurate account of their own, local connection with global or (at least) international money than the concept of risk. If Berger's idea of known probabilities necessarily means known by *someone*, we could say that one person's risk is another's uncertainty. This is not to suggest that most of us, for at least some of the time, may not seek to know more about the financial world in so far as it affects us. But what we do know, or at least think we know, about the complexities of offshore markets and their impact on us tends to be mediated by experts, not based on experience.

As I shall discuss later on, this is also true for governments and regulators. The uncertainties presented by international monetary networks are not self-evident. Their characterisation as such is a consequence of the production, interpretation and contestation of expert knowledge. There is plenty of scope for research here, not only from the perspective of the sociology of knowledge, into the production and dissemination of information in and around the financial system but also (in social psychology) on the attribution of trust *in* knowledge. (For example, in the broader area of life-style risks some psychologists suspect that we take more notice of second-hand information drawn from known, immediate and particular cases – a grandfather who has smoked all his life for example – than from what the experts tell us.)

In the context of offshore currencies, it is useful to distinguish between uncertainty and complexity where the role of information is concerned. Briefly, uncertainty implies that we have insufficient or imperfect information, whereas complexity suggests that we have too much. A series of theoretical and empirical questions is raised by this distinction. For example, Luhmann employs a similar definition of complexity in order to argue that trust reduces complexity within a social system; whereas Michael Power's research into the audit society suggests that the monitoring systems employed within institutions – what he calls the technology of mistrust – may, in so far as they are illusory (i.e. they sometimes increase our trust in the system without good reason), in fact increase risk (which, in Luhmann's terms, probably suggests more, not less, complexity). In another context (geography), Thrift has argued that the plethora of information available in financial institutions – much of it expensive, confusing and contradictory – has reinforced rather than weakened the importance of interpersonal and spatially defined relationships within financial markets which, according to conventional wisdom, are becoming more abstract, spatially elastic and impersonal.

But we should not merely be interested in the information available to and disseminated by experts and non-experts in the context of international money. What must be of considerable interest in this area concerns the reflexivity of information, that is to say, its role not merely in describing but in changing a particular environment or system. For example, Giddens writes about the way in which information about social practices may constitutively alter the character of those practices (Giddens 1990: 38–9). In the more specific context of financial markets, Soros puts forward a similar definition of reflexivity: 'financial markets attempt to predict a future that is contingent on the decisions people make in the present. Instead of just passively reflecting reality, financial markets are actively creating the reality that they, in turn, reflect' (Soros 1998: xxiii). This has important ramifications not only for the way we approach the question of uncertainty in relation to international money, but for research into the regulatory problems which arise from it.

With regard to uncertainty, I want to propose a heuristic distinction which has some bearing on the reflexivity of information. In relation to money, uncertainty (in so far as it affects trust) is twofold. First, it arises from the sheer openness of a future which, by definition, is unknowable. But in so far as some futures are less knowable than others, a second form of uncertainty refers to the quality or quantity of the information available to us, and on the basis of which we acquire weak inductive knowledge about the institutions, systems and processes around us. This distinction can be translated into two very basic definitions of uncertainty:

- *Uncertainty I* is inherent within a complex system, and may arise from instability within that system, or from an unforeseeable combination of elements within that system (i.e. its emergent properties).

- *Uncertainty II* arises by virtue of the fact that we do not know enough about how a system works, although it is knowable and others may control or mediate the information we require in order to know more.

I will not pretend for a moment that the distinction is watertight. The concept of reflexivity, as I have just discussed it, means that there must be some overlapping between each type. The point I am driving at, however, concerns whether it is possible to argue that a system – such as international money – is inherently uncertain (or risky, complex, and so on) or whether the problem arises partly (or largely) as a function of what we do, and above all do not, know about it. In so far as the first type of uncertainty exists, research into the regulation and control of international monetary networks would need to investigate structural or systemic weaknesses such as grey areas of regulation which enable banks to become over-exposed or which expose others to their mistakes. The second definition of uncertainty – what (we think) we do not know – raises further important research questions, for example, about the production of financial expertise; about the role of knowledge and information in the regulatory process; and about the management of confidence at times of banking collapse or failure. Let me now expand on these points.

National and international regulation: research questions

To recall Caveat II from the earlier discussion of globalisation, the idea that international monetary networks transcend nation-state borders in any real sense is difficult to verify. This is not least because the idea of transcendence in this context could mean either increasing openness between monetary systems or increasing interdependence between them. Either condition might be taken to suggest that offshore monetary networks lie beyond the reach of national regulators. In the sociology of law and regulation, however, research is being undertaken into the emergence of a new form of international regulation. Here, we are not talking about the mere existence of international regulations (such as treaties) – as if talking about the mere existence of any law could tell us much about the role of law in society – but, in much more depth and detail, about the way in which regulations are drafted, implemented and enforced. This suggests another, perhaps less worrying, way in which nation-states may have been (or will eventually be) superseded, i.e. by international or transnational bodies which are taking over their functions. But detailed study of what Hawkins and Hutter call the regulatory process – i.e. the emergence, drafting, implementation, enforcement and impact of regulation – at international or transnational level does not suggest either that the nation-state has been superseded by organisations higher up or, more seriously from our point of view, that there are processes and institutions which operate beyond the scope of regulators altogether.

I do not want to suggest that there is simply no problem concerning the regulation and control of international monetary networks; that when a banking or financial crisis in one country has consequences for another – or others – we should not be interested in asking why, and in understanding whether those consequences could have been avoided. What I am saying, however, is that we should exercise caution before assuming that such consequences are necessarily the result of the globalisation of money. If globalisation is taken to mean the interdependence of local and global processes and institutions, research is needed into the relationship between national regulators and international monetary networks, as well as into the even more tricky area of international regulation itself.

With regard to the emergence of international and transnational regulation, there are at least two main avenues for further research. The first of these stems from the first definition of uncertainty, i.e. it concerns systemic weaknesses in the relationship between national (and/or international) regulators on the one hand, and offshore monetary networks on the other. There are a number of different players involved in the regulatory process at this level. These include transnational organisations, non-governmental organisations, nation-states and state agencies, state officials, professionals such as lawyers, economists and scientists (see Jasanoff, 1990), international banks and multinational companies. To take the example of international banks, research needs to be undertaken into the nature of the sector concerned – its importance, regulatory capacity and degree of organisation – and how this affects its relation to other key players. It would be mistaken to assume, for example, that there is a straightforward relationship between the size of a financial sector and its regulatory capacity. This raises the broader question of power differentials, for example, the extent to which international banks are able to exert pressure on governments, and vice versa; the extent to which nation-states are able to influence other nation-states; and the internal pressures within the state which determine how the national interest is publicly defined (Olsen, 1992).

A second avenue for research into the emergence of international and transnational regulation concerns the characterisation of problems perceived to require a regulatory solution. This stems from the second definition of uncertainty. For research purposes, such problems cannot be treated as given. Questions must be raised about the relationship between the level of understanding of particular problems and the degree of international contestation over available information regarding those problems (Smith and Wynne, 1988). For example, it cannot be assumed that those problems that are most contested internationally are necessarily those that are least well understood. If the Russian default crisis of 1998 demonstrates anything, it is that even supposedly sophisticated – or information-rich – investors did not fully understand the nature and extent of the risks they were taking, or the dangers to which they were exposed. It may well be true that the international financial system enables the consequences of such a problem to be transmitted across state borders more rapidly than ever, but that should not detract from the possibility that the root of the problem is cognitive, not systemic. If so, it would be premature either to confirm *or* deny the observation of even so experienced a practitioner as Soros that 'financial markets are *inherently* unstable' (Soros 1998: 176; italics added). Research into this area must therefore take account of both the perceived severity of a problem (such as the market in derivatives) and its degree of complexity, for example, whether its origins (and/or consequences) are perceived as falling within the jurisdiction of one or a number of nation-states.

As I have already suggested, however, it is far from clear whether we can talk of international regulation in a straightforward way. Where international regulations are drafted – for example, in international treaties, which may be a loose conglomeration of signatories, or the much tighter organisation of a body such as the EU with its member states – evidence supporting the view that international regulatory organisations are superseding national regulatory regimes is most likely to be found where formal institutional arrangements have been set up to support particular agreements. But even in respect of the EU, the case for regarding this as an instance of integration is debatable. The EU, in so far as it provides a forum for the setting of agreed regulations and standards among member states, may be viewed as an instance of increasing identity, i.e. similarity in characteristics between two or more countries. But the participants within such a forum are, in the first instance, state representatives. So if it is to be argued that this stage of the regulatory process has undergone increasing integration, i.e. a new form of international regulation has emerged, evidence would be required that these representatives are acting in an increasingly autonomous fashion, i.e. without reference to national governments or interests. But little is known about the extent to which state representatives negotiate and adapt their position about rule-making, rule-framing and policy-making at the level of international forums. And nothing can be known about this until the process is examined directly, i.e. through detailed empirical research. What, for example, lay behind the contested IMF policy during 1998 of supporting the currencies of Brazil, Indonesia and Russia at a level that many thought to be artificial, therefore continuing the exposure of those economies to fluctuations in the confidence of markets elsewhere? Note, in passing, that this is a question about the practice of policy-intervention from outside, not the principles behind it. It is also a question which revolves around the reflexive impact of information – and confidence – within and across financial markets.

If we want to understand the extent of the problems posed by offshore monetary networks for national regulators, we have to look more closely at the process of the implementation or enforcement of regulations, whether or not these regulations were actually drafted nationally or internationally. We should begin by acknowledging that, even in respect of international treaties, states remain primarily responsible for their implementation and enforcement. This and further issues, such as regulatory shopping – basically, where banks or corporations play off national regulatory regimes against each other – cannot properly be addressed until we know more about how international banks operate, their understanding of regulations with respect to requirements, enforcement, why they do or do not comply, and the role of regulation in their choice of location. But this also depends on what is known by those who participate in the regulatory process or, more accurately, what the participants think they know.

Conclusion

I have suggested that we should be cautious when talking about the risks generated by international monetary networks. Not, thankfully, because we (as social scientists) could do much damage to public confidence by what we say about economic matters – although particular individuals involved with policy and regulation certainly can – but because we should as far as possible resist complicating what is already a complex picture. More specifically, I have expressed a preference for the concept of uncertainty as opposed to risk in the context of international monetary networks because this enables us to investigate, as a research question, the extent to which the uncertainties of international money arise from a lack of understanding or agreement among experts, and further, the extent to which the contestation of knowledge or information at this level constitutively alters the operation of international monetary networks themselves. As social scientists, we ought to exercise caution and resist defining globalisation and risk in such as way that the former seems necessarily to generate an increase in our exposure to the latter. It is a matter for research, not theory or the definition of concepts, whether the global uncertainties of money are more apparent than real, or at least, not fundamentally distinctive from problems already faced by national regulators where money and finance are concerned. In this chapter, I have tried to suggest some terms in which we might undertake such research.

Acknowledgements

Some of the ideas discussed in this paper, particularly the material on international and national regulation, have been formulated through ongoing collaborative work with Bridget Hutter, also of the Department of Sociology at the LSE.

Bibliography

Aliber, R.Z. (1985) 'Eurodollars: An Economic Analysis', in P. Savona and D. Sutija, eds, *Eurodollars and International Banking*, Basingstoke: Macmillan: 77–98.

Aliber, R.Z., ed. (1987) *The Reconstruction of International Monetary Arrangements*, Basingstoke: Macmillan.

Archer, M. (1990) 'Theory, culture and post-industrial society', in M. Featherstone, ed. *Global Culture*, London: Sage: 97–119.

Bauman, Z. (1998) *Globalisation: The Human Consequences*, Cambridge: Polity Press.

Beck, U. (1992) *Risk Society: Towards a New Modernity*, London: Sage.

Beck, U. (1995) *Ecological Enlightenment: Essays on the Politics of the Risk Society*, New Jersey: Humanities Press.

Beck, U. (1998) *Democracy Without Enemies*, Cambridge: Polity Press.

Berger, J. (1994) 'The Economy and the Environment', in N. Smelser and R. Swedberg, eds, *The Handbook of Economic Sociology*, Princeton: Princeton University Press: 766–97.

Clarke, W.M. (1979) *Inside the City*, London: George Allen & Unwin.

Cooper, R.N. (1986) *Economic Policy in an Interdependent World*, Cambridge, Mass: MIT Press.
Davis, S.I. (1979) *The Management of International Banks*, London: Macmillan.
Dodd, N. (1994) *The Sociology of Money: Economics, Reason and Contemporary Society*, Cambridge: Polity Press.
Dodd, N. (1995) 'Money and the nation-state: contested boundaries of monetary sovereignty in geopolitics' *International Sociology* 10, 2: 139–54.
Dodd, N. and Hutter, B. (1997) 'Geopolitics and the regulation of economic life: the decline of the nation-state?', manuscript available from Department of Sociology, London School of Economics, Houghton Street, London, WC2A 2AE, England.
Dunn, J., ed. (1990) *The Economic Limits to Modern Politics*, Cambridge: Cambridge University Press.
Emery, R.F. (1984) *The Japanese Money Market*, Lexington, MA: Lexington Books.
Featherstone, M. (1990) 'Global culture: an introduction,' in M. Featherstone, ed. *Global Culture*, London: Sage: 1–14.
Franklin, J. (1998) *The Politics of Risk Society*, Cambridge: Polity Press.
Friedman, J. (1990) 'Being in the world: globalisation and localization,' in M. Featherstone, ed. *Global Culture*, London: Sage: 311–28.
Gambetta, D., ed. (1988) *Trust*, Oxford: Blackwell.
Giddens, A. (1985) *The NationState and Violence*, Cambridge: Polity Press.
Giddens, A. (1990) *The Consequences of Modernity*, Cambridge: Polity Press.
Giddens, A. (1991) *Modernity and Self-Identity*, Cambridge: Polity Press.
Giddens, A. (1994) *Beyond Left and Right*, Cambridge: Polity Press.
Gilpin, R. (1987) *The Political Economy of International Relations*, Princeton: Princeton University Press.
Goodhart, C.A.E. (1985) 'Carli: "Eurodollars: Policy Analysis"' in P. Savona and D. Sutija, eds, *Eurodollars and International Banking*, Basingstoke: Macmillan: 161–5.
Hall, J.A., ed. (1986) *States in History*, Oxford: Basil Blackwell.
Hamada, K. and Horiuchi, A. (1987) 'The Political Economy of the Financial Market' in K. Yamamura and Y. Yasubo, eds, *The Political Economy of Japan*, vol. I, Stanford, CA: Stanford University Press: 223–60.
Harvey, D. (1989) *The Condition of Postmodernity*, Oxford: Blackwell.
Hawkins, K. (1984) *Environment and Enforcement: Regulation and Social Definitions of Pollution*, Oxford: Clarendon Press.
Hawkins, K.H. and Hutter, B. M. (1993) 'The Response of Business to Social Regulation in England and Wales: An Enforcement Perspective' *Law and Policy* 15, 3: 199–225.
Hayek, F. (1990) *Denationalization of Money*, London: Institute of Economic Affairs.
Held, D. (1989) *Political Theory and the Modern State*, Cambridge: Polity Press.
Higonnet, R.P. (1985) 'Eurobanks, Eurodollars and International Debt,' in P. Savona and D. Sutija, eds, *Eurodollars and International Banking*, Basingstoke: Macmillan: 15–52.
Hintze, O. (1975) *The Historical Essays of Otto Hintze*, ed., F. Gilbert, New York: Oxford University Press.
Hont, I. (1990) 'Free Trade and the Economic Limits to National Politics: Neo-Machiavellian Political Economy Reconsidered', in J. Dunn, ed. *The Economic Limits to Modern Politics*, Cambridge: Cambridge University Press: 41–120.
Hopwood, A.G. and Miller, P., eds, (1994) *Accounting as Social and Institutional Practice*, Cambridge: Cambridge University Press.
Hutter, B.M. (1988) *The Reasonable Arm of the Law?: The Law Enforcement Procedures of Environmental Health Officers*, Oxford: Clarendon Press.
Hutter, B.M. (1997) *Compliance: Regulation and Environment*, Oxford: Clarendon Press.

Ingham, G. (1984) *Capitalism Divided?* Basingstoke: Macmillan.

Inoguchi, T. and Okimoto, D.I., eds, (1987) *The Political Economy of Japan* vol II, Stanford, CA: Stanford University Press.

Jasanoff, S. (1990) *The Fifth Branch: Science Advisors as Policymakers*, Cambridge, Mass.: Harvard University Press.

Kennedy, P. (1988) *The Rise and Fall of the Great Powers*, London: Fontana Press.

Keohane, R.O. (1984) *After Hegemony*, Princeton: Princeton University Press.

Keohane, R.O. and Nye J.S. (1977) *Power and Interdependence: World Politics in Transition*, Boston: Little, Brown.

Kindleberger, C.P. (1984) *A Financial History of Western Europe*, London: George Allen & Unwin.

Kindleberger, C.P. (1987) *International Capital Movements*, Cambridge: Cambridge University Press.

King, M. (1989) 'International Harmonization of the Regulation of Capital Markets', *Special Paper no. 19, LSE Financial Markets Group.*

Knapp, G.F. ([1905] 1924) *The State Theory of Money*, London: Macmillan.

Lash, S. and Urry, J. (1987) *The End of Organized Capitalism*, Cambridge: Polity.

Leyshon, A. and Thrift, N. (1997) *Money/Space: Geographies of Monetary Transformation*, London: Routledge.

Little, J.S. (1985) 'Higonnet: "Eurobanks: Policy Analysis" – Comment', in P. Savona and D. Sutija, eds, *Eurodollars and International Banking*, Basingstoke: Macmillan: 165–8.

Luhmann, N. (1988) 'Familiarity, confidence, trust: problems and alternatives' in D. Gambetta, ed. *Trust*, Oxford: Blackwell: 94–107.

Mann, F. ([1938] 1992) *The Legal Aspect of Money*, 5th edition, Oxford: Clarendon Press.

Mann, M. (1986a) 'The Autonomous Power of the State: Its Origins, Mechanisms and Results', in J.A. Hall, ed. *States in History*, Oxford: Basil Blackwell: 109–36.

Mann, M. (1986b) *The Sources of Social Power*, vol. I, Cambridge: Cambridge University Press.

Murakami, Y. (1987) 'The Japanese Model of Political Economy', in K. Yamamura and Y. Yasubo, ed. *The Political Economy of Japan*, vol. I, Stanford, CA: Stanford University Press: 33–90.

Muramatsu, M. and Krauss, E.S. (1987) 'The Conservative Policy Line and the Development of Patterned Pluralism' in K. Yamamura and Y. Yasubo, eds, *The Political Economy of Japan*, vol. I, Stanford, CA: Stanford University Press: 516–54.

OECD (1977) *Towards Full Employment and Price Stability*, (The McCracken Report) Paris: OECD.

Ogus, A. (1994) *Regulation: Legal Form and Economic Theory*, Oxford: Clarendon Press.

Olsen, P. (1992) *Six Cultures of Regulation*, Copenhagen: Handelshøjskolen I København.

Panić, M. (1988) *National Management of the International Economy*, Basingstoke: Macmillan.

Pocock, J.G.A. (1990) 'The Political Limits to Premodern Politics' in J. Dunn, eds, *The Economic Limits to Modern Politics*, Cambridge: Cambridge University Press: 121–41.

Poggi, G. (1978) *The Development of the Modern State*, London: Hutchinson.

Power, M. (1994) 'The Audit Society' in A.G. Hopwood and P. Miller, eds, *Accounting as Social and Institutional Practice*, Cambridge: Cambridge University Press: 299–316.

Power, M. (1997) *The Audit Society: Rituals of Verification*, Oxford: Clarendon Press.

Risse-Kappen, T., ed. (1995) *Bringing Transnational Relations Back In*, Cambridge: Cambridge University Press.

Savona, P. and Sutija, D., ed. (1985) *Eurodollars and International Banking*, Basingstoke: Macmillan.

Scott, A., ed. (1997) *The Limits of Globalisation: Cases and Arguments*, London: Routledge.
Shafer, J.R. (1987) 'The Theory of the Lender of Last Resort and the Eurocurrency Markets', in R.Z. Aliber, ed. *The Reconstruction of International Monetary Arrangements*, Basingstoke: Macmillan: 281–304.
Shinkai, Y. (1988) 'The Internationalisation of Finance in Japan' in T. Inoguchi and D.I. Okimoto, eds, *The Political Economy of Japan* vol. II, Stanford, CA: Stanford University Press: 249–71.
Smelser, N. and Swedberg, R. eds, (1994) *The Handbook of Economic Sociology*, Princeton: Princeton University Press.
Smith, A.D. (1986) 'State-Making and Nation-Building,' in J.A. Hall, ed. *States in History*, Oxford: Basil Blackwell: 228–63.
Smith, R. and Wynne, B. ed. (1988) *Expert Evidence: Interpreting Science in the Law*, London: Routledge.
Soros, G. (1998) *The Crisis of Global Capitalism: Open Society Endangered*, London: Little, Brown and Company.
Spero, J.E. (1990) *The Politics of International Economic Relations*, London: Unwin Hyman.
Spindler, J.A. (1984) *The Politics of International Credit*, Washington DC: Brookings Institution.
Thrift, N. (1995) *Spatial Formations*, London: Sage.
Thrift, N. and Leyshon, A. (1994) 'A Phantom State? The de-traditionalization of money, the international financial system and international financial centres' *Political Geography* 13, 4: 299–327.
Tsoukalis, L. (1985) 'The new international monetary "system" and prospects for reform', in L. Tsoukalis, ed. *The Political Economy of International Money*, London: Sage: 283–304.
Vogel, D. (1995) *Trading Up: Consumer and Environmental Regulation in a Global Economy*, Cambridge, Mass: Harvard University Press.
Wallerstein, I. (1974) *The Modern World-System*, vol. I, New York: Academic Press.
Wallerstein, I. (1990) 'Culture as the ideological battleground of the modern world system', in M. Featherstone, ed. *Global Culture*, London: Sage: 31–55.
Yamamura, K. and Yasubo, Y., eds, (1987) *The Political Economy of Japan*, vol. I, Stanford, CA: Stanford University Press.

11 The logic of giving up national currencies

Lessons from Europe's monetary union

Amy Verdun

As the millennium is drawing to a close, Europe stands at the eve of a major change, i.e. the introduction of a single European currency. A large majority of European Union (EU) countries have adopted a supranational currency, the Euro, in the year 1999 and, provided no major political upheaval occurs in the coming years, they will be fully replacing their national currencies with new Euro banknotes and coins floating from 2002. The European case of abolishing national currencies and creating a supranational currency for an area of as many as eleven countries stands out as a single case in the contemporary world. Of course, due to so-called 'globalisation', 'internationalisation' and 'financial market integration', various countries across the globe are aiming at international monetary co-operation and keeping exchange rates stable. Yet, nowhere else in the world are countries as serious about giving up their national currencies and replacing them by a new, previously non-existent supranational currency.

When examining why the Member States decided to create an Economic and Monetary Union (EMU), which sets out to create a single currency in the EU, some scholars have pointed to economic and political factors that have favoured the general European integration process. But why was it deemed necessary to give up national currencies as part of this process? The introduction of a single currency in Europe far precedes the creation of a European nation-state. The decision to give up national currencies is particularly puzzling because a considerable portion of the citizens in a number of countries oppose the idea of abolishing their national currency in favour of a European currency, and in other countries only a minority supports the Euro.[1]

This chapter examines why European national currencies, some of them internationally respectable ones, are seemingly 'easily' given up, in favour of a supranational currency. In order to understand what made this currency revolution possible the chapter looks at the specific circumstances under which the EMU project took off and the broader context in which this development has taken place. The structure of the chapter is as follows. The first section gives a brief history of currency co-operation in Europe. The second section discusses the various economic reasons for the creation of a European single currency. As that section argues, there are good economic reasons for adopting a single currency in Europe. However, in order to understand fully why a single currency, and not another scenario, was envisaged, political factors will be explored. This is done in the third section. The fourth section briefly looks into the reasons behind the political and popular opposition to the single currency. The final section draws some conclusions.

Historical background

In order to understand the crossroads at which European nation-states stand it is important to have some sense of their history. This section discusses the general European integration process with particular emphasis on monetary co-operation and the circumstances under which EMU came on the European agenda.

Currencies in European nation-states have had multiple functions over the past centuries (see the Introduction and chapters in the first part of this volume). During some periods they were considered less important political symbols than at other times. Sometimes multiple currencies circulated in any given country. Even monetary unions were created.[2] It was not until the nineteenth century that European nation-states began to have fully developed national monetary systems, with a national currency being exclusive legal tender, and not until the early twentieth century that such national monetary systems became the norm across all of Europe.

After the Second World War government involvement in the economy increased dramatically. A larger proportion of Gross Domestic Product (GDP) was redistributed or spent by the government. The role that national currencies played in each country's national collective identity intensified at this point. State power over the economy made national monetary authorities keen on exerting control over the national currency and they limited or banned the use of foreign currencies. Yet, it was recognised that fixing exchange rates *vis-à-vis* the currencies of neighbouring countries could be beneficial, especially in a geographical area with significant cross-border trading. Fixed exchange rates would increase international trade and economic transactions. Also, it was considered important that traders remain confident that currencies would retain their value. Finally, it was thought that fixed exchange rates could well expand the political power of the area.

However when the first post-1945 multilateral economic co-operation occurred in Western Europe, no reference was made to fixed exchange rates or a monetary union. The European Economic Community (EEC)[3] focused on trade and aimed at setting up a customs union. It was only in 1971 that the first plan was adopted to create an Economic and Monetary Union (EMU) in the EC. It was to achieve irrevocably fixed exchange rates, with perhaps a single currency. There would be free movement of goods, services, labour and capital (four freedoms). In addition, some macroeconomic policies would have to be co-ordinated.

The decision to adopt the EMU plan in 1971 was in response to a number of factors. Considerable success had been achieved by 1968 in creating the customs union. At the same time one of the most important common EEC policies, the

Common Agricultural Policy (CAP), was working successfully. But it was clear that the CAP would benefit most from guaranteed fixed exchange rates (Tsoukalis, 1977; Ungerer, 1997). Towards the late 1960s it was clear that for a variety of reasons fixed exchange rates were the preferred option of the EC Member States. As a result, in December 1969 the EC national governments proposed at the European Council meeting in The Hague to investigate the creation of a monetary union. A group of experts, the so-called 'Werner Group', was asked to draft a report. The resulting EMU blueprint (Werner Report 1970) was a messy compromise of two different approaches to achieve EMU: to obtain macroeconomic policy convergence and subsequently fix exchange rates, and vice versa. Their plan was adopted in 1971.

That EMU did not take off that decade was due to unfavourable international circumstances which occurred in the 1970s, i.e. the end of the Bretton Woods System, the 1973 oil crisis, inflation and recession, and, importantly, the diverging national responses to these challenges (Kruse, 1980). At the same time, the performance of the Keynesian Welfare State was becoming the subject of debate and with it a fundamental discussion about the role of the state in economic matters, the role of inflation and the causes of unemployment. By the late 1970s the tides had turned and anti-inflationary monetary policies came to steer monetary policies, most clearly in some countries such as West Germany, the Netherlands and the UK, and further into the 1980s in other countries such as France and Italy.[4]

Meanwhile, after the collapse of the Bretton Woods system the EC Member States had achieved some success in maintaining fixed exchange rates in Europe. In the 1970s a system known as 'the Snake' was adopted to fix the EC currencies. The Snake worked well for West Germany and a handful of smaller EC and non-EC countries, but Britain and France left the Snake. Britain left the Snake in June 1972, only three months after its initiation. France withdrew in January 1974, rejoined in July 1975 and withdrew once and for all in March 1976. Towards the end of the decade the EC countries wanted to re-create the Snake as an EC institution and give it a new start (Ludlow, 1982; Walsh, 1994). By 1979 the European Monetary System (EMS) was born. It contained an Exchange Rate Mechanism (ERM) similar to the Snake arrangement. All EC Member States joined the full EMS arrangement, except the UK that joined the EMS but stayed out of the ERM.[5]

At the outset in 1979 the EMS was not seen as a very promising project. Indeed it had a turbulent start with many currency realignments. But an important domestic turn-around in France in 1983 gave the EMS its first firm foundation, with the French socialist government adopting more stringent monetary policies (Goodman, 1989; Hall, 1986). From the mid 1980s most EC national governments had pegged their national currency *de facto* to the Deutschmark, which resulted in fewer currency alignments.

In response to a widespread view that Europe was losing competitiveness *vis-à-vis* the rest of the world the European integration process was revived in the mid-1980s. A new initiative was launched, the so-called '1992 programme', which would complete the creation of the EC Internal Market by the end of 1992. The aim was to abolish all remaining non-tariff barriers as well as harmonise standards so that trade could flow freely in the EC. The 1992 programme was translated into the 1985 Single European Act (SEA). The SEA mentioned the possible re-launch of EMU. In 1988 the European Council in Hannover instructed a group of experts to draft a possible blueprint for EMU. Commission President Jacques Delors presided over this expert committee which was composed of mostly central bank presidents.

The Delors Committee presented its report in April 1989 (Delors Report, 1989). Having learnt from the problems encountered by the Werner Group, it made clear choices about the minimum degree of institutional change and convergence needed before the exchange rates could be fixed. EMU would entail: (a) the 'four freedoms', i.e. freedom of goods, services, labour and capital; (b) a common competition policy; (c) binding rules and procedures on budgetary policy; (d) a single monetary policy based on price stability; (e) the creation of an independent European System of Central Banks which would consist of the existing central banks and a new European central bank (the ESCB would become solely responsible for EC monetary policy); and (f) irrevocably fixed exchange rates. The Delors Committee expressed a preference for a single currency to be introduced in the EC but left it to the politicians to determine whether that would be politically desirable.

The European Council in June 1989 adopted the Delors Report. It was used as the basis for the intergovernmental negotiations which were necessary to change the EEC Treaty. During these intergovernmental conferences (IGC) the Delors Committee's preference to adopt a single currency and abolish the national currencies found large support. A British proposal to have a parallel currency or 'hard ECU' (HM Treasury 1989) was considered, but soon abandoned.[6] The next item on the IGC agenda was to determine the criteria for entry, i.e. the macroeconomic and monetary conditions which countries needed to fulfil to join EMU. The EC Monetary Committee, in which monetary authorities of all EC member states are represented, decided to base the criteria for entry on purely monetary criteria: performance on exchange rates, inflation rates, budgetary deficits and public debts. These became known as the 'convergence criteria' (see Italianer, 1993). Privately a number of monetary experts in the 'core' countries thought that these criteria would keep the 'weaker' countries (e.g. the Mediterranean countries) from joining EMU at the outset (Verdun forthcoming). The institutional framework of EMU was eventually incorporated in the *Treaty on European Union*.[7] It envisaged a three-stage road to a single currency and specified the criteria for joining it, i.e. the convergence criteria.

Economics of EMU

The historical background in the previous section shows that European monetary integration is embedded in the larger European integration process as well as more general developments in the global economy. But these two factors alone only partly explain why EMU occurred. In addition, there is a complex set of other economic and political factors that led to Member States' enthusiasm for EMU. The following sections differentiate between so-called 'economic' and 'political' factors, even though these categories are to a certain degree artificial. This section highlights the economic reasons for the choice of EMU and analyses to what extent these factors can explain why the introduction of a single currency became the preferred option. As will be argued, a mere economic analysis does not fully explain the outcome. Political factors need to be taken into consideration as well, which is done in the next section.

First of all, EMU was a reaction to a successful EMS and the effort of European national governments to fix exchange rates among most of the European states ever since the end of the Second World War. This aim had wide support. It was considered good for trade and an excellent tool to reduce inflation. Member States wanted to give a strong signal to the markets that terms of trade between Member States would continue to be fixed. Irrevocably fixed exchange rates do not give such a strong signal to the markets as a single currency does. Most Member State governments were strengthened in this conviction when the Exchange Rate Mechanism (ERM) virtually collapsed as a result of exchange rate turmoil in 1992–93 (Gros and Thygesen, 1998).[8] Moreover, the European single currency would further reduce transactions costs on intra-European trade (Taylor, 1995).

The EMS experience also made clear to national Member States, that monetary sovereignty in a regime of fixed exchange rates is strongly restricted, especially in an atmosphere of high capital mobility. This was true even for West Germany, although to a lesser extent. In the last instance Member States could pursue deviating policies, but increasingly they perceived national sovereignty over monetary policies as having been lost. The experience of France in the mid-1980s and Italy during the 1980s had made that sufficiently clear (Blanchard and Muet, 1993). Hence the step from EMS to EMU was not such a large step. EMU to a certain extent would institutionalise choices made under EMS. These choices had increasingly led European governments to prioritise the same low inflation objectives.

Reinforcing this trend was the fact that by the late 1980s, two economic ideas had been abandoned (Marcussen, 1997; McNamara, 1998). One was the notion that there was a trade-off between inflation and unemployment. The other was the belief that competitive devaluations were good for economic development. Capital markets would 'punish' currencies which could potentially devalue, and European governments frequently experienced that devaluations led to inflation due to the way higher import prices fed through in prices and wages (Gros, 1996). In other words, monetary policy learning had occurred, and economic ideas about inflation and devaluation had changed and converged (Goodman, 1992).

At the same time, the institutional structure of central banks and the variety of success in monetary policy as a factor of the institutional structure became the focus of attention. It became clear that capital markets judged national monetary policy on the basis of its past track-record, as well as on the probability that the monetary authorities in power would cause inflation. Countries which had independent central banks, that is, whose central bank presidents could not be instructed by elected politicians (e.g. those of the German and Dutch central banks) could more easily convince capital markets that they were truly committed to low inflation. As a result a lower risk premium was paid, lowering interest rates. The experiences of the 1980s highlighted the importance of credibility and stability of monetary policies and emphasised the value of placing monetary policies out of the hands of national politicians (Woolley, 1992).

In other words, for a variety of economic reasons Member State governments wanted to safeguard fixed terms of trade. So far this goal had been based on the EMS. In addition they wanted to achieve price stability. Successful monetary policies had been conducted by those countries that had an independent central bank and where an anti-inflationary monetary policy was pursued, the leading example being Germany. Hence when considering progress towards more European monetary integration it was going to be based on both the general principles of European integration, but take as model the successful West-German institutional structure (an independent central bank) and German monetary policy practices (maintaining price stability). Hence the Euro and the European Central Bank will not be fully alien entities. On paper they are new but as far as political culture, policy objectives and institutional structure are concerned, Germany has been taken as the model.

The economic objectives of creating fixed terms of trade to increase trade and welfare, and achieving price stability could have been achieved in more than one way. A single currency was not the only remedy. Member States could have just maintained the fixed exchange rate regime while strengthening certain elements of the EMS, or they could have introduced a new parallel currency, as the British suggested, or even an existing parallel currency. So the puzzle remains: why were Member States so convinced of the need to create an EMU, i.e. why give up national sovereignty and replace well-functioning currencies with a previously non-existent supranational currency when in theory other options were possible? To find the answer one needs to look at political reasons behind the creation of EMU, to which we now turn.

Politics of EMU

Let us turn to those other options and analyse whether they would have been politically feasible. First of all, it could have been possible to introduce a new parallel currency, as the British government proposed. Yet, most other national governments realised that the British government put forward this alternative to distract other Member States from seriously considering the adoption of a single currency. Moreover, except for the British government, everybody was convinced a thirteenth currency would not be used as it would circulate parallel to well-functioning existing currencies. Especially if the aim was to have it replace the existing currency, this was not a viable solution. There would be no interest in changing to the new currency. In contrast to what happened for example in Eastern Europe, where the Deutschmark and the dollar had often taken over the functions of the national currencies, there was nothing wrong with the national currencies of the EC Member States.

Another alternative would have been to adopt the Deutschmark as legal tender besides the national currencies in the rest of Europe. This so-called parallel adoption of the leading currency is typically what happens in countries where the national currency is weak (Central and South America, and Eastern Europe). Yet, for two reasons the adoption of the Deutschmark as a parallel currency would not be acceptable to the EC Member States.

A first important political reason is that it is unacceptable in Europe to have one country dominate the other Member States. Europe is made up of small and medium-sized countries and no single country has a clear leadership over all other countries in terms of size or clear economic dominance. The adoption of the Deutschmark might well create the impression that the other nations are subordinated by Germany. Moreover, the EC was created to make the countries of Europe co-operate and not be dominated by one country.

In addition, the adoption of the Deutschmark would not be attractive because Member States would want a common currency to be managed by all Member States via a *European* institution – not by having one nation's central bank determine its monetary policy. If the Deutschmark were adopted it would not be easy to achieve a truly European institutional framework. The German central bank (the Bundesbank) would not voluntarily start sharing the responsibility to monitor the Deutschmark with the governments of the other Member States.

Another powerful political reason why EMU came to the fore was that for many Member States the status quo became less tolerable. Though the EMS was very successful during the 1980s it had increasingly become centred around the Deutschmark. Dominance by any single EC country is difficult to accept within the European context, but German dominance is for historical reasons even less acceptable. In addition to the asymmetry in the EMS, almost all Member States had meanwhile learnt the lesson that monetary policies deviating from those in Germany were punished by financial markets. National monetary authorities had decided that fixed exchange rates and low inflation comprised the desired regime, that small deviations were undesirable, and that following German policies was a successful strategy. In other words the status quo displayed a clear dependence on German monetary policies and practices.

Thus, the countries that had been closely following German monetary policies, such as France and the Benelux countries, wanted to create a more formal European institutional framework in which monetary polices were conducted at the European level. That way the system would remain *de facto* the same, but they would have formal decision-making power. Monetary policy would not purely be based on German domestic politics. The economically 'weaker' countries, i.e. Spain, Portugal, Ireland and Greece, also wanted to make sure that they could join the 'club'. At the same time they bargained for larger transfer payments from the richer to the poorer regions in parallel with arrangements on monetary union (Martin, 1993).

More generally, with the anticipated completion of the Internal Market and the successful functioning of the EMS up to the late 1980s, those in favour of European integration saw EMU as a project that would keep the integration process going. They felt that the EC was in need of a clear political symbol of European unity. A single currency would provide such a symbol. A functional mode of reasoning could have been in the back of the minds of some; the single currency would make clear the need for further political integration. Without gradual integration, and step-by-step integration, it is impossible to move a step further towards European unity – so the functional argument goes (cf. Sandholtz, 1993). Others had more realistic objectives; by having its own single currency and integrating its countries even further, the EU would become a more powerful player in the world. The Euro would possibly become a leading trade and reserve currency, competing with the dollar (Verdun, 1998a). In addition there would be seigniorage gains for Europe from this development (De Grauwe, 1997). In other words, the creation of the Euro would be one way to try to combat Europe's lost international political and economic power.

Let us now turn to the countries with a more sceptical attitude towards European integration, such as the UK and Denmark. The reasons for this scepticism are described in the next section, but why did the governments of these countries agree to participate in the EMU negotiation process? The UK government participated in the EMU negotiation process because they wanted to avoid a repetition of history.[9] Once the British government realised that a critical mass was considering EMU it made sure that it fully participated in EMU negotiations and did not obstruct an agreement that all countries wanted. At the same time British negotiators tried to limit the extent of political integration that would accompany the introduction of a single currency and safeguard their own opt-out. The Danish case is quite different. In Denmark the government and the political elites are in favour of EMU. Here it is the Danish citizens that are sceptical about EMU (Iversen and Thygesen, 1998).

If it is clear that several Member States favoured EMU because they wanted to Europeanise a *de facto* dominance by Germany, it is interesting to turn to Germany itself. Why was Germany in favour of EMU?[10] There are several reasons. The German government favoured increased monetary integration, because of its genuine pro-European stance. Also, it had been favouring in particular monetary integration provided the conditions were right (i.e. convergence before fixing exchange rates). In fact, the German government supported the 1988 proposal to investigate the creation of EMU. Second, as some observers emphasised, German monetary policies noticed the effects from other countries following German monetary policies. By setting European-wide standards for monetary policies, everyone would be pursuing policies that the German monetary authorities considered best. Finally, after the Cold War ended and Germany reunified, the German government felt an even stronger need to show its commitment to European integration. It must be noted, however, that the German government was in favour of EMU even before it was clear that the Iron Curtain would be lifted and the Wall would be torn down. Thus, the German government's positive attitude can only be explained by assuming that the Germans were in favour of the integration project more generally, confident that EMU would resemble a German model of monetary policy-making, and that countries not yet ready to join would be kept out.

Resistance to EMU

Let us now turn to some sources of resistance to the introduction of a single currency, problems with the institutional design and the specific role of national currencies for national identity in some Member States.

Let us first examine some general reasons for resistance to EMU. There is the problem that the European currency will be introduced representing a 'half way house'. The European Union is more than an international organisation, but less than a nation-state. Where it particularly falls short is in providing a democratically elected government that runs the economy on a day-to-day basis. The EU's budget is close to negligible (1.27 per cent maximum of EU GDP). There is a clear asymmetry built into the design of EMU. It will feature a fully developed monetary policy and yet macroeconomic policy will remain the responsibility of individual Member States (Verdun, 1996). There will be a European Central Bank responsible for a single monetary policy, yet at the EU level there will be no 'economic government' to flank this monetary institution.[11] This design stands in large contrast to what is the case in individual nation-states, be they federal or unitary states. Yet, Member State governments have not been opposed to this institutional design. On the contrary, almost all have opposed transfer of sovereignty over macroeconomic and fiscal policy to the EU level.

The EU national governments seem to be of the opinion that EMU will imply a pure institutionalisation of policies already pursued in Europe today, and do not anticipate major change. By contrast, many citizens are unsure about what this means for the governability of the country. They want to know the costs and benefits of EMU. Even if EMU were good in the long run, they wonder who will pay for the adjustment in the short and medium term. Citizens of low-inflation countries are afraid of higher inflation. In richer countries they fear eventually having to agree to larger transfer payments to poorer Member States. In poorer Member States citizens are concerned that restructuring would in the short run imply higher unemployment and slower growth. Connected to this is the general public's lack of understanding of the EU integration project. Some think EMU would imply more political integration, which they dread. Others think that political integration will still take some time, and are concerned about insufficient political integration.

Basically, citizens concerned about EMU worry that they would not any more be able to rely on their national governments to look after their specific interests. They are confused about the powers of the European Union, how the EU is governed, and are concerned about the EU not being able to safeguard their specific as well as general interests such as economic growth and employment (Verdun, 1998b). Some are concerned that EMU would lead to more equal spread of the costs and benefits of European integration. Others fear the exact opposite, i.e. the fair spread of costs and benefits throughout the EU!

Next to these general concerns that citizens have, the general public in some countries are more reserved about EMU than in others. National currencies do not have the same meaning for national identity in all countries. This is of course also true in Europe (cf. Helleiner, 1998). Let us examine the role of the national currency in Germany, the UK, and Scandinavia.

Germany is a particular case. The role of the Deutschmark for the German people cannot easily be compared to that of any other nation in Europe. After having suffered hyper-inflation in 1923, its citizens were very much opposed to inflation. In addition, the First and Second World Wars shattered Germany's self-image, leaving many Germans ashamed of their German nationality. It was difficult to re-create the state and a sense of national identity with very few things in recent history to be proud of (see Engelmann *et al.*, 1997). The German Deutschmark and German *Wirtschaftswunder* (economic miracle) became the core of German identity. It is therefore no surprise that the Deutschmark is not easily given up. Over the past 70 years Germany went through many currency changes. Now that it has a successful formula citizens are unhappy to give it up. Moreover, they only recently experienced German reunification in which the Ost-Mark was abolished and converted to the Deutschmark on a one-to-one basis. The Germans in former Eastern Germany in particular have been subject to major political and economic changes this century. One of their main motivations for reunification had been to acquire the Deutschmark.[12]

The UK is another case whereby the national currency has symbolised more than just legal tender (Helleiner, 1998). Less than a century ago, the pound sterling was the world's leading currency. Moreover, the British government has been filled with 'reluctant Europeans' ever since the EC was founded. To replace the British national currency by a European currency is just one bridge too far for the UK government and for many of the British people. This opposition to the abolition of the pound is based on more than just opposing the fact that the 'Queen's Head' will be taken off the banknotes; the pound sterling is a political and economic institution. The more sceptical voices also emphasise that the British economy is often half a year ahead of the business cycle in continental Europe. Advocates of EMU in Britain, in turn, point out that most of British trade is with the rest of Europe. Hence staying outside EMU seems unwise.

The Scandinavian countries are the other countries in which strong opposition to EMU has been voiced.[13] These countries have an interesting history. They co-operated long before they joined the EU. As regards international politics they have tried to stay neutral whenever possible. The Scandinavian nation-states have a strong sense of national identity and sovereignty. The reason that both Denmark and Sweden do not want to join EMU at the outset is that public support for transfer of monetary sovereignty to the European level is lacking. By contrast, the political elites in these countries are generally in favour of participation in EMU (Moses, 1998b; Iversen and Thygesen, 1998). Public opinion in Finland, by contrast, is more pro-European mainly for political reasons. There is support for continuing a process of economic restructuring that has been going on since the 1990s, which EMU will intensify. There is a widespread public belief that monetary policies are currently 'made in Germany' and that participation in EMU will imply a larger Finnish say over monetary policies than is currently the case (Moses, 1998a).

Yet, even though some citizens are more sceptical about the introduction of the Euro, the Member State governments seem to have much less difficulty abandoning national currencies. The difference is that the national governments have evaluated the *de facto* limit on monetary policymaking, and do not appear to see the symbolic value of a currency as being all that important. By contrast, the citizens, who may not have a lot of time and interest to comprehend fully what state sovereignty implies in contemporary Europe, and who may not have realised how little nation-state sovereignty has been exercised in the monetary area in recent years, still *do* have a desire for political symbols and identity. Many are weary of change. They are happy with their national currency and do not see the problem that a single currency will allegedly have to solve.

Ultimately the single currency may help to accelerate political integration in Europe, and contribute to building a European identity. Yet, many citizens of the fifteen EU Member States do not feel solidarity and fraternity towards neighbouring citizens in other European Member States. This absence of a European identity makes them more sceptical towards giving up their currency. Many Europeans are also concerned about the open-endedness of what is coming, as well as the realisation that to regain national monetary sovereignty implies putting the European integration project at risk. Despite these general concerns, most national governments of the EU Member States push ahead with EMU because of the important economic and political reasons outlined in the previous section.

Conclusions

This chapter has examined why European currencies will be abandoned and replaced by a supranational currency. The introduction of a single currency in Europe can only be understood if one takes into account the exact circumstances and conditions under which the process has been taking place.

History shows that European monetary integration is a gradual process which has taken place in the second half of the twentieth century. A number of reasons explain why the adoption of a single currency was the logical step forward. EMU followed the successful exchange rate co-operation in the EC, the 1992 initiative to complete the Internal Market, and the idea that Europe needed to integrate further to cope with globalisation and increased international competitiveness. Economic and Monetary Union in Europe is thus happening partly because European countries wanted to move ahead in a process of economic and political integration.

The status quo was also no longer acceptable for other reasons. An important factor was that German monetary policy was *de facto* determining other

Member States' national monetary policies. This was politically an undesirable situation for many countries, though economically they were convinced of its usefulness. Member State governments thought that only limited *real* sovereignty would be transferred to the European level if they moved towards EMU, as they had already chosen to gear monetary policies towards those pursued in Germany.

Furthermore it was widely believed that monetary sovereignty had been an illusion for several decades. In an integrated market, the pursuit of independent national monetary policies would be punished by capital markets. Monetary authorities had already made the choice for fixed exchange rates and low inflation. The question that remained was how to safeguard those choices. Hence, a single monetary policy and a single currency were not considered a great sacrifice of national sovereignty.

To create EMU the German model has been copied relentlessly. National Member State governments have made educated guesses that this institutional structure will safeguard the independent conduct of monetary policy and thus guarantee price stability. They assume that their interest will remain convergent and that price and exchange rate stability (a single currency) will continue to be their number one priority.

Problems with EMU occur because it is unclear whether its institutional design is adequate to sustain monetary integration in the years to come. In addition, national currencies and national monetary policy remain important elements of national collective identity for many people. In most European countries public opinion favours the introduction of a single currency. Yet, public opinion is opposed to EMU in countries where the national currency has formed an important part of national identity or where general scepticism exists towards the broader European integration project.

The logic of giving up national currencies in Europe is that EMU is carefully designed to institutionalise at the European level a regime of monetary policy-making which has existed in Europe since the 1980s which to date has been dominated by Germany. In addition, EMU is linked to the broader process of accelerating European integration. But the introduction of the Euro remains an unprecedented step and there are many sources of opposition to it. Only time will tell whether Europe's single currency will survive the tests of time.

Acknowledgements

The author would like to thank Michaela Dabringhausen, Eric Helleiner and Paul Schure for useful comments on an earlier draft. The usual disclaimer applies.

Notes

1 According to *Eurobarometer*, at the end of 1996 a majority of the citizens in Denmark, Sweden, the UK and Finland were against the introduction of a single currency. On average in these countries roughly 60 per cent was against the

introduction of a single currency, 30 per cent was in favour and 10 per cent held no opinion. In other countries, such as Austria, Germany and Portugal, support for the single currency was less than 50 per cent of the citizens. However, if the citizens of the 15 Member States are taken together the picture changes: 51 per cent favours the introduction of the single currency, 33 per cent is opposed and 16 per cent has no opinion (European Commission, 1997). In the spring of 1997 support for the single currency dropped. Now 47 per cent was in favour, 40 per cent against and 13 per cent had no opinion (European Commission, 1998).

2 Examples of monetary unions – in which member countries allow other member countries' coins to circulate – included the Latin Monetary Union set up in 1865 and the Scandinavian Monetary Union set up in the early 1870s (see Dyson, 1994). These monetary unions were established without political union. Monetary unions also occurred when states were unified. Examples are German and Italian unification in the nineteenth century, and German reunification in 1990. In these cases political and monetary unification went hand in hand.

3 The EEC was set up in 1957 by the Benelux countries, France, Italy and West Germany. The EEC, the European Atomic Energy Community and the European Community for Coal and Steel formed the three European Communities (EC). In 1993 they were incorporated into the Treaty of European Union (TEU) which created the European Union (EU).

4 West Germany had been pursuing anti-inflationary monetary policies for several decades.

5 Most Member States' currencies could float 2.25 per cent from a given parity. Some currencies, e.g. the Italian lira, were given a wider band of 6 per cent.

6 ECU = European Currency Unit, the term used for the European single currency prior to the official decision in 1996 to name it the 'Euro'. The ECU was the unit of account used in the ERM and EMS.

7 The Treaty on European Union, the so-called 'Maastricht Treaty', changed the EEC Treaty in a number of important ways. It incorporated the three original EC Treaties and extended the possible area of activity so as to include a Common Foreign and Security Policy as well as Justice and Home Affairs.

8 Many economists warned during the 1980s and early 1990s that although the EMS had become a political symbol of successful European integration, the underlying real economic 'fundamentals' did not support the exchange rates. They warned that eventually a re-adjustment would be necessary. They proved to be right. In 1992–93 and again in 1996, exchange-rate turbulence struck the European currency markets, resulting in a stretching of the small margins of fluctuation from ±2.25 to ±15 (with the exception of the Deutschmark/Guilder parity which remained unchanged).

9 In the 1950s the UK government did not want to join the EC. When the UK first applied for membership the French president De Gaulle vetoed British EC membership for at least a decade. During that period rules and codes of conduct had been made. Once they joined they had to accept the entire package which they had obviously not helped shape.

10 The German foreign minister Hans-Dietrich Genscher was among the first to re-launch the EMU initiative. Chancellor Helmut Kohl soon picked up the idea. The German Bundesbank was long quite sceptical of the idea. It feared that monetary policies could become more relaxed if countries with less strong commitment to price stability joined EMU.

11 The French in particular favoured the establishment of a European 'economic government'.
12 It was the fear of mass migration that led the German Chancellor Helmut Kohl to agree to a speedy German reunification (political union), and that German monetary union would occur with an exchange rate favourable to the East Germans.
13 None of the Scandinavian countries was among the founding fathers of the EC. Denmark joined in 1973 whereas Finland and Sweden joined in 1995. Norway is not a member because its citizens rejected membership in a referendum (see Sciarini and Listhaug, 1997).

Bibliography

Blanchard, O.J. and Muet, P.A. (1993) 'Competitiveness through disinflation: an assessment of the French macroeconomic strategy' *Economic Policy* 16: 11–56.

Commission of the EC (1977) *Report of the Study Group on the Role of Public Finance in European Integration*, vols 1 and 2 'MacDougall Report', Brussels, Commission of the European Communities, Doc II/10/77, April.

De Grauwe, P. (1997) *The Economics of Monetary Integration*, 3rd edition, Oxford: Oxford University Press.

Delors Report (1989) *Report on Economic and Monetary Union in the European Community* (Committee for the Study of Economic and Monetary Union), Luxembourg: Office for Official Publications of the E.C.

Dyson, K. (1994) *Elusive Union: The Process of Economic and Monetary Union in Europe*, London and New York: Longman.

Eichengreen, B. (1993) 'Is Europe an optimum currency area?', in S.Silvio and H.Grubel, eds, *The European Community after 1992: Perspectives from the Outside*, London: Macmillan: 138–61.

Engelmann, D., Knopf, H-J, Roscher K. and Risse-Kappen, T. (1997), 'Identity politics in the European Union: the case of Economic and Monetary Union', in P.Minkkinen and H.Patomäki, eds, *The Politics of Economic and Monetary Union*, Boston/Dordrecht/London: Kluwer: 105–32.

European Commission (1993a) 'The economics of community public finance', *European Economy* 5.

European Commission (1993b) 'Stable money – sound finances: Community public finance in the perspective of EMU' *European Economy* 53.

European Commission (1997) *Eurobarometer Public Opinion in the European Union, Report Number 46*, Brussels: European Commission.

European Commission (1998) *Eurobarometer Public Opinion in the European Union, Report Number 47*, Brussels: European Commission.

Genscher, H-D. (1988) 'Memorandum für die Schaffung eines europäischen Währungsrampes und einer europäischen Zentralbank' *Diskussionsgrundlage*, Bonn, 26 February.

Goodman, J.B. (1989), 'Monetary policy in France, Italy, and Germany: 1973–85', in P. Guerrieri and P.C. Padoan, eds, *The Political Economy of European Integration: States Markets and Institutions*, New York: Harvester Wheatsheaf: 171–201.

Goodman, J.B. (1992) *Monetary Sovereignty: The Politics of Central Banking in Western Europe*, Ithaca and London: Cornell University Press.

Gros, D. (1996) 'Towards Economic and Monetary Union: problems and prospects' CEPS

Paper No. 65, Brussels: CEPS.

Gros, D. and Thygesen, N. (1998) *European Monetary Integration: From the European Monetary System to Economic and Monetary Union*, 2nd edition, Harlow Essex/New York: Longman.

Hall, P.A. (1986) *Governing the Economy: The Politics of State Intervention in Britain and France*, New York: Oxford University Press.

Hall, P.A. (1994), 'Central bank independence and co-ordinated wage bargaining: their interaction in Germany and Europe' *German Politics and Society* 31 (Spring): 1–23.

Helleiner, E. (1998) 'National currencies and national identities', *American Behavioral Scientist* 41, 10: 1409–36.

Henning, C. R. (1994) *Currencies and Politics in the United States, Germany, and Japan*, Washington D.C.: Institute for International Economics.

HM Treasury (1989) 'An evolutionary approach to EMU', mimeo, November.

Italianer, A. (1993) 'Mastering Maastricht: EMU Issues and how they were settled', in K. Gretschmann, ed. *Economic and Monetary Union: Implications for National Policy-Makers*, Maastricht: European Institute of Public Administration: 51–115.

Iversen, T. and Thygesen, N. (1998), 'Denmark: from external to internal adjustment', in E. Jones, J. Frieden and F. Torres, eds, *Joining Europe's Monetary Club: The Challenges for Smaller Member States*, New York: St Martin's Press: 61–82.

Kennedy, E. (1991) *The Bundesbank: Germany's Central Bank in the International Monetary System*, London: Pinter.

Kruse, D.C. (1980) *Monetary Integration in Western Europe: EMU, EMS and Beyond*, London and Boston: Butterworths.

Ludlow, P. (1982) *The Making of the European Monetary System: A Case Study of the Politics of the European Community*, London: Butterworth Scientific.

McNamara, K.R. (1998) *The Currency of Ideas: Monetary Politics in the European Union*, Ithaca: Cornell University Press.

McNamara, K.R. and Jones, E. (1996) 'The clash of institutions: Germany in European monetary affairs' *German Politics and Society* 14, 3: 5–30.

Marcussen, M. (1997) 'The role of "ideas" in Dutch, Danish and Swedish economic policy in the 1980s and the beginning of the 1990s', in P. Minkkinen and H. Patomäki, eds, *The Politics of Economic and Monetary Union*, Boston/Dordrecht/London: Kluwer: 76–104.

Martin, L. (1993) 'International and domestic institutions in the EMU process' *Economics and Politics* 5, 2: 125–45.

Moses, J.W. (1998a), 'Finland and EMU' in E. Jones, J. Frieden and F. Torres, eds, *Joining Europe's Monetary Club: The Challenges for Smaller Member States*, New York: St Martin's Press: 83–104.

Moses, J.W. (1998b), 'Sweden and EMU' in E. Jones, J. Frieden and F. Torres, eds, *Joining Europe's Monetary Club: The Challenges for Smaller Member States*, New York: St Martin's Press: 203–24.

Sandholtz, W. (1993) 'Choosing union: monetary politics and Maastricht' *International Organization* 47, 1: 1–39.

Sciarini, P. and Listhaug O. (1997) 'Single cases or a unique pair? The Swiss and Norwegian "No" to Europe' *Journal of Common Market Studies* 35, 3: 407–38.

Taylor, C. (1995) *EMU 2000? Prospects for European Monetary Union*, London: Royal Institute of International Affairs.

Tsoukalis, L. (1977) *The Politics and Economics of European Monetary Integration*, London: George Allen and Unwin.

Ungerer, H. (1997) *A Concise History of European Monetary Integration: From EPU to EMU*, Westport CT/London: Quorum Books.

Verdun, A. (1996) 'An "asymmetrical" Economic and Monetary Union in the EU: perceptions of monetary authorities and social partners' *Journal of European Integration/Revue d'Integration Européenne* 20, 1: 59–81.

Verdun, A. (1998a) 'The international aspects of the EU's exchange rate policy: European integration and dollar dominance', in A. Cafruny and P. Peters, eds, *The Union and the World*, London: Kluwer: 175–89.

Verdun, A. (1998b) 'The Institutional Design of EMU: A Democratic Deficit?' *Journal of Public Policy* 18, 2: 107–32.

Verdun, A. (forthcoming) *European Responses to Globalization and Financial Market Integration. Perceptions of Economic and Monetary Union in Britain, France and Germany*, London: Macmillan, New York: St. Martin's Press.

Wallace, H. (1993) 'European governance in turbulent times' *Journal of Common Market Studies* 31, 3: 293–303.

Walsh, J. (1994) 'Politics and exchange rates: Britain, France, Italy, and the negotiation of the European Monetary System' *Journal of Public Policy* 14, 3: 345–69.

Werner Report (1970), 'Report to the Council and the Commission on the realization by stages of Economic and Monetary Union in the Community', Council and Commission of the EC, *Bulletin of the EC*, Supplement 11, Doc 16.956/11/70, 8 October.

Woolley, J.T. (1992) 'Policy credibility and European monetary institutions', in A.Sbragia, ed. *Europolitics*, Washington DC: Brookings Institution: 157–90.

12 Conclusion – the future of national currencies?

Eric Helleiner

Introduction

National currencies are neither the necessary nor the inevitable outcome of the historical development of money. As the first part of this volume illustrates, money was organised quite differently before their emergence. Moreover, even as national currencies became the predominant form of organising money in the nineteenth and twentieth centuries, they have never been completely homogenous. Various forms of alternative currencies have often circulated alongside national currencies, and national currencies have also been earmarked in various ways, undermining their apparent homogeneity. Also, some countries – such as the African members of the CFA franc zone – have never had a national currency. Others do not have as absolute a national currency as is sometimes suggested; for example, in their proud defence of Great Britain's national currency, many in England forget that private banks still issue different 'national' notes only for circulation in Scotland.

If the historical perspective of the chapters in the first part of this volume reminds us that national currencies – like the nation-states that contributed to their production – are the deliberate social construction of a certain period, the chapters in the second part discuss various ways in which these national currencies are now increasingly challenged across the world. Let us briefly review these various challenges.

One challenge comes from proposals to create supranational currencies. The best known initiative of this kind exists in Europe, where eleven members of the European Union have agreed to eliminate their national currencies altogether in favour of a supranational currency by 2002 (see Chapter 11). Proposals for similar initiatives have also been discussed in other regions too, such as in North America (e.g. Federal Reserve Bank of Kansas City, 1991), East Asia (Lucas, 1998), and among the countries of Mercosur: Brazil, Argentina, Uruguay and Paraguay (see Giambiagi, 1998). Many nationalist movements today seeking separation from nation-states in these regions – as, for example, in Scotland or Quebec – are also strong supporters of these supranational currency proposals, thus signalling an interesting departure from most historical nationalist movements that have traditionally understood the creation of a new national currency as an integral part of their political project to build a nation-state.

The growing use of foreign currencies alongside domestic currencies within national territories represents the second challenge; we might refer to this as a 'transnational' – as opposed to 'supranational' – threat to national currencies. One example of this phenomenon is the increasingly widespread currency substitution that has taken place in many countries across the 'South' and in the ex-Eastern bloc over the last two decades (see Chapter 7). In some countries, foreign currencies – usually US dollars – are used primarily as a unit of account or as a store of value. In other cases where currency substitution is very pervasive, they also become an important means of exchange even at the retail level. Indeed, currency substitution is so pervasive in some places today that foreign currencies make up the bulk of the country's money supply. Some 'Southern' countries – such as Argentina – have also recently introduced currency boards which institutionalise the practice of currency substitution by encouraging the use of a foreign currency alongside the domestic currency as a key element of monetary reform.

Another example of the growing use of foreign currencies involves the dramatic rise of 'eurocurrency' financial activity since the 1960s (see Chapters 9 and 10). Eurocurrency activity involves financial activity denominated in a currency other than that issued by the country in which the activity takes place. In the early years of the growth of the eurocurrency market, this primarily involved dollar-based activity in London. But today it also involves yen, sterling and many other currencies in financial centres around the world. Eurocurrency markets are no longer just marginal segments of the global financial system as they were in the early days of the market's growth; rather, they have now become among the most important financial markets in the world.

The final kind of challenge to national currencies is a subnational one. To date, the prime example of this kind of challenge involves the emergence of the 'local currencies' that are mentioned briefly by a number of the contributors to this volume (see Chapters 4, 7 and 9). Since the early 1980s, hundreds of these subnational currencies have been created in countries ranging from Australia and Sweden to Japan and Canada. In most cases, the local currencies are forms of money that are denominated in a national currency but are not convertible into it. They serve simply as a means of exchange within a clearly defined local community network. In some instances – such as the well-known 'Ithaca Hours' – local currencies are issued in a physical form as a paper note. In many other instances – such as the popular Local Exchange Trading Systems (LETS) – the currency exists primarily just as a book-keeping entry usable only by the local network of hundreds of 'local currency' members (e.g. Solomon, 1996).

One other kind of private currency is increasingly being discussed as a possible challenge to national currencies. This would be issued not by communities only for local use but rather by private corporations or banks for use by the public at large. To date, this kind of private money has not yet emerged on a large scale anywhere in the world. But as is discussed below, the emergence of 'electronic money' is touted by some as the key catalyst enabling this kind of private currency to be issued in a widespread manner in ways that would challenge the state's monopoly over money (Kobrin, 1997).

It is clear, then, that we live at a time when serious questions are being raised about the future of national currencies. What are the sources of these increasing challenges to national currencies today? And what is the significance of the erosion of national currencies for the nation-state? The chapters in the second half of this volume make clear that these questions are difficult to answer at a general level because the nature of these challenges differs considerably in various parts of the world. The causes and implications of the introduction of a supranational currency in Europe may be quite different from those associated with currency substitution in Latin America or the growing use of local currencies in other regions. Also complicating the analysis is the varying intensity of the challenges to national currencies in different parts of the world. While many European countries are well on their way to abandoning national currencies altogether, new nation-states in Eastern Europe and the ex-Soviet Union are often quite committed to defending the national currencies that they have only recently introduced.

Despite these complexities, the fact that national currencies are being called into question in such a widespread manner in this era does call out for a more general analysis of the causes of this phenomenon and its implications for the nation-state. In this concluding chapter, I seek to present this kind of analysis as a way of tying together many of the themes raised by the chapters in this volume. In addition to drawing upon many of the arguments raised in the chapters in the second half of the volume, I suggest that the historical themes outlined in the introductory chapter and the first half of the volume about the relationship between the emergence of national currencies and nation-states are useful in this task.

Why are national currencies being challenged in such a widespread way?

As was argued in the introductory chapter of this book, the origins of national currencies can be located in many of the broader historical processes that accompanied the rise of nation-states in the nineteenth and twentieth centuries; the growth of the state's administrative capacity, the rise of industrial capitalism, expanding fiscal needs of the state, and emerging nationalist sentiments. If national currencies are being called into question today, some causes are likely to found by exploring the extent to which these earlier historical processes, and the historical structures that they created, are being transcended and transformed.

Challenges to the administrative power of the nation-state, for example, are clearly playing a role in encouraging many of the contemporary currency transformations. It is not coincidental that currency substitution is often most prevalent today in those 'Southern' countries where the state's capacity to regulate and influence the activities of its citizens has been eroded (see Chapter

8). In some countries, this erosion has resulted from internal challenges to the state's authority, while in others external economic pressures have played the key role (particularly in the context of the international debt crisis that began in the early 1980s). In these situations, it is not just that states have been increasingly unable to enforce legal tender laws or influence monetary choices through their presence in the everyday economic activities of citizens. Equally important, the citizenry have often lost 'trust' in the state's ability to manage the national currency effectively, especially in the aftermath of experiences of high inflation. Indeed, a desire to recultivate this lost trust has been behind initiatives, such as that in Argentina, to allow a foreign currency – such as the US dollar – to circulate alongside the national one. The move is designed to send a signal to the population about the seriousness of the government's intent to reestablish the 'trustworthiness' of the national currency and state monetary managers by subjecting them to the 'competition' provided by a more 'credible' foreign currency.

In different ways, the growth of the offshore eurocurrency markets, the supranational currency in Europe, and local currencies have also benefited from the changing administrative capacity of states. As indicated in Chapter 10, the eurocurrency markets rely to a considerable extent on the decisions of leading states to cooperate in extending to the markets various regulatory frameworks and lender-of-last-resort activities (see also Kapstein, 1994). These practices have emerged in the context of increasingly intensive inter-state cooperation between financial and monetary officials from the dominant economic countries since the mid-1970s in bodies such as Bank for International Settlements. This 'internationalisation' of the state's administrative capabilities (Cox, 1987) has played a key role in encouraging private market actors to have confidence in the stability and trustworthiness of the new form of money, particularly in the wake of some key crisis moments over the past two decades.

More obviously, the supranational currency project in Europe is also linked to a broader integration process involving the expanding administrative capacity of regional Europe-wide institutions above individual nation-states. The Euro is, after all, to be managed on a day-to-day basis by a new European central bank. Trust in this institution's ability to manage the money has been cultivated in various ways, including a guarantee of its independence from government officials and the incorporation of clear principles by which the currency must be managed within its constitution. The various means to print money have also been standardised across participating nation-states to ensure the highest levels of security and quality. Regional bodies, such as the European Commission, have also actively promoted the Euro in various ways, such as soliciting feedback on the social and cultural impact of the introduction of the Euro from experts of different nationalities in the fields of psychology, history, law, economics, etc. Among those pilot schemes designed by the Commission to help integrate the Euro are those initiated to improve the public's financial literacy with tools for training and information, schemes that have also sought to target more vulnerable groups of people such as the illiterate.[1]

The growth of local currencies has also been linked in some contexts to the changing administrative capacity of the state. It is not that states have been unable to curtail the growth of these private subnational currencies. Most of the states where these currencies have proliferated certainly have the capacity to eliminate these forms of money if they so choose. That they have instead allowed their growth has been related in some countries to the recognition that local currencies can help to supplement the state's social service role *vis-à-vis* the unemployed in a period of budget constraints and government cutbacks. In Australia, for example, where local currencies have become very widespread, the state has actively encouraged their use for this reason (Williams, 1996).

A second important change fostering challenges to national currencies has been in the economic realm. If the emergence of national currencies was linked to the rise of industrial capitalism, alternative monetary arrangements emerging today are being encouraged by a dramatic restructuring of capitalism over the last two decades. This can be seen first by examining the changing technology of money itself.

The information technology revolution has played a key role in the recent restructuring of capitalism and information technologies have been applied more extensively to the monetary and financial sector than to any other sector of the world economy. These technologies first began to be used in a prevalent manner during the 1970s and 1980s in order to increase the efficiency of processing, storing and transmitting money at the wholesale level by large financial institutions. More recently, they have also come to play a vital role in retail financial transactions (e.g. credit and debit cards). As their use has become more and more extensive, money has come increasingly to be an electronic blip on a computer screen or in a data base.

Just as 'industrially produced money' was important to the emergence of national currencies, the growing use of 'electronic money'[2] is playing a role in encouraging new currency arrangements to emerge. There is no doubt, for example, that the advent of 'electronic money' has encouraged the growth of eurocurrency activity. As soon as money could be moved reliably and rapidly via telecommunications channels between London and New York in the 1960s, it became easy for US banks to conduct dollar transactions offshore in London simply as bookkeeping operations (Strange, 1976). Enthusiasts of 'currency substitution' also argue that 'smart cards' and other kinds of electronic money might enable consumers to operate more efficiently in several different currencies simultaneously at the retail level by reducing transaction costs associated with complex exchange rate calculations (Hayek, 1990). Advanced software programs have also been used by LETS supporters to facilitate the bookkeeping operations associated with the local currencies' multilateral barter network (Tibbett, 1997).

In the last few years, information technologies have also begun to be used to create entirely new monetary devices carrying electronic representations of prepaid value, such as stored value cards (or 'electronic purses') and software products that can be used to make payments across computer networks (sometimes referred to as 'digital cash'). In contrast to credit or debit cards, these devices do not access a bank account or credit line but rather represent general liabilities of the issuer. The importance of these new forms of money therefore is that they may challenge state control over the domestic money supply, since anyone can potentially issue these new forms of money. Private issuers may even decide to provide customers with a choice of different national currencies – or even an entirely new private currency – in which to conduct banking or even retail transactions. The creation and use of these new forms of electronic money is only in a state of infancy at the moment. But potential issuers – both banks and non-banks – are investing large amounts of money and time in order to develop them (Kobrin, 1997).

For this reason, some are predicting a kind of 'back to the future' (Craig, 1996) scenario in which we return to a world that existed before states began to monopolise the creation of money in the nineteenth century when private issuers of currency were often prominent. This kind of prediction should be regarded cautiously, however, since it underestimates the capacity for states to respond to these new monetary innovations either by regulating the issuers of this money or even by assuming the issuing of these new forms of money themselves (Helleiner, 1998a). Still, what may be significant is the coincidence of the birth of these new forms of 'e-currency' with an era in which the appropriate monetary role for the state is being questioned more generally. Specifically, we can already see how this technological development has given 'free banking' advocates a useful opportunity to raise key questions about the relationship between states and markets in the monetary sector.

The recent restructuring of capitalism has also been characterised by a dramatic globalisation of economic activity. This, too, has played a role in encouraging monetary innovations that challenge national currencies. One way it has done this is by encouraging a disenchantment with the constraints and limitations of national economic spaces, a sentiment that has extended to the national currencies that complement these spaces.

The early growth of the eurocurrency market, for example, derived much of its support from private financiers and firms that were seeking a new kind of economic space to match their increasingly transnational operations. As Chapter 10 highlights, these private agents were particularly frustrated by the constraints of various domestic regulations and policies, and they embraced the way that eurocurrency activity provided them with an 'offshore' or 'transnational' economic space beyond such national controls. Indeed, Ronen Palan (1998) has shown well how the creation of this kind of 'offshore' economic space has in fact been a major feature of the recent restructuring of global capitalism not just in the monetary realm, but also in the realm of production (e.g. the spread of regulation-free special export zones). As Chapter 9 indicates, support for eurocurrencies also came from key figures in the City of London who perceived the potential of this monetary innovation to the rebuilding of the City's traditional cosmopolitan orientation in face of the national exchange controls designed to defend the British national currency.

In Europe, support for the Euro has also come from policymakers seeking to free up firms from the limitations of national economic spaces and national regulations in that region. By reducing transaction costs associated with region-wide economic activities, the supranational money is seen to be a key part of their broader project to construct a more coherent regional economic space designed to enable firms to become more competitive in the new global economic environment. Not surprisingly, the Euro has also been actively supported by transnational private interests across Europe for the same reason (Eichengreen and Frieden, 1994).

Support for local currencies has also been linked to the changing conceptions of economic space. Unlike supporters of the eurocurrencies or supranational currencies, however, the local currency advocates are often reacting against the new globalised nature of economic life (Tibbett, 1997). Many of these advocates are inspired by 'green' political ideas that emphasise the various benefits of small-scale economic life, such as the closer sensitivity to environmental issues and the greater possibilities for meaningful democratic participation and community involvement (Helleiner, 1996). These benefits are thought to have been lost in the larger economic spaces that are being created by the latest phase of capitalist restructuring. Whereas supranational currencies are designed to reduce transaction costs associated with long-distance economic activities, local currencies are actually designed to increase them, thus fostering intra-local trade and local self-sufficiency (e.g. Williams, 1996).

Economic globalisation has also encouraged challenges to national currencies in a second way that is related to a growing disillusionment with the kinds of activist national macroeconomic policies that became popular after the 1930s. This disillusionment has emerged partly out of the experiences of inflation in many 'Northern' countries in the 1970s – and other more recent experiences in other regions of the world – which were blamed by many on activist Keynesian macroeconomic management. The success of the rational expectations revolutions in the discipline of economics over the last two decades further undermined intellectual support for activist, discretionary monetary management. Also encouraging the abandonment of this kind of monetary policy, however, have been the difficulties of pursuing it in the new environment of globalised financial markets (Andrews and Willett, 1997).

The declining support for activist national macroeconomic planning has not encouraged a rejection of national currencies in all instances. In many countries, it has simply led to a more orthodox management of the national currency, closer to that pursued in the pre-1930s era than the Keynesian era. But in countries where this option has been more difficult to pursue for various political reasons, support for alternatives to national currencies has often emerged. In parts of the 'South' which have experienced very high rates of inflation, for example, currency substitution has increasingly been seen as a tool to discipline national macroeconomic policymakers and societal groups. In Europe, as Chapter 11 illustrates, some support for EMU has also had a similar motivation, particularly in economic liberal circles: abandoning the national currency in favour of the

Euro will prevent national policymakers from pursuing 'outdated' Keynesian macroeconomic policies in an environment of high capital mobility.

It is not just those opposed to activist national macroeconomic policies who back these alternatives to national currencies. Support has also come from traditional advocates of activist macroeconomic management who have concluded that the nation-state's capacity to pursue this kind of management in an age of global financial integration has been curtailed. One response to this situation has been a defeatist one: embracing currency substitution as a way of signalling to the markets that national macroeconomic trends will be disciplined by currency competition. A less defeatist response has been to support the delegation of power to a supranational authority such as the European central bank which might be able to challenge the markets more effectively, as Chapter 11 highlights.

The creation of local currencies also represents one further such response; supporters regard local currencies as able to promote macroeconomic priorities that the nation-state is no longer believed to be capable of performing. According to their proponents, these forms of money help reduce the vulnerability of local communities to the global financial 'casino' and also act as a kind of local form of 'capital control' by encouraging money to remain within the local community. Moreover, by facilitating economic transactions in poor communities that are starved of cash, local currencies are also seen to provide a primitive macroeconomic 'stimulus' to such communities. These currencies are also often used to promote community values (e.g. pricing goods and services not by market but by the hours of work involved in providing them), thus encouraging what Leyshon and Thrift call an 'alternative morality' of money to that promoted by global financial markets. Advocates of local currencies are, in other words, seeking to restoring a sense of social 'embeddedness' to the functioning of money, a characteristic that national currencies appear to have increasingly lost in the contemporary global financial environment.[3]

If the changing administrative capacity of states and the restructuring of capitalism have played a key role in encouraging challenges to national currencies, a departure from the fiscal goals of the state that helped to produce national currencies in the past might also be expected to be significant. David Glasner (1989), for example, offers one speculative example of this point in his recent book advocating 'free banking' as an alternative to homogenous, state-controlled national currencies. He suggests that the declining importance of mass warfare in the late twentieth century may be creating a political environment in which governments are more willing to abandon the seigniorage benefits that national currencies provide and consider alternative forms of money.

In a different way, pan-European fiscal arrangements are also clearly encouraging challenges to national currencies in that region. Whereas European policymakers in the nineteenth century sought to lower transaction costs associated with administering emerging national-scale bureaucracies, their counterparts today worry about the impact of intra-European exchange rate movements on the operations of the Europe-wide fiscal arrangements. Particularly important are the operations of the Common Agricultural Policy (CAP) which still make up such a large portion of the European Union's budget. In an environment when national currencies have fluctuated dramatically against each other, the functioning of the CAP has been rendered very complicated. A desire to avoid these complications has played a significant role in prompting European governments to consider ways to eliminate intra-regional exchange rates.

Finally, since national currencies were created partly to bolster nascent national identities historically, we can expect that a reconfiguration of identities that de-emphasises the role of the nation might also be infusing some of the new monetary arrangements.[4] This is clearly the case in the European context. Verdun illustrates how enthusiasts of European integration, for example, often see EMU as a tool to promote a greater sense of European unity. It can also help explain some of the enthusiasm for currency substitution and private currencies in the current age. This is an age in which economic liberalism has emerged as a dominant ideology around the world, and, as I explain in Chapter 8, some of the enthusiasm for these new monetary structures stems from economic liberal circles where individualistic and cosmopolitan ideals have always held higher priority than nationalistic ones. A reconfiguration of identities is also playing a role in encouraging the growth of local currencies where local currency advocates often favour local affiliations over and above nationalist predilections. They trust local currencies to promote such local affiliations partly by fostering local economic interaction and partly in a symbolic sense; local currencies, when they exist in a physical form, are usually emblazoned with imagery and slogans that reflect local values (Helleiner 2000).

In sum, many of the causes behind the rising challenges to national currencies can be found in the reconfiguration of the historical processes and structures that produced national currencies in the first place. This is not to suggest that these changes provide a complete explanation of contemporary developments. Circumstances unique to specific regions must also be drawn upon to account for developments in that area, as Verdun does in Chapter 11 with respect to the historical relationship between Germany, for example, and its neighbours in the case of the Euro. Moreover, to explain the different ways that national currencies are being challenged and the different intensities of these challenges in each country, we must move away from this general level of explanation to examine regional and country-specific variations in the factors cited above. Still, these factors do provide a useful way of beginning to account for the widespread phenomenon of challenges to national currencies in the contemporary age.

Implications for the nation-state?

Despite the many challenges to national currencies that I have outlined above, it cannot be forgotten that there are equally those who are resistant to these challenges (see Chapters 8 and 11). Support for national currencies remains tenacious in many parts of the world. Particularly prominent examples can be found in regions where nation-states are in the process of being constructed, such as the new republics created by the break-up of the USSR, Czechoslovakia and Yugoslavia. In each of these instances, new national currencies have been created alongside the new nation-states as a central component of the new independent political status of these countries. Indeed, in these cases the relationship between money and nation-states is being harnessed as a cornerstone of nation-state formation, recalling a much earlier period in the history of national currencies and the beginning of their consolidation in the early nineteenth century.

The motivations for the resistance to the erosion of national currencies are understandable since the potential consequences for nation-states are considerable. Drawing on the previous analysis, we can identify three important features of the nation-state that may be challenged. The first is the coherent and exclusive sense of homogenous national economic space that has been so characteristic of the age of the nation-state. National currencies were recognised early on by state policymakers as a key tool in fostering this economic territoriality of the nation-state. By eliminating the heterogeneous and rather chaotic nature of pre-national monies, national currencies reduced domestic transaction costs in ways that promoted internal economic coherence. At the same time, national currencies also strengthened the nation-state's economic territoriality in an external sense by creating a clear monetary boundary between the nation-state and the world.

Local currencies and the growing use of foreign currencies in domestic monetary systems each can play a role in eroding the internal economic territoriality of the nation-states. The former are in fact explicitly designed to increase internal transaction costs across the economic space of the nation-state by fostering intra-local trade among their users at the expense of trade with the rest of the nation. The latter can also have the effect of increasing internal transaction costs, particularly in cases where currency substitution has become pervasive at the retail level.

Supranational currencies, such as the Euro, on the other hand, can challenge the nation-state's external economic territoriality. They are in fact being promoted by those who seek to construct a more supranational kind of economic space in which the transaction costs and exchange rate risks associated with the crossing of national monetary borders are eliminated. In the European context, for example, a single 'price language' is being created, giving people a sense of living in a new single economic territory that the popular press has dubbed 'Euroland'. The significance of the nation-state's external economic border is also undermined in a similar, though less dramatic, way by the growth of eurocurrency activity and currency substitution within its territory. By blurring the traditional distinction between domestic and foreign economic activities, these phenomena contribute to what Saskia Sassen (1996: ch.1) calls the 'denationalisation' of domestic territory in the contemporary era.

A second feature of the nation-state to be challenged by the new currency arrangements is the 'direct' nature of the link between state and domestic society that distinguishes nation-states from previous historical forms of state (Tilly 1990: 25; Hobsbawm 1992: 80–1; Giddens, 1985). This link was forged partly from above in the nineteenth century as public authorities sought to expand what Michael Mann (1986) calls the 'infrastructural' power of the state as a means of bolstering their internal power, projecting power externally or promoting modern economic development. It also came from below as the new sense of national citizenship encouraged domestic social groups and individuals to make direct claims on the state. The creation of national currencies was one of the many institutional innovations that helped create this new direct link between state and domestic society by providing a macroeconomic tool for the state to serve domestic society more directly, and by bolstering the state's ability to extract resources directly from the people it governed through seigniorage revenues.

Alternative currency arrangements emerging in the contemporary era threaten to weaken the close state–society relationship that national currencies helped to create. Not only will the state's extractive abilities be eroded if seigniorage benefits are reduced through the diminished use, or elimination, of the national currency but also the state's ability to serve the citizens directly by manipulating the domestic money supply or exchange rate policy will be diminished. Both changes can already be seen in countries experiencing considerable currency substitution (see Chapter 7). The latter change is being experienced even more dramatically in Europe where the introduction of the Euro is removing monetary and exchange rate policies as a macroeconomic tool of nation-states altogether. In this context, individual European nation-states must fall back on other tools of macroeconomic management, such as fiscal policy or wages and incomes policies, which are often less flexible or effective. Indeed, fears that these alternatives may be insufficient to enable smooth adjustment to external shocks have led many European policymakers to conclude that it may be necessary to strengthen region-wide fiscal arrangements – such as transfer payments – to offset these shocks as has been done traditionally by individual nation-states, thus further accelerating the shift of power to supranational authorities.

A final feature of the nation-state that may be weakened by challenges to national currencies is the sense of collective identity that binds inhabitants of a nation-state to each other. In Benedict Anderson's (1981) phrase, citizens of a nation-state feel themselves to be linked as members of an 'imagined community' that is not only limited to a particular territory and sovereign but also bound by a kind of 'horizontal comradeship'. As several of the contributors to this volume have argued, national currencies have played a role in cultivating this sense of national identity in many countries. For this reason, their erosion may also be significant in encouraging alternative senses of identity to emerge.

How significant these changes are is a question that would require much more research on a country-by-country basis. But judging by the comments of opponents of the common currency project in Europe, national symbols on money remain significant sources of identification for some people in the contemporary era. The Archbishop of Canterbury, for example, recently noted, 'I want the Queen's head on the banknotes. The point about national identity is a very important one' (quoted in Goodhart 1995: 455). The attention paid to the imagery to be placed on the new European notes as well as the money of new states in Eastern Europe also highlights the continuing significance of the symbolic role of currencies.[5]

It may not just be at the level of imagery that identities are altered by new monetary arrangements. These new forms of money may influence identities by creating new 'price languages', thus altering the mental universe of monetary calculations that an individual makes every day. A recent publication from the European Commission (1995: 48–9) makes this point quite effectively: 'In at least one respect, adjusting to it [the Euro] is somewhat like learning a language – it takes time and practice before it is possible to 'think' in the new currency. . . . For some people, the change will feel almost like a change of identity. . .'.

Similarly, people may lose the sense of participating in a shared community of fate when they no longer share the same common national monetary experiences as they did in the age of national currencies. In 'Southern' countries experiencing widespread currency substitution, for example, wealthier citizens who hold many of their assets in dollars and work frequently with the US currency will experience a devaluation of the domestic currency as a less significant event than will the poor who continue to live and work only with the domestic currency. Whereas a national currency may remind rich and poor that they are members of the same nation, this denationalised monetary structure may reinforce the sense of distance between the two groups and the more 'internationalised' identity of the former.

In the EU, too, collective national monetary experiences will also be lost with the elimination of national currencies. Presently, when one region of a European country experiences a sudden decline in its exports to other EU countries, the entire nation experiences this change and adjusts accordingly, with perhaps a devaluation or a tightening of national monetary policy. After the introduction of the Euro, however, this region will be forced to find alternative adjustment mechanisms, perhaps a decrease in wages or migration. These new adjustment mechanisms will be region specific and will not directly involve other citizens of that country, just as similar adjustments within existing national currency zones are regionally specific. With this change may be lost the sense of togetherness brought about by being in the same national 'monetary boat' or by the experience of sharing a monetary destiny at the national level.

National identities may also be altered in one further way. Modern forms of monies have no intrinsic 'commodity value' and thus rest ultimately on trust; the value and use of one's money is dependent on the trustworthiness of the state and community that issues and accepts it. In cases where a national currency has proved very trustworthy and stable in value, it has often become an important, almost mystical, symbol of the nation's trustworthiness and stability. The Deutschmark in postwar West Germany represents a good example of this phenomenon (Helleiner, 1998b). Alternative currency forms that prove trustworthy may, in a similar way, encourage alternative forms of identification, as trust is cultivated in communities at the local (in the case of local currencies), supranational (for example, Europe in the case of the Euro) or even transnational levels (for example, foreigners' 'trust' in the US dollar).

To sum up, three central features of nation-states may be challenged by the erosion of national currencies: their economic territoriality, the direct link between state and domestic society, and the sense of collective national identity that binds the members of nation-states. Indeed, the erosion of national currencies is often made possible only because these features are being challenged already for various reasons, some of which have been briefly mentioned earlier in this chapter. Just as the emergence of national currencies historically was intricately connected with broader processes that gave rise to the nation-state, their decline may thus also be closely tied in complicated ways to broader challenges to the nation-state in the contemporary era. And as we have highlighted, these challenges are very uneven and heterogeneous in form, making a prediction of the strength of the trends outlined above very difficult in global or general terms.

It is also important to reiterate that these trends should not be understood in absolutist terms. A number of the contributors to this volume have reminded us that national currencies were historically rarely as homogenous as is sometimes assumed. Thus, in many instances, the kinds of challenges described above – to the nation-state's territoriality, its state–society relations and its identities – are not always as new as one might expect. They are perhaps better seen as degrees of change rather than as dramatic and entirely new kinds of change.

Conclusion

The widespread nature of the challenges to national currencies is one of the more interesting phenomena in the contemporary world. Perhaps because these challenges are so uneven geographically and heterogeneous in form in the contemporary age, scholars have not devoted much attention to the development of a general analysis of the causes of this phenomenon and its consequences for the nation-state. Drawing on many of the contributions to this volume, I have suggested that one way to examine these causes is to explore the extent to which the broader historical processes that helped create national currencies in the first place – the growth of the state's administrative capacity, the rise of industrial capitalism, expanding fiscal needs of the state, and emerging nationalist sentiments – are being transcended and transformed. To analyse the consequences for the nation-state of these challenges, I have argued that attention needs to be paid to three central features of the nation-state: its economic territoriality, its direct link between state and domestic society, and the sense of collective national identity that binds the members of nation-states.

This analysis does not pretend to be at all comprehensive. Rather, my goal – like that of this volume as a whole – is to raise questions and issues in the hope that others will be encouraged to do further research in this area. Indeed, the absence of an extensive literature on this topic to date is surprising given the importance of this issue in the contemporary world. It may, however, simply reflect the fact that analyses of money have been traditionally dominated by economists who have been inclined to view money primarily as an economic phenomenon. As this chapter and the others in the volume have shown, the study of the relationship between money and nation-states requires a wider perspective on money, one that views it also as an historical, geographical, political, social and cultural phenomenon. By offering this wider, more interdisciplinary approach, the contributors to this volume have helped to set a new research agenda in this field. We only hope that these essays serve to foster more work on the relationship between nation-states and money in ways that help us better to understand the past, present and future of national currencies.

Acknowledgements

I am grateful to Emily Gilbert for her comments.

Notes

1 I am grateful to Emily Gilbert for these last two points.
2 Some writers use the phrase 'electronic money' in a narrow way to refer only to the new 'electronic purses' or 'digital cash' discussed briefly below. I am using it here in a broader sense to refer to money that is stored, moved, and processed in electronic form.
3 It is also worth noting that many supporters of local currencies in fact believe that national currencies never reflected social priorities effectively or served local communities well, even before this age of global financial integration. They are often critics of the inflexibility of centralised national macroeconomic planning who seek to decentralise policymaking below the level of the nation-state, as Maruyama illustrates in the Japanese case (Chapter 4).
4 This point should not be overemphasised. In contexts such as Quebec and Scotland, as already mentioned, nationalists are also supporters of alternative monetary structures.
5 Almost all the new states in Eastern Europe have introduced national currencies with images and names of currencies that evoke the distant past of the nation, thus legitimising the historical lineage of the new nation-state through the iconography of the currency. See for example Murphy (1992).

Bibliography

Anderson, B. (1981) *Imagined Communities*, London: Verso.
Andrews, D. and Willett, T. (1997) 'Financial Interdependence and the State' *International Organization* 51, 3: 479–511.
Cox, R. (1987) *Power, Production and World Order*, New York: Columbia University Press.
Craig, B. (1996) 'Competing Currencies: Back to the Future?' *Economic Commentary* Federal Reserve Bank of Cleveland, 15 October.
Eichengreen, B. and Frieden, J., eds, (1994) *The Political Economy of European Monetary Unification*, Boulder: Westview.
European Commission (1995) *Green Paper: On the Practical Arrangements for the Introduction of the Single Currency*, Brussels: European Commission.
Federal Reserve Bank of Kansas City, ed., (1991) *Policy Implications of Trade and Currency Zones*, Kansas City: Federal Reserve Bank of Kansas City.

Giambiagi, F. (1998) 'Una Propuesta de Unificacion Monetaria Para Los Paises Del Mercosur' Published at *http://www.cefir.org.uy/docs/dt25/04giambi.htm*

Giddens, A. (1985) *The Nation-State and Violence*, Cambridge: Polity.

Glasner, D. (1989) *Free Banking and Monetary Reform*, Cambridge: Cambridge University Press.

Goodhart, C. (1995) 'The Political Economy of Monetary Union' in P. Kenen, ed. *Understanding Interdependence*, Princeton: Princeton University Press.

Hayek, F. (1990) *The Denationalisation of Money – The Argument Refined* 3rd edition, London: Institute for Economic Affairs.

Helleiner, E. (1996) 'International Political Economy and the Greens' *New Political Economy* 1, 1: 59–77.

Helleiner, E. (1998a) 'Electronic Money: A Challenge to the Sovereign State?' *Journal of International Affairs* 51, 2: 387–410.

Helleiner, E. (1998b) 'National Currencies and National Identities' *American Behavioral Scientist* 41, 10: 1409–36.

Helleiner, E. (2000) 'Think globally, transact locally: green political economy and the local currency movement' *Global Society* (January).

Hobsbawm, E. (1992) *Nations and Nationalism Since 1780*, 2nd edition, Cambridge: Cambridge University Press.

Kapstein, E. (1994) *Governing the Global Economy*, Cambridge: Harvard University Press.

Kobrin, S. (1997) 'Electronic Cash and the End of National Markets' *Foreign Policy* 107: 65–77.

Lucas, L. (1998) 'Asian Monetary Union is Mooted' *Financial Times*, 31 December.

Mann, M. (1986) *Sources of Social Power, v.1*, Cambridge: Cambridge University Press.

Murphy, C. (1992) 'A License to Print Money' *The Atlantic* 269, 6: 26–8.

Oedel, D. (1997) 'Why Regulate Cybermoney?' *The American University Law Review* 46, 4.

Palan, R. (1998) 'Trying to Have Your Cake and Eating It: How and Why the State System Created Offshore' *International Studies Quarterly* 42, 4: 625–44.

Sassen, S. (1996) *Losing Control? Sovereignty in an Age of Globalization*, New York: Columbia University Press.

Solomon, L.D. (1996) *Rethinking Our Centralized Monetary System: The Case for a System of Local Currencies*, Westport, CN: Praeger.

Strange, S. (1976) *International Monetary Relations*, Oxford: Oxford University Press.

Tibbett, R. (1997) 'Alternative Currencies: A Challenge to Globalisation?' *New Political Economy* 2, 1: 127–35.

Tilly, C. (1990) *Coercion, Capital and European States, AD 990–1990*, Cambridge: Basil Blackwell.

Williams, C. (1996) 'The New Barter Economy: An Appraisal for Local Exchange and Trading Systems' *Journal of Public Policy* 16, 1: 85–101.

Index